Italian Holiday Cooking

Italian Holiday Cooking

A COLLECTION OF

150 TREASURED RECIPES

Michele Scicolone

WILLIAM MORROW

An Imprint of HarperCollinsPublishers

To Charles

HarperCollins books may be purchased for educational, business, or sales promotional use. For information please write: Special Markets Department, HarperCollins Publishers Inc., 10 East 53rd Street, New York, NY 10022.

FIRST EDITION

Printed on acid-free paper

Designed by Pei Loi Koay

Photographs by Ellen Silverman
Food styling by Anne Disrude
Prop styling by Betty Alfenito

Library of Congress Cataloging-in-Publication Data

Scicolone, Michele.
    Italian holiday cooking : a collection of 150 treasured recipes / Michele Scicolone.
    —1st ed.
        p.   cm.
      ISBN 0-06-019991-1
      1. Cookery, Italian.   2. Holiday cookery.   I. Title.

TX723 .S3663   2001
641.5'68—dc21

                                                                            2001030461

01   02   03   04   05   QWF   10   9   8   7   6   5   4   3   2   1

Contents

ACKNOWLEDGMENTS   VII

INTRODUCTION   1

Antipasti   5

Bread and Savory Pies   21
PANE E PIZZE

Soups   41
MINESTRE E ZUPPE

Sauces and Ragus   55
SALSE E RAGÙ

Pasta, Risotto, and Polenta   75

Fish and Seafood   133
PESCE E FRUTTI DI MARE

Meat and Poultry   159
CARNE E POLLAME

Vegetables   195
VERDURA

Cakes and Tarts   217
TORTE E CROSTATE

Cookies, Fruit, and Nuts   237
BISCOTTI, FRUTTI, E NOCI

Desserts   271
DOLCI

SOURCES   296

BIBLIOGRAPHY   297

RECIPES BY HOLIDAYS, FEAST   298
DAYS, AND CELEBRATIONS

RECIPE INDEX   301

Acknowledgments

Tante grazie to all my family, friends, students, and acquaintances who gave me recipes or shared their memories with me for this book. They include my mom, Louise Tumminia, Loretta Balsamo, Millie Castagliola, Dora Marzovilla, Mauro Mafrici, Lars Leicht, Aileen Riotto Sirey, Barbara Riotto Garodnick, Phil and Jackie Cicconi, Antoinette Sisti, Mary Ann Esposito, Linda Carucci, Arthur Schwartz, Maurizio di Rosa, Donnatella Arpaia, Nancy Weber, Leona Ancona Cantone, Rose Di Dio, Tony Di Dio, Sal Agro, Arlyn Blake, Anne Amendolara Nurse, Margaret Scicolone, Sara Beleckis, Mary Ann Amico, Susan Sarao Westmoreland, Kevin Benvenuto, and Donna Boland—who not only gave me her recipe but was kind enough to recheck some of the others for me.

Special thanks to Harriet Bell, my editor, for her patience and clear thinking. I can't believe this is our seventh book together.

Judith Weber, my agent, who always gives me good advice and wise guidance. Ellen Silverman took the evocative, stylish photos, as she has in the past for some of my other books. Anne Disrude and Betty Alfenito are the food and prop stylists whom I know I can count on to visually capture the feeling of my work. As Harriet says, "They just get it."

Thanks to the team at Morrow: Roberto de Vicq de Cumptich, for the jacket; Judith Sutton for her careful reading and copyediting of the manuscript; and Ann Cahn, production editor; Karen Lumley, production manager; and Leah Carlson-Stanisic, design manager, for creatively pulling the book together from manuscript to bound book; Karen Ferries, who takes care of all the details, as well as Carrie Weinberg.

Introduction

Sometimes when you least expect it, the idea for a book is born. In the case of this book, it happened one summer day at the Union Square Greenmarket in New York City. I had been asked to help promote the Greenmarket by bringing some food samples and signing copies of my books. A man stopped, picked up a book, and began flipping through the pages. I asked him if he was looking for anything in particular, and he replied, "Yes, *vecchiarelle.*"

Vecchiarelle means little old ladies, so I asked him just what he meant. He explained that they were a type of deep-fried cookie flavored with red wine and dipped in honey that his Sicilian grandmother used to make. He described how she made them by rolling the dough over a cheese grater, like gnocchi. He hadn't tasted them in years, he said, a little sadly. No one had thought to write down his nonna's recipe and he could not find it in any Italian cookbook.

As he spoke, I felt like a cartoon character who suddenly has a lightbulb flash on over her head. I remembered eating those same cookies, and, in fact, my mother and I used to make them together. But I did not have a recipe and I had not eaten them for years either. I had completely forgotten about them until his description jogged my memory. I could hardly wait to call my mom.

When I reached her later that day, Mom remembered the cookies too. We called them red wine *struffoli,* to distinguish them from the Neapolitan-style struffoli that were traditional in our family. The red wine version was given to my mother by a neighbor, who had learned it from her Sicilian mother-in-law, though, as far as we know, she did not call them *vecchiarelle* either. But Mom couldn't find the recipe. Disappointed, I found myself thinking, "Somebody should write down these great old family favorites before they are lost completely."

After many phone calls, I tracked down the recipe. My aunts did not have it. But finally, my sister, Annette, asked our mother's oldest friend, "Aunt" Millie, if she remembered it. Sure enough, she had it in her recipe file, written in my mother's elegant handwriting on pink notepaper imprinted with my sister's maiden name. Judging by the notepaper, it had to be more than forty years old. I made a batch of the red wine *struffoli* as soon as I could and they were as good as we remembered them.

I began making lists of the recipes that my friends, students, and relatives were always asking me for: a good lasagne like my mother's, *sfinci* for Saint Joseph's Day, stuffed mushrooms, *zeppoli*, and a creamy Italian-style cheesecake. Friends suggested others: *cremolata, pastiera,* and a pasta sauce with meatballs, sausages, and braciole with tomato sauce the way it used to be made every Sunday. Then there were my personal favorites: seven-layer cookies, ragu Bolognese, and ravioli. My husband spoke longingly about his grandmother's special pasta timbale that had never been written down and no one knew how to make anymore.

Family, friends, acquaintances, and even complete strangers gave me some of the most delicious recipes. My friend Aileen Riotto Sirey generously offered me her Aunt Josie Clemente's precious cookbook, filled with carefully written family recipes. Dora Marzovilla, whose family owns I Trulli Restaurant in New York City, came to my kitchen and showed me how she makes her special Saint Joseph's Day pasta. Phil and Jackie Cicconi, who knew me only through having read my book *Savoring Italy,* sent me several recipes that were traditional in their family, from the Marches region. They wrote that they were glad to have a reason to finally set the recipes down on paper so that they could be passed on to their children and future generations.

Again and again, people I spoke to told me that since their grandmother, father, aunt, or mother always made these special dishes, no one had ever thought to write down the recipes. Now that they were gone, there was no way to re-create those cookies, pastas, or special soups, and they regretted it. "If only we had paid more attention and written it down," was the lament I heard over and over again, "we could honor their memory by preparing that special dish. It would be like having Grandma here with us again."

While researching to find the best examples of these dishes, I realized that there were endless variations depending on where the recipe originated and that the dishes had different associations in every area. Family tastes were issues too. Uncle Nicky does not like garlic, or Aunt Mary can't eat green peppers, meant that ingredients were omitted or substitutions were made to suit their needs.

Why were certain dishes related to specific days, such as snails for Saint John's Day? Particular foodstuffs were probably associated with a holy day simply because they happened to be abundant at the time of the year. Ages ago, when people lived close to the land, the appearance of fat snails might seem like a gift of God—or a plague if they were devouring the crops. It was only natural to seek to explain it. Thus people rationalized that the snails were really devils, because they had horns, and eating them disposed of the devils and the problems they created.

Many of the traditions can be traced back to pre-Christian times. Saint's day feasts and celebrations often coincide with what were once pagan holidays.

When the Church imposed its calendar, Christian holidays came to be substituted for the pagan rites and rituals. Saint John's Day (June 23) is celebrated at the summer solstice and Saint Lucy's Day (December 13) coincides with what was originally the winter solstice. Both were traditionally days when it was believed that witches and spirits roamed the earth. All Souls' Day (November 2) falls on the Celtic feast of Samain, when the spirits of the dead were believed to rise up and walk the earth again. The early church fathers assigned saints and holy rituals to these pagan holidays to disguise any traces of paganism without depriving the people of the customary celebrations of the day.

Many of the traditions Italian Americans hold so dear are no longer remembered in Italy, while others are as popular now as they were a hundred years ago, when Italian immigrants introduced them here. I asked friends in Italy what dishes they serve today for special occasions and added them to my collection. Sadly, though, several told me that "no one in Italy takes the time to cook anymore." I find it very interesting that there are many traditions being kept safe here in American families that have completely disappeared in Italy.

As my recipe collection began to grow, it was easy to spot recipes that had been adapted to American kitchens and ingredients. True, many adaptations were made out of necessity when the original ingredients could not be found, but genuine Italian cooking is simple and uncomplicated and derives its appealing flavors from the combination of a few quality ingredients. If a dish is made with packaged bread crumbs, jarred tomato sauce that is invariably oversweetened and overspiced, and grated cheese from a can, it cannot possibly taste authentic or be "just like Grandma's." Good olive oil, Parmigiano-Reggiano, pecorino romano, imported canned tomatoes, and fresh mozzarella may take more effort to shop for and, occasionally, prepare, but there is no substitute for their flavor and quality. There is no excuse for using garlic powder, dried herbs, and flavored bread crumbs from a can. I rejected recipes that had strayed unreasonably from their Italian origins.

I remember shopping with my grandmother, who would walk long distances to buy freshly killed chicken or rabbits, the best produce, the crispest breads, or the type of cheese she preferred. Although we all have less time today, only if cooks make the special effort to buy the best ingredients can they ever hope to capture the authentic flavors of Italian cooking.

I tried as best I could to reconstruct these recipes from the often scanty information that I was provided. Often the dishes were meant to feed large extended families. My grandmother's *pastiera*, or wheat berry cheesecake, was baked in an enormous aluminum pan 14 inches wide and 6 inches deep—and she always made other smaller pies at the same time to give to friends and family. I scaled down her recipe to fit a standard 9-inch springform pan.

In addition, preparing holiday foods such as *struffoli, cuccidati,* and the like was traditionally a family enterprise. Mothers, aunts, and cousins would get together to make these foods in assembly-line fashion. One mixed and kneaded, another stuffed and sealed, another fried. The men cracked the nuts or peeled and chopped the fruits. Children dusted desserts with sugar or sprinkled them with colored candies. These are the key ingredient that made these foods so special—the anticipation, the togetherness, the jokes and stories, families getting together, if only once a year, to celebrate.

Reconnecting with and preserving our past not only enhances the special occasion, it ensures that we will be remembered in the future. We might recall a dear aunt's kindness or an uncle's jokes, but they become all the more real when we prepare and share that aunt's recipe for stuffed artichokes, or that uncle's incomparable pizza. Celebrating special occasions not only helps us to remember, but lifts us out of the everyday, and brings joy to our lives.

If you are so fortunate as to have treasured family recipes, whatever your heritage, I hope you will be inspired to write them down too. Ask other family members what they remember of these lost dishes and re-create them, just as I did with my husband's grandmother's pasta and many other recipes in this book.

While Grandma or Auntie may have cooked with a pinch of this and handful of that, her food tasted so good because her repertoire of dishes was probably very limited and she made them all the time. Practice makes perfect. Even if the cook never used standard cup and spoon measurements (which are still rare today in Italy and many other places), you might be able to find a similar recipe and tinker with it until it tastes as you remember it.

Use this book to discover lost traditions, or create new ones. These are recipes to make and give and share. I hope you will enjoy them.

Antipasti

An antipasto whets the appetite for the meal to come. The word means that which is outside a meal, or comes before a meal, and since these small bites are eaten in small quantities, antipasti are often more highly flavored than the rest of the meal. While most Italians would not serve an antipasto before an everyday meal, holiday and special-occasion dinners usually begin with one.

A simple antipasto can be easily assembled. Sliced dried or cured meats like prosciutto, salami, and dried sausages of all kinds are typical. Though most here are made from pork, in Italy you might find cured meats and sausages made from wild boar, venison, or goose, depending on the region. Although cheese is usually eaten after a meal, southern Italians serve a small wedge of sharp provolone or sweet and milky fresh mozzarella as an antipasto, plain or with olives and pickled peppers.

It is easier to say what is not eaten as an antipasto than what is. Fresh meats—such as a steak or roast—would not be served, nor would pasta in any form. Vegetables rule as antipasti, though not often fruits, except ripe figs and sweet cantaloupe or honeydew melon, classically paired with silky pink prosciutto. Salads are popular, especially those made with vegetables, seafood, and, occasionally, chicken. Eggs may be stuffed or made into a frittata. Fried foods, like vegetables or seafood in a light crispy coating, are often served as antipasti, especially in southern Italy.

A more elaborate antipasto would be an assortment of fried or baked stuffed vegetables. These can double as side dishes, and a number of them can be found in the vegetable chapter.

Cherry Bombs

PEPERONCINI RIPIENI

I always forget how addictive these little stuffed peppers can be. Buy the smallest, one-bite-size peppers, but be careful—they are hot! Serve at room temperature with salami and wedges of sharp provolone cheese.

SERVES 8 TO 12

One 32-ounce jar hot pickled cherry peppers (about 25 small to medium), drained, juice reserved

1 cup dry bread crumbs, preferably homemade

6 anchovy fillets, chopped

2 tablespoons capers, very finely chopped

1 small garlic clove, finely chopped

Extra virgin olive oil

1. Slice off the tops of the peppers. With a small spoon, scoop out the seeds.

2. Combine the bread crumbs, anchovies, capers, and garlic. Add about 3 tablespoons olive oil, or enough to moisten the crumbs. Add 1 to 2 tablespoons of the reserved pepper juices to taste.

3. Fill the cherry peppers with the crumb mixture, packing it in lightly. Refrigerate until serving time.

4. Just before serving, drizzle the peppers with a little oil, if desired.

WINE MATCH: Falerno Bianco, Villa Matilde

Stuffed Olives from the Marches

OLIVE ASCOLANA

When my book Savoring Italy *was published, I received a letter from a reader, Mrs. P. Cicconi. She was disappointed that I mentioned* olive ascolana *in the book but did not include a recipe. She told me she made stuffed olives all the time. I wrote back that though I had eaten the olives in Italy, I had never made them. I asked her for the recipe, and she and her husband, Phil, kindly sent it to me, along with several others in this book.*

Here is what the Cicconis wrote: "Stuffed olives were served on all major holidays. . . . Mom spent hours peeling large green olives into a continuous strand that she would use to wind around a ball of the meat mixture. She ground the meat using a kitchen meat grinder (she also would put a sign of the cross on the completed stuffing). We have changed the process slightly to make it less labor-intensive. We use a food processor for the meat grinding and large pitted green olives that we split and put around the meat mixture. (The sign of the cross is optional.)"

Leftover cooked chicken or pork can be substituted instead of making the meats from scratch. The Cicconis do not recommend using beef or lamb, however, since their flavors are too different. You will need about two cups of cooked meat. If you do make the meats from scratch, the cooking sauce is a bonus that can be used for pasta.

Making these olives is a bit of a production, though well worth the effort. Enlist a helper or two to assist with the stuffing and coating.

This recipe makes a lot, but they freeze well and are good to have around for snacks or parties.

The Cicconis also recommend the stuffing as a filling for ravioli. The ravioli are served "white"—that is, simply boiled and rolled in grated cheese, no tomato sauce—or fried until golden brown and sprinkled with sugar.

MAKES ABOUT 65

MEATS

¼ cup olive oil

2 small pork chops (12 ounces)

1 bone-in chicken breast (8 ounces)

Salt and freshly ground black pepper

1 medium onion, finely chopped

1 celery rib, finely chopped

1 carrot, finely chopped

1 garlic clove, finely chopped

3½ cups peeled, seeded, and chopped fresh
   tomatoes or one 28- to 35-ounce can
   Italian peeled tomatoes, chopped

2 or 3 basil leaves

FILLING

2 large eggs
½ cup chopped green olives
½ cup freshly grated Parmigiano-Reggiano
1 teaspoon ground cinnamon
½ teaspoon freshly grated nutmeg
½ teaspoon ground allspice
½ teaspoon grated lemon zest
Freshly ground black pepper

Four 7-ounce jars extra-large pitted green
   olives (about 65)
3 large eggs
1 cup all-purpose flour
2 cups fine dry bread crumbs
Vegetable oil for frying

1. To cook the meats, heat the oil in a large skillet over medium heat. Add the pork chops and chicken breast and brown well on all sides. Remove from the pan and sprinkle with salt and pepper.

2. Add the onion, celery, carrot, and garlic to the skillet. Cook, stirring often, until the vegetables are tender, about 10 minutes. Add the tomatoes, basil, and salt and pepper to taste. Return the meats to the pan and bring to a simmer. Cook over low heat, stirring occasionally, until the meats are tender and the sauce is thickened, about 1 hour.

3. Remove the meats from the sauce. Reserve the sauce for another dish. Remove the skin and bones and cut the meats into 1-inch chunks. You should have about 2 cups meat.

4. Put the meat in a food processor and coarsely chop. Add the eggs, olives, cheese, spices, lemon zest, and pepper to taste; process until the mixture is fine and the ingredients are well blended. (If you prefer, you can pass the meat and olives through a meat grinder and mix together with the remaining ingredients in a bowl.) Cover and refrigerate until ready to use.

5. Rinse the olives and pat dry. Cut lengthwise in half.

6. Beat the eggs in a shallow bowl. Spread the flour on a sheet of wax paper, and spread the bread crumbs on another sheet. Place a large wire rack on a baking sheet.

7. Pinch off a teaspoon or so of the meat filling and shape it into a ball slightly smaller than an olive. Place the ball of filling between two olive halves and press them gently together. Roll the olive in the flour, dip it in the eggs, and then roll it in the

bread crumbs, being sure to coat it completely. Place the olive on the wire rack so that the coating will dry and set. Repeat with the remaining olives.

8. Pour about 2 inches oil into a deep heavy saucepan or a deep fryer. Heat over medium heat to 370°F on a deep-frying thermometer, or until a small drop of the beaten eggs sizzles and moves about the pan quickly when dropped in the oil.

9. Add a few olives to the pan and cook, turning occasionally, until golden brown and crisp, about 2 minutes. Remove the olives with a slotted spoon and drain well on paper towels. Keep warm in a low oven while you fry the remainder. Serve immediately.

NOTE: To freeze the olives after frying them, cool completely on wire racks. Place in a heavy-duty freezer bag and freeze for up to 1 month. To serve, place on a baking sheet in a preheated 350°F oven and bake for 15 to 20 minutes, or until heated through.

WINE MATCH: Prosecco Rustico, Nino Franco

Chickpea-Flour Fritters

PANELLE

Sicilians love these little chickpea-flour fritters, served at every special-occasion dinner, as well as on feast days such as Saint Lucy's Day (December 13) and Saint Rosalie's Day (July 13).

When I was growing up in Brooklyn, they were a specialty of the Sicilian restaurants known as focaccerie. Even today, you can enjoy traditional panelle at Joe's Focacceria on Avenue U or Fernando's on Union Street. Panelle are served hot, either plain as a snack or appetizer or stacked in soft Sicilian-style rolls, topped with a scoop of fresh ricotta and a generous sprinkle of sheep's milk cheese.

SERVES 4

1 cup chickpea flour
Salt

Vegetable oil for frying

1. Have ready a large cookie sheet and a flexible metal spatula.

2. In a heavy medium saucepan, whisk the chickpea flour into 1½ cups cold water until smooth. Add ½ teaspoon salt. Place the saucepan over medium heat and cook, stirring constantly with a wooden spoon, just until the mixture begins to thicken. Watch carefully so that it does not scorch. Remove from the heat and continue to stir until smooth.

3. Immediately scrape the mixture onto the cookie sheet. Working quickly (the mixture sets up as it cools), spread it as evenly as you can to a thickness of ¼ inch or less. (The mixture can be made ahead; cover with plastic wrap up to 1 hour.)

4. With a small knife, cut the chickpea mixture into 2-inch squares.

5. In a deep heavy skillet, heat about 1 inch oil to 370°F or until a small piece of the chickpea mixture sizzles and moves around the pan rapidly when added to the hot oil. Peel a few panelle off the cookie sheet and carefully slip them into the hot oil. Do not

crowd the pan or they may stick together. Cook, turning the pieces often, about one minute until golden brown and slightly puffy. Remove with a slotted spoon and drain well on paper towels. Repeat with the remaining panelle. Serve hot, sprinkled with salt.

VARIATION: Add 2 tablespoons chopped flat-leaf parsley and a generous grind of black pepper to the panelle batter.

TIP: Chickpea flour is available in health food stores and Middle Eastern markets, as well as Italian groceries. If you buy it in an Indian market, look for the unroasted kind.

WINE MATCH: Inzolia, Valle dell'Acate

Golden Rice Balls

ARANCINI

Because of their round shape and golden color, Sicilians call these crusty balls of rice with a core of meat and tomato sauce arancini, *meaning little oranges. In some parts of Sicily, they are made in cone or oval shapes and filled with cheese and* besciamella, *the thick white sauce.*

Beloved by Sicilians, arancini are found everywhere, in corner coffee bars, markets, and take-out shops. They are always served at parties and on feast days, especially Saint Lucy's Day, December 13.

MAKES 18

FILLING

2 tablespoons olive oil
½ cup very finely chopped onion
1 garlic clove, finely chopped
8 ounces ground veal or beef

1½ cups chopped fresh tomatoes or canned
  Italian peeled tomatoes
Salt and freshly ground black pepper
½ cup fresh or frozen peas

RICE SHELLS

5 cups chicken broth
¼ teaspoon saffron threads, crumbled
2 cups (1 pound) medium-grain rice, such as
  Arborio
3 tablespoons unsalted butter
Salt
1 cup freshly grated Parmigiano-Reggiano
4 large egg yolks

5 large egg whites
1 cup all-purpose flour
2 cups fine dry bread crumbs
4 ounces sharp provolone or caciocavallo, cut
  into small dice
Olive or vegetable oil for frying

1. To make the filling, put the oil and onion in a medium skillet, set over medium heat, and cook, stirring, until the onion is soft, about 5 minutes. Stir in the garlic.

2. Add the veal or beef and cook, stirring to break up the lumps, until the meat is no longer pink. Stir in the tomatoes and salt and pepper to taste and bring to a simmer.

Reduce the heat to low and cook, stirring occasionally, until the sauce is thick, about 30 minutes.

3. Add the peas and cook for 5 minutes more. Scrape the sauce into a bowl and let cool.

4. To make the rice, bring the broth to a boil in a large pot. Crumble in the saffron. Stir in the rice, butter, and salt to taste. Cover, reduce the heat to low, and cook for 15 to 18 minutes, or until the rice is tender.

5. Spoon the rice into a bowl and stir in the cheese. Let cool slightly, then stir in the egg yolks.

6. To assemble the rice balls, beat the egg whites in a shallow bowl until frothy. Spread the flour on a sheet of wax paper and the bread crumbs on another. Set a wire rack over a baking sheet.

7. Dip your hands in cool water to prevent the rice from sticking. Scoop up about ⅓ cup of the rice mixture. Holding it in the palm of one hand, poke a shallow hole in the center of the rice, press about 1 tablespoon of the filling into the hole, and add a piece of cheese. Cup your hand slightly, molding the rice over the filling to enclose it completely; add a little more rice if necessary to cover the filling. Very gently squeeze the ball together to compact the rice. Carefully roll the rice ball in the flour, then in the egg whites, coating it completely. Roll the ball in the bread crumbs, being sure not to leave any spots uncovered. Place the rice ball on a rack to dry.

8. Continue with the remaining ingredients, to make a total of 18 rice balls, rinsing your hands between each to prevent the rice from sticking. When all of the rice balls have been made, place the rack on a baking sheet in the refrigerator for 30 minutes, to dry the coating and help the rice balls to keep their shape.

9. Pour about 2 inches oil into a deep fryer or a deep heavy saucepan (there should be enough oil to cover the balls by 1 inch, with plenty of room to allow for the oil to bubble up). Heat the oil to 370°F on a deep-frying thermometer, or until a drop of the egg whites sizzles when it is added to the oil.

10. With a slotted spoon or skimmer, lower a few of the arancini into the oil. Do not crowd the pan. Cook until golden brown and crisp all over, 3 to 4 minutes. Transfer to paper towels to drain, then keep warm in a low oven while you fry the remainder. Serve hot or warm.

TIP: To get the rice balls all the same size, scoop up the prepared rice with a ⅓ cup dry measure.

WINE MATCH: Cerasuolo di Vittorio, Valle dell'Acate

Olives with Fried Bread Crumbs

OLIVE FRITTE

Heating olives brings out their flavor, but it can also make them seem very salty. For baking or cooking, use a mild, less salty olive, like the large green or black cerignola variety. Crunchy, spicy bread crumbs are a delicious topping for these.

SERVES 8

¼ cup olive oil
2 tablespoons chopped flat-leaf parsley
1 garlic clove, minced
1 tiny dried peperoncino, crumbled, or a pinch
  of crushed red pepper

2 cups mild black or green olives, drained
1 tablespoon vinegar
½ cup fresh bread crumbs, preferably
  homemade

1. In a small skillet, heat the oil with the parsley, garlic, and peperoncino over medium heat. Add the olives and vinegar and cook, shaking the pan, until the olives are warm, 2 or 3 minutes.

2. Remove the olives with a slotted spoon and set aside. Add the bread crumbs to the pan and cook, stirring constantly until evenly toasted.

3. Toss the olives with the bread crumbs and serve warm.

WINE MATCH: Verdicchio Casal di Serra, Umani Ronchi Osimo

Asparagus and Prosciutto Frittata

FRITTATA DI ASPARAGI E PROSCIUTTO

Frittatas are especially popular in the springtime, and they are always on the menu for traditional Easter Monday picnics. They are good hot, room temperature, or cold for breakfast, brunch, or dinner. Serve a wedge of frittata as part of an antipasto assortment or sandwich it between two slices of crusty bread. Practically anything can be cooked with the eggs. Try sautéed peppers and onions, fried potatoes, sliced sausages, cooked drained spinach, cheeses, salami, or mushrooms—I could go on.

The first time I tried flipping a frittata was a disaster: it slipped right off the plate and all over the stove. Be sure to protect your hands with oven mitts and keep a firm grip on the plate and skillet. (You might want to flip the frittata over a roasting pan as insurance until you feel comfortable with the motion.) If you prefer, you can just slide the pan under the broiler rather than flipping it.

SERVES 4

1 pound asparagus	Freshly ground black pepper
Salt	3 ounces prosciutto, cut into narrow strips
8 large eggs	2 tablespoons olive oil
¼ cup freshly grated Parmigiano-Reggiano	1 tablespoon unsalted butter

1. Wash the asparagus and snap off the base of the stems.

2. Bring a large shallow pan of water to a boil. Add the asparagus and salt to taste. Cook until tender, 5 to 10 minutes, depending on the thickness of the asparagus. Drain the asparagus, and, when cool enough to handle, cut them into 2-inch pieces.

3. In a bowl, beat the eggs with the cheese and pepper. Stir in the prosciutto.

4. In a 9-inch skillet, heat the olive oil and butter over medium heat. Add the asparagus, spreading it in an even layer. Pour on the egg mixture. Reduce the heat to low and cook, lifting the edges two or three times to allow the uncooked egg to slide under the cooked portion, until the frittata is set around the edges but still moist in the center, about 10 minutes.

5. To flip the frittata, invert a large plate over the skillet. Holding the skillet and plate firmly together, quickly invert the frittata onto the plate. Slide the frittata back into the pan to finish cooking, 2 to 3 minutes more.

6. Slide the frittata onto a serving plate. Cut into wedges to serve.

Baked Clams

VONGOLE ARAGONATE

Small hard-shell clams baked under a light, crispy coating of tasty crumbs were always one of the starters for our Christmas Eve feasts. My father soaked the clams briefly and scrubbed them with a stiff brush. Then he opened each one with his well-worn clam knife, holding the clams over a bowl and carefully preserving every bit of the juice.

The clam juice had two purposes: it was used as a rinse for the clams if they appeared sandy or had a bit of broken shell inside, and then the strained juice was drizzled over the clams in their shells to keep them moist and flavorful while they baked. My job was to spoon on the topping, and heaven help me if I put too much on or packed it down. My father said the secret to tasty baked clams was a light touch with the coating, so that the flavor of the clams could shine through. And he was right.

Sometimes I add a tablespoon or two of grated cheese to the topping. Oysters are also good prepared this way.

SERVES 4 TO 6

2 dozen littleneck or other small hard-shell clams
⅓ cup fine dry bread crumbs
2 tablespoons chopped flat-leaf parsley
1 small garlic clove, very finely chopped

Pinch of salt
Freshly ground black pepper
Extra virgin olive oil
Lemon wedges

1. With a stiff brush, scrub the clams well under cold running water. Discard any clams that have broken shells or that don't close up tightly when handled.

2. Working over a bowl to catch the juices, and protecting your hand with a thick towel or pot holder, grasp a clam, with the hinged side out, and gently but firmly push a dull-bladed knife into the crevice between the top and bottom shells. Slide the knife through the hinge that holds the shells together. Separate the shells, first scraping the clam meat away from the top shell, then cutting the clam away from the muscle that anchors it to the bottom shell. Place the clam in a small bowl, and repeat with the remaining clams.

3. Place a cake rack in a large rimmed, shallow baking pan, such as a jelly-roll pan (the rack will prevent the clams from tipping). Arrange half the clams shells on the rack; discard the rest. If the clam meat looks sandy, rinse it in the clam juices in the bowl. Place a clam in each half-shell. Strain the juices through a paper coffee filter or

a piece of cheesecloth. Drizzle a little juice over each clam. (The clams can be assembled up to 1 hour ahead; cover and refrigerate.)

4. Preheat the broiler. Combine the bread crumbs, parsley, garlic, salt, and pepper to taste, adding just enough oil to moisten the crumbs. Spoon a little of the mixture over each clam. Drizzle each with a few more drops of oil.

5. Place the clams about 4 inches beneath the heat source. Broil until the crumbs are lightly browned and crisp, about 4 minutes. Serve immediately, with lemon wedges.

WINE MATCH: Greco di Tufo, Feudi di San Gregorio

Opening Clams

Have you ever gone to a clam bar and watched the shuckers at work? Armed with just a stubby knife with a sturdy blade, they zip the clams open with ease. But there is a knack to it, and if you are like me, a couple of dozen clams can take all day to open. Another alternative is to steam the clams open, which does little to change their flavor.

Place the clams and ½ cup water in a large pot. Cover and cook over high heat for 3 minutes, or until steam begins to seep out of the pot. Remove any opened clams. Cover and let the remaining clams steam just until they open. Check frequently, so that you can remove the clams as they open. Do not let the clams overcook. Twist off the top shell and discard it. Loosen clams from bottom shells. Arrange the clams on the rack as described above. Strain the juices in the pot and drizzle them over the clams.

Bread Crumbs

Homemade bread crumbs are easy to make from leftover slices of Italian or French bread. Do not use sliced white bread—it is soft and spongy and contains sugar and other ingredients you don't want.

Lay the slices on a baking sheet and toast them in a low oven until very dry. Let cool, break up, then grind the slices in a food processor. Store the crumbs in a tightly sealed plastic bag in the refrigerator or freezer.

Stuffed Easter Eggs

UOVA RIPIENE PASQUALI

Antipasti are a specialty in the Piemonte region in northern Italy. Banquets sometimes begin with as many as thirty different kinds. While traveling there at Easter time, we were served several egg dishes as antipasti, including these delicious stuffed eggs.

SERVES 8

8 large eggs
One 7-ounce can tuna in olive oil, drained
2 green onions, trimmed and cut into 1-inch
  pieces
2 tablespoons freshly grated Parmigiano-
  Reggiano

1 tablespoon drained capers
2 or 3 celery leaves
2 or 3 basil leaves
Salt and freshly ground black pepper
2 tablespoons extra virgin olive oil, or to taste
Chopped flat-leaf parsley for garnish

1. Place the eggs in a medium saucepan with water to cover and bring to a boil. Immediately turn off the heat. Leave the eggs in the pan until the water is cool enough to touch.

2. Drain the eggs and remove the shells. Cut them lengthwise in half, scoop out the yolks, and put them in a food processor or blender. Place the egg whites cut sides up on a serving plate.

3. Add the tuna, green onions, cheese, capers, celery, and basil to the egg yolks and chop fine. Add salt and pepper to taste. Drizzle in the olive oil and process until smooth. Taste for seasoning.

4. Spoon the egg yolk mixture into the egg whites. Sprinkle with parsley. Cover and chill until serving time.

WINE MATCH: Arneis, Vietti

Bread and Savory Pies

PANE E PIZZE

One of Italy's best-kept food secrets is its vast range of flavored breads and savory pies. Some of them are probably not well known because they were afterthoughts, something to be made with the extra bit of bread dough and left-over vegetables or meat. These recipes have remained strictly regional and subject to endless variations.

Easter breads and pies were devised as ways to use up the eggs and cheese not consumed during the long Lenten season. *Pizza rustica, fiadone,* and *torta pasqualina* are just three of the many types of savory pies eaten around this time of year.

Tuscan Rosemary Raisin Bread

PAN DI RAMERINO

Bread flavored with rosemary, raisins, and olive oil and decorated with a cross was once made especially for Holy Week, preceding Easter. It was sold at the door of churches in Tuscany for the faithful to take home to share with their families. A prayer was said before consuming it, and throwing any away was considered a sacrilege: the bread was eaten down to the last crumb.

This is a lovely bread to serve with cheese, or as an afternoon snack with tea or sweet wine. It is made with a starter, a mixture of yeast, flour, and water, that gives it a deeper flavor and helps it to keep longer, so plan ahead.

MAKES 2 ROUND LOAVES

STARTER

1 package (2½ teaspoons) active dry yeast or instant yeast

1 cup unbleached all-purpose flour

DOUGH

3 to 3½ cups unbleached all-purpose flour

¼ cup sugar

1 teaspoon salt

1 tablespoon rosemary leaves, very finely minced

3 tablespoons olive oil, plus more for brushing the loaves

1 cup golden raisins

1. To make the starter, sprinkle the yeast over 1 cup warm (100° to 110°F) water, let stand until creamy, then whisk. Stir in the flour. Cover with plastic wrap and leave at room temperature for at least 1 hour, or overnight. The mixture will become thick and bubbly. The longer the starter sits, the better the flavor will be; after 24 hours, you can refrigerate the starter for up to 3 days.

2. To make the dough, combine 3 cups flour, the sugar, salt, and rosemary in a large bowl. Scrape the starter into the bowl, add the olive oil, and stir until a soft dough forms. Turn the dough out onto a lightly floured surface and knead until smooth and elastic, about 10 minutes. (The dough can also be made in a heavy-duty mixer with a dough hook. Add a little more flour if necessary to prevent the dough from sticking.) Knead in the raisins.

3. Lightly oil a 4- to 6-quart bowl. Scrape the dough into the bowl. Cover with plastic wrap and let rise in a warm, draft-free place for 1½ hours, or until doubled in volume.

4. Oil a large baking sheet. Turn the dough out onto a lightly floured surface. Flatten it with your hands to eliminate the air bubbles. Cut the dough into 2 pieces. Shape each piece into a smooth ball. Place the pieces on the prepared baking sheet, leaving room between them for the dough to expand. Cover with plastic wrap and let rise for 45 minutes, or until doubled.

5. Preheat the oven to 400°F.

6. Brush the loaves with olive oil. With a sharp knife or razor, cut a cross about ½ inch deep in the tops of the loaves. Bake the loaves for 25 to 30 minutes, or until golden. Transfer to wire racks and let cool completely before slicing.

The Blessing of the Throats

For the day of Saint Blaise, San Biagio, on February 3, the priest blesses the throats of the faithful with a pair of crossed candles. Saint Blaise is recognized as the protector against illnesses of the throat because he once saved the life of a boy who had swallowed a fish bone. Blaise is believed to have been a bishop in Asia Minor during the fourth century.

In some areas, people bring an apple or loaf of bread to the church to be blessed. In our church, when I was growing up, we were given a small loaf of blessed bread to take home with us. The blessed food is to be divided among family members and eaten to protect their throats from illness all the rest of the year.

Sicilians make a grasshopper-shaped bread called *cavaduzzi* for San Biagio Day because it is believed that the saint saved the wheat crop from an infestation of the insects.

Olive Rolls

I love how when Italians meet, the conversation invariably turns to food!

When my husband and I were selling our house, I got to talking with the real estate agent, Mary Ann Albano. I mentioned that I was working on a book about Italian family holiday recipes. She asked me if I had ever heard of the olive-filled little rolls her mother made on special occasions. I had not, so she told me how her family made them, and they sounded delicious. The recipe originally was from her grandmother Mamie Albano, who came from the town of Porto Imperico in Sicily.

For rolling out piecrusts and the like, I have a long, heavy rolling pin. But for making these, I use a small, lightweight pin. It is easier to maneuver and makes shaping the little rolls a breeze. Serve the rolls as an appetizer or with salad or soup.

MAKES 1 DOZEN

FILLING

1 large onion, chopped
2 tablespoons olive oil
1 small dried peperoncino, crumbled, or a pinch
   of crushed red pepper

2 cups oil-cured black olives, pitted and
   chopped

DOUGH

1 package (2½ teaspoons) active dry yeast
3 to 4 cups unbleached all-purpose flour

2 teaspoons salt
¼ cup olive oil

1. To make the filling, combine the onion, oil, and peperoncino in a large skillet. Cook over low heat until the onion is tender and golden, about 10 minutes. Stir in the olives and cook 5 minutes more. Let cool.

2. To make the dough, sprinkle the yeast over 1 cup warm (100° to 110°F) water. Let stand for 5 minutes. Stir until dissolved.

3. In a large bowl, stir together 3 cups flour and the salt. Add the yeast mixture and olive oil and stir until a soft dough forms, adding more flour as necessary. Turn the dough out onto a lightly floured surface and knead until smooth and elastic, about 10 minutes. (Or make the dough in a heavy-duty mixer, food processor, or bread

machine.) Shape the dough into a ball and place it in a large oiled bowl. Cover and let rise until doubled, about 1½ hours.

4. Oil two baking sheets. Turn the dough out onto a floured surface and flatten it with your hands. Cut the dough into 12 equal pieces.

5. With a floured rolling pin, flatten one piece into a 6 × 4-inch rectangle. Starting at one short end, spread the dough with a heaping tablespoon of the olive mixture, leaving a ½-inch border at the other short end. Roll up the dough from the covered end, moisten the uncovered edge with a little water, and press to seal the roll. Repeat with the remaining dough and olive mixture.

6. Arrange the rolls several inches apart, seam side down, on the prepared baking sheets. Cover with plastic wrap. Let rise for about 45 minutes, until doubled.

7. Preheat the oven to 450°F.

8. Bake the rolls for 15 to 20 minutes, or until golden. Serve warm.

TIP: Most yeast breads have a better texture if the dough is left slightly moist, so add as little flour as possible when kneading.

Instead of saying someone is as "good as gold," Italians say a person is *"buono come il pane,"* good as bread.

Prosciutto Bread

PANE DI PROSCIUTTO

In the Cobble Hill section of Brooklyn, several bakeries were well known for their excellent Italian-style breads and pastries. Each had its specialty, but Cammareri's and Mazzola's were renowned for their prosciutto bread. Breads similar to this, filled with chunks of prosciutto, cooked ham, salami, and cheese, are eaten only at Eastertime in Naples and other places in southern Italy, but in Brooklyn, you can find them year-round.

Cammareri's Bakery became briefly famous when it was featured in the movie Moonstruck. Nicholas Cage played the melancholy, romantic baker Johnny Cammareri, who falls in love with the Italian-American woman portrayed by Cher. Those characters may have lived happily ever after, but Cammareri's is closed. Mazzola's continues to turn out prosciutto bread.

I once bought a prosciutto loaf and left it on the kitchen counter, planning to serve it for lunch. I returned a short time later to find that my cat, a big Tuxedo Tom who never said no to temptation, had torn the bag and the loaf to shreds and eaten all the meat and cheese chunks. Luckily, I hadn't opened the bottle of red wine I was planning to serve with it, or my connoisseur cat might have tried to sample that too.

MAKES 1 ROUND LOAF

1 package (2½ teaspoons) active dry yeast
1 tablespoon melted lard or olive oil
About 2½ cups unbleached all-purpose or
 bread flour
½ teaspoon salt

½ teaspoon coarsely ground black pepper
4 ounces prosciutto, sliced ¼ inch thick and
 diced (or a combination of prosciutto and
 salami, cut into small dice)
2 ounces provolone, cut into small dice

1. Sprinkle the yeast over 1 cup warm (100° to 110°F) water in a large bowl and let stand for 5 minutes. Stir until the yeast is dissolved.

2. Add the lard and 2 cups flour, the salt, and pepper and stir until a soft dough forms. Turn the dough out onto a lightly floured surface and knead until smooth and elastic, about 10 minutes, adding more flour as necessary to make a moist, but not sticky, dough. (Or make the dough in a heavy-duty mixer, food processor, or bread machine, following the manufacturer's directions.)

3. Oil a large bowl. Put the dough in the bowl, turning it once to coat the top. Cover with plastic wrap and let rise in a warm spot until doubled in volume, about 1 hour.

4. Oil a large baking sheet. Place the dough on a lightly floured surface and flatten it with your hands to eliminate the air bubbles. Scatter the meat and cheese over the surface. Fold the dough over to enclose the ingredients. Flatten the dough and fold it over several times, until the meat and cheese are evenly distributed.

5. Cut the dough in half. Roll each piece between your palms into a 24-inch rope. Loosely twist the two ropes together, then form them into a circle on the baking sheet. Pinch the ends together to seal them. Cover with oiled plastic wrap and let rise until doubled, about 1 hour.

6. Preheat the oven to 400°F.

7. Bake the loaf for 30 minutes, or until golden brown. Slide the bread onto a wire rack to cool slightly. Serve warm.

TIP: Keep a separate board for kneading bread and pasta dough. If the board has been used for cutting garlic or onions, the odor can be transferred to the dough and ruin its flavor.

Savory Easter Pie

PIZZA RUSTICA

Leona Ancona Cantone, a friend from my high school days, comes from a family of great cooks, and she inherited their passion for good food. Despite her busy life and running a thriving business, Leona cooks for her friends and family. She finds cooking relaxing, a pleasant change from work, and she relies on recipes that she learned from her mother and aunt.

Leona says that according to her family, it wouldn't be Easter without her mom's pizza rustica, so she makes a double batch of this double-crusted, savory pie and bakes it in one roasting pan or two smaller springform pans.

Pizza rustica is sometimes called pizza chiena, *a dialect term meaning stuffed or full pie. Full it is, brimming with sausages, cheeses, and salumi. Leona's recipe also contains sautéed onions, a delicious addition. She uses store-bought pizza dough for her crust, though I give a recipe for a homemade version flavored with black pepper.*

Traditionally, pizza rustica is made on Good Friday to be eaten on Easter Sunday, or to be taken on the traditional Easter Monday picnic.

SERVES 10 TO 12

DOUGH

1 package (2½ teaspoons) active dry yeast
2 tablespoons olive oil
3 to 4 cups unbleached all-purpose flour

1 teaspoon salt
½ teaspoon freshly ground black pepper

FILLING

2 tablespoons olive oil, plus more for brushing
2 large onions, thinly sliced
8 ounces sweet Italian sausage meat
3 large eggs
One 32-ounce container whole-milk or part-skim ricotta
¼ cup freshly grated pecorino romano or Parmigiano-Reggiano

¼ cup chopped flat-leaf parsley
8 ounces mozzarella, sliced or chopped
4 ounces sliced Swiss cheese, cut into narrow strips
8 ounces cooked ham, cut into narrow strips
4 ounces sliced Genoa salami, cut into narrow strips
3 ounces sliced pepperoni, cut into narrow strips

1. To make the dough, sprinkle the yeast over 1½ cups warm (100° to 110°F) water in a large bowl. Let stand until the yeast is creamy. Stir to dissolve. Stir in the oil. Add 3½ cups of the flour and the salt and pepper; stir until a dough forms.

2. Turn the dough out onto a lightly floured surface and knead, adding more flour as needed, until smooth and no longer sticky. Shape the dough into a ball. Place it in a large oiled bowl, turning once to coat. Cover with plastic wrap and let rise in a warm place for 1 to 1½ hours, until doubled in size.

3. Preheat the oven to 375°F.

4. To make the filling, combine the olive oil and onions in a large skillet and cook over medium heat, stirring, until the onions are tender and golden, about 10 minutes. Remove the onions from the pan.

5. Add the sausage meat to the pan and cook until it is no longer pink. Transfer the meat to a colander to drain.

6. In a large bowl, beat the eggs until blended. Add the ricotta, grated cheese, and parsley and stir well. Stir in the mozzarella and Swiss cheeses, the onions, sausage, and sliced meats.

7. Turn the dough out onto a lightly floured surface and press it down to eliminate air bubbles. Cut the dough into 2 pieces, one about three times as large as the other.

8. Roll out the larger piece of dough to a 16-inch circle. Transfer the dough to a 9-inch springform pan, pressing it smoothly against the bottom and up the sides. Scrape the filling into the pan.

9. Roll out the remaining piece of dough to a 9-inch circle. Place it over the filling. Pinch the edges of the top and bottom layers of dough together to seal. With a small knife, make several small slits in the top of the dough to allow steam to escape. Brush the dough with olive oil.

10. Bake the pie in the center of the oven for 60 to 75 minutes, or until a toothpick or cake tester inserted in the center comes out clean. Cool the pie on a wire rack for 10 minutes. Remove the sides of the pan and let cool completely.

WINE MATCH: Copertino Riserva, Cantina Sociale Copertino

Easter Pie from Abruzzo

FIADONE

Savory pies rich with eggs and cheese became popular as a way to use up all of the ingredients that were not eaten during the long Lenten fast. This Easter cheese pie from Abruzzo is made with a rich egg dough. Serve it as an appetizer with a glass of wine or for lunch with a green salad. There are many variations. Some cooks use a sweet pie dough for this recipe. It is often shaped like a calzone or into a rectangle rather than a round pie.

SERVES 10 TO 12

DOUGH

2 cups unbleached all-purpose flour

1 teaspoon baking powder

½ teaspoon salt

2 large eggs

2 tablespoons olive oil

FILLING

One 16-ounce container ricotta

½ cup freshly grated pecorino romano

¼ cup chopped flat-leaf parsley

Pinch of freshly grated nutmeg

Freshly ground black pepper

1 egg yolk, beaten with 1 tablespoon water, for egg wash

1. To make the dough, stir together the flour, baking powder, and salt in a large bowl. Beat the eggs and olive oil in a small bowl. With a wooden spoon, stir the eggs into the dry ingredients. Add 2 tablespoons water, more if needed, and stir until the dough begins to come together.

2. Turn the dough out onto a floured surface and knead until smooth and well blended, about 2 minutes. Divide the dough into 2 pieces and shape each one into a disc. Wrap in plastic and let rest at room temperature for 30 minutes.

3. To make the filling, place the cheeses in a large bowl. Add the remaining ingredients, mixing well with a rubber spatula.

4. Preheat the oven to 350°F. Grease and flour a large baking sheet or pizza pan.

5. Lightly flour a board or countertop. With a rolling pin, roll out one piece of dough to an 11-inch circle, turning it from time to time and flouring it if it seems sticky. Place the circle of dough on the prepared pan. Spread the filling over the dough, leaving a ½-inch border.

6. Roll out the remaining piece of dough the same as the first. Center the dough over the filling. With your fingertips, firmly press the edges of the dough together to seal them. Fold the edge over and press it again. Brush the top of the pie with the egg wash. With a small sharp knife, cut 6 slits in the top.

7. Bake the *fiadone* for 30 minutes. Turn off the oven and leave the pie inside for 10 minutes, then slide the pie onto a rack to cool. Serve warm or at room temperature, cut into thin slices.

WINE MATCH: Montepulciano d'Abruzzo, Illuminati

San Vito's Focaccia

FOCACCIA DI SAN VITO

According to legend, San Vito, or Saint Vitus, grew up in Mazara del Vallo in Sicily in the fourth century. When his family objected to his devotion to Christianity, he left home and became famous as a holy man and healer. The Emperor Diocletian in Rome sent for him to cure his epileptic son. Although the son was cured, the emperor, jealous of the holy man's powers, ordered him to be tortured and killed. As a martyr, he became venerated throughout Europe as the patron saint of epileptics and others who suffer from similar diseases.

June 15 is recognized as San Vito's Feast Day in Italy, and celebrations in his honor are held throughout the month. In Mazara, a silver statue of the saint is carried in a dawn procession to the shore to commemorate his departure in a boat guided by an angel.

The nuns of the Convent of San Vito in Palermo were known for the delicious savory pies they made and sold to the public. This version, a double-crusted pizza with a filling of anchovies, onions, tomatoes, and cheese, is one of several that they made.

SERVES 8

DOUGH

1 envelope (2½ teaspoons) active dry yeast

2 tablespoons olive oil

2 large eggs, beaten

About 3½ cups unbleached all-purpose flour

1 tablespoon sugar

1 teaspoon salt

FILLING

¼ cup olive oil

2 medium onions, chopped

2 or 3 fresh tomatoes, chopped, or 2½ cups canned Italian peeled tomatoes, drained and chopped

½ teaspoon dried oregano

Salt and freshly ground black pepper

One 2-ounce tin anchovies, drained and chopped

¼ cup raisins

2 tablespoons pine nuts

4 ounces caciocavallo or provolone, thinly sliced

1 tablespoon olive oil

2 tablespoons dry bread crumbs

1. To make the dough, sprinkle the yeast over 1 cup warm (100° to 110°F) water in a large bowl. Let stand until the yeast is creamy.

2. Stir to dissolve the yeast, then stir in the olive oil and eggs. Add 3 cups flour, the sugar, and salt. Stir until a soft dough forms.

3. Turn the dough out onto a lightly floured surface and knead until smooth and elastic, about 10 minutes. Add the additional flour a little at a time if the dough feels sticky (but remember that a soft moist dough is better than a firm dry dough). Shape the dough into a ball.

4. Oil a large bowl and add the dough, turning it once to oil the top. Cover and let rise in a warm place for 1 to 1½ hours, until doubled in size.

5. While the dough is rising, make the filling. In a large skillet, combine the oil and onions and cook over medium heat until the onions are soft and translucent, about 7 minutes. Stir in the tomatoes, oregano, and salt and pepper to taste. Cook 10 minutes, or until the liquid is evaporated. Stir in the anchovies. Let cool.

6. Place a rack in the center of the oven and preheat the oven to 400°F. Oil a 12-inch pizza pan.

7. Turn the dough out onto a floured surface and divide it in half. Roll one piece into a 12-inch circle. Center the dough on the prepared pan. Spread the onion mixture over the dough, leaving a ½-inch border all around. Sprinkle with the raisins and pine nuts. Arrange the cheese slices on top.

8. Roll out the remaining dough, to a 12-inch circle. Drape it loosely over the rolling pin and center it over the filling. Fold the edge of the bottom dough over the top and pinch the edges together to seal. Brush the top with the oil. With a small knife, make several slits in the surface. Sprinkle with the bread crumbs.

9. Bake for 35 to 40 minutes, or until golden brown. Slide the pizza onto a rack to cool. Serve warm or at room temperature, cut into wedges.

TIP: If you are concerned about the freshness of your yeast, try proofing it. Mix the yeast with the warm water as described above, adding ½ teaspoon sugar. If the yeast is still usable, it will form bubbles. If nothing happens, the yeast is dead, and you need to start over with fresh yeast.

WINE MATCH: Rosso del Soprano, Palari

Grandma's Easter Egg Wreath

CIAMBELLA DI PASQUA ALLA NONNA

A large braided wreath of this beautiful sweet bread always graced my grandmother's Easter table. We ate the bread fresh or toasted, for breakfast or with tea. Grandma flavored the bread with orange zest, but lemon is good too. My Aunt Anna reminded me that my grandmother used fresh homemade lard, but I use butter instead.

Decorating the eggs with food coloring is optional. If you like, the unbaked loaves can be sprinkled with colored candy shot just before baking.

MAKES 2 RING-SHAPED LOAVES

DOUGH

1 envelope (2½ teaspoons) active dry yeast

3 large eggs, at room temperature

⅔ cup sugar

8 tablespoons (1 stick) unsalted butter, melted and cooled

½ cup warm (100° to 110°F) milk

2 teaspoons vanilla extract

1 tablespoon grated orange zest

5 to 5½ cups unbleached all-purpose flour

1 teaspoon salt

6 whole (uncracked) eggs, colored if desired

1 egg yolk beaten with 1 tablespoon water, for egg wash

Colored candy sprinkles, optional

1. To make the dough, in a small cup, sprinkle the yeast over ½ cup warm (100° to 110°F) water. Let stand until creamy, about 5 minutes. Stir until dissolved.

2. In a large bowl, beat the eggs until blended. Beat in the sugar. Stir in the butter, milk, vanilla, and orange zest. Stir in the yeast mixture. Add 5 cups of the flour and the salt. Stir until a soft dough forms. Gradually add just enough of the remaining flour to make a smooth, slightly sticky dough.

3. Transfer the dough to a lightly floured surface and knead it for a minute or so, until it is very smooth. Shape the dough into a ball. Place it in a large buttered bowl. Cover with plastic wrap and let rise in a warm place until doubled in bulk, about 1½ hours.

4. Butter two baking sheets. Punch down the dough and cut it into 4 pieces. Roll out one piece under your palms into a rope about 20 inches long. Repeat with another piece of dough. Lay the ropes side by side and loosely braid them together. Lift the

braid onto the prepared baking sheet and bring the ends together to form a ring. Pinch the ends to seal. Place 3 eggs at intervals around the wreath, tucking them in between the ropes of the dough.

5. Repeat with the remaining dough and eggs. Cover the wreaths with plastic wrap and let rise for about 45 minutes, or until doubled in size.

6. Preheat the oven to 350°F.

7. Brush the yolk mixture over the wreaths. Scatter the candy sprinkles on top, if using. Bake them for about 30 minutes, or until golden brown, reversing the position of the pans in the oven halfway through the baking time. Transfer the bread to racks to cool completely.

TIP: A long rasp-type grater is perfect for removing orange or lemon zest, the colored part of the skin, without any of the bitter white pith.

Easter Baby Dolls

PUPI CON L'UOVA

In many southern Italian families, sweet breads are traditional gifts for children at Easter time. The breads are shaped into different figures, though little boys are likely to receive birds or chickens, which represent masculinity, while the girls are given baby dolls. Other familiar shapes are wreaths, baskets, hearts, and horses, which can be quite imaginative. Each figure is decorated with at least one whole egg in its shell, held in place with crossed strips of dough.

In Puglia, tradition calls for tinting the eggs red either with cochineal, a coloring extract made from insects, or a dye made from pine bark. Superstitious people considered red a powerful color that could destroy evil forces. In addition, the cakes had to be decorated with an uneven number of eggs, because uneven numbers were believed to have favorable or conciliatory influences. In some areas, an engaged girl traditionally made a large bread called la scarcella decorated with twenty-one eggs that she would present to her betrothed on Easter Sunday.

Many Italian-American families I have spoken to get creative with shaping the dough into Easter bunnies and teddy bears. Make these with or give them to your favorite children, and you will have lots of fun.

The texture of this bread is like a firm dry cake or scone.

MAKES 4

4 cups unbleached all-purpose flour

⅔ cup sugar

1 tablespoon baking powder

1 teaspoon salt

3 large eggs, at room temperature

2 teaspoons vanilla extract

1 teaspoon grated lemon zest

6 tablespoons (¾ stick) unsalted butter, melted and cooled

About ⅔ cup milk

4 whole (uncracked) eggs, colored if desired, at room temperature

Raisins and pine nuts or slivered almonds for garnish

1 egg beaten with 1 tablespoon water, for egg wash

1 tablespoon colored candy sprinkles, optional

1. In a large bowl, stir together the flour, sugar, baking powder, and salt.

2. In a medium bowl, beat together the eggs, vanilla, and lemon zest. With a wooden spoon, stir the mixture into the dry ingredients, along with the butter. Gradually stir

in just enough of the milk to form a dough. Remove the dough from the bowl and shape it into a ball. Wrap in plastic wrap for 1 hour and refrigerate.

3. Preheat the oven to 350°F. Butter and flour two large baking sheets.

4. Transfer to a work surface and divide it into 4 pieces. Work with one piece of the dough at a time. To make a doll, pull off a portion of dough the size of an egg and set it aside. Shape the remainder into 3 balls, each ball slightly smaller than the next. Arrange the balls next to one another on the prepared baking sheet, as if you were making a snowman, and flatten each one slightly. Press a whole egg (in its shell) into the bottom, or apron section, of the doll. Pinch off a piece of the reserved dough, divide it in half, and form it into 2 thin ropes. Crisscross the ropes over the egg, pressing the ends against the dough. Use the remaining dough to make arms and a mouth. Use raisins for the eyes and pine nuts or almonds for hair.

5. To make a bird, take a piece of the dough and pull off an egg-size portion; set aside. Divide the remainder into two parts, one two times as large as the other. Shape the larger portion into a thick rope about 8 inches long. Curve it into an open S shape and place it in the baking sheet, leaning to the right, to form the "body"—imagination required here! Pinch the ends slightly to form the beak and tail. Shape the smaller piece of dough into a 3-inch rope. Bend it in half to form a V shape, and press these "wings" into the back of the body. Press a whole egg (in its shell) into the belly of the bird. Pinch off a piece of the reserved dough, divide it in half, and form it into 2 thin ropes. Crisscross the ropes over the egg, pressing the ends against the dough. Insert a raisin for the eye and a pine nut for the beak.

6. Repeat with the remaining portions of dough. Brush the egg wash over the figures. Decorate with colored sprinkles, if desired.

7. Bake for 30 minutes, or until nicely brown. Slide onto wire racks to cool.

Ligurian Easter Tart

TORTA PASQUALINA

Ligurians love to debate about the proper way to make a torta pasqualina. *Some make layers of the filling, alternating it with paper-thin sheets of pastry. (Of course, the number of layers is a matter of debate as well, some claiming that twenty-four are sufficient, while others go for thirty-three, representing Jesus' age at his death.) Some cooks make the torta with a mixture of greens. Swiss chard is the most common, but spinach, arugula, and beet greens, as well as artichokes, are all typical. In Liguria, a slightly sour fresh cheese known as* prescinsceua *or* quagliata *is used in place of ricotta.*

This torta is a modern version, made with just two layers of dough, forming the top and bottom crusts. Although it was originally made only at Easter time, it is now so popular that you can find it in restaurants and bakeries in Liguria all year round.

SERVES 8 TO 10

DOUGH

2½ cups unbleached all-purpose flour
½ teaspoon salt

¼ cup olive oil

FILLING

1 pound Swiss chard, washed and trimmed
1 pound spinach, washed and trimmed
Salt
1 tablespoon unsalted butter
1 medium onion, chopped
Pinch of ground cloves
6 large eggs
1 cup ricotta

½ cup plus 1 tablespoon freshly grated
    Parmigiano-Reggiano
1 tablespoon chopped freshly marjoram or
    ½ teaspoon dried
⅛ teaspoon freshly grated nutmeg
Freshly ground black pepper
Olive oil

1. To make the dough, combine the flour and salt in a large bowl. Stir in the oil and ½ cup water, or just enough to make a smooth, nonsticky dough. Knead very briefly. Divide the dough into 2 pieces, one three times the other, and shape each into a ball. Wrap the dough in plastic wrap and let rest for at least 30 minutes at room temperature.

2. To make the filling, combine the Swiss chard and ½ cup water in a large pot. Cover and cook over medium heat until tender and wilted, about 10 minutes. Add the spinach and salt to taste. Cook for 5 minutes, or until the spinach is tender. Drain the greens and let cool.

3. Wrap the greens in a kitchen towel or a piece of cheesecloth and squeeze to extract the moisture. Place the greens on a cutting board and chop fine.

4. In a small saucepan, melt the butter. Add the onion and cloves. Cover and cook over medium heat until the onion is tender, about 7 minutes. Remove from the heat.

5. In a large bowl, beat 2 of the eggs until blended. Add the greens, onion, ricotta, ½ cup of the Parmigiano-Reggiano, the marjoram, nutmeg, and salt and pepper to taste. Mix well with a wooden spoon. Set aside.

6. Set an oven rack in the center of the oven and preheat the oven to 375°F. Oil a 9-inch springform pan.

7. On a floured surface, roll out the larger piece of dough to a 16-inch circle. Center the dough in the pan and press it against the bottom and up the sides. Scrape the filling into the dough.

8. With the back of a spoon, make four evenly spaced indentations in the filling. Break an egg into a small cup, then carefully slide the egg into one of the indentations. Repeat with the remaining eggs. Sprinkle with the remaining 1 tablespoon Parmigiano.

9. Roll out the smaller piece of dough and center it on top of the filling. Trim the edges of the dough to about 1 inch. Fold the bottom over the top, pinch the edges together, and press down firmly around the side of the pan to seal. Brush the top of the dough with olive oil. With a small sharp knife, cut several slits in the top.

10. Bake the torta for 45 minutes, or until browned. Cool on a wire rack 10 minutes, then remove the sides of the pan. Serve hot or at room temperature.

TIP: Bread dough can be kneaded by hand or in a food processor, heavy-duty mixer, or bread machine. But always finish by kneading the dough for a minute or so by hand to be sure that it has the right consistency.

When kneading dough in a food processor, remember that the heat of the motor can cause the dough to get too warm and then rise too quickly. Process the dough only as long as is needed to develop the elasticity. Knead in any raisins and nuts by hand, after removing the dough from the machine.

WINE MATCH: Pigato, Colle dei Bardellini

Soups

MINESTRE E ZUPPE

Italian soups can be as humble as a few vegetables simmered together in water with a handful of rice or broken pasta, or as complex as a rich broth made from capon or mixed meats with tiny handmade tortellini. They can be thick or thin, clear or creamy, chunky or smooth. Soups have always been a mainstay of Italian cooks and they are eaten by everyone, young and old, rich and poor, on special occasions or for everyday meals.

Legume-based soups are popular from the Veneto to Sicily, though different kinds of beans, peas, or lentils are favored in each area. The Venetian versions are smooth and creamy, made with cranberry or borlotti beans. The Tuscans favor cannellini beans or chickpeas, while the Sicilians lean toward lentils. Soups tend to be chunky with vegetables in southern Italy, though the Neapolitans like to add leafy greens such as escarole.

One of the interesting discoveries I made in researching this book was the many chicken-soup-and-egg variations served for holidays. Starting with chicken broth as a base, there are numerous ways to vary the soup with eggs, from egg drops and grated cheese to fried bread slices soaked in eggs to a cheese omelet to a surprising and very special souffléd egg-and-cheese topping.

For holidays and other celebrations, Italians serve soup as a first course instead of pasta or risotto. At other times, soup may be served as the evening meal.

Chicken Soup and Broth

ZUPPA DI POLLO

Serve this simple chicken soup on its own or use it as the broth for risotto or the broth-based soups that follow. The flavor will be even better if you use an older chicken, called a fowl or stewing hen. Sometimes I add a couple of turkey wings to the broth, but don't use too much, or the flavor will be overwhelming.

SERVES 6 TO 8 (MAKES ABOUT 3 QUARTS BROTH)

1 chicken (about 3½ pounds)

1 pound chicken backs and wings (or turkey parts)

2 medium carrots, plus 2 more if making soup

2 celery ribs, plus 2 more if making soup

2 onions, peeled, plus 1 more if making soup

6 sprigs flat-leaf parsley

6 peppercorns

Salt

1. Remove the liver and reserve for another use. Rinse the chicken and chicken parts well. Place in a 6-quart pot. Add 4 quarts cold water. Bring to a simmer over medium heat. Lower the heat and cook for 30 to 60 minutes. Skim off the foam and any fat that rises to the surface.

2. Add the vegetables, herbs, peppercorns, and a little salt. Cook for 2 hours. Let cool slightly.

3. Strain the broth. Remove the chicken from the bones, discarding the skin and bones. If you are serving the broth as soup, return it to the rinsed-out pot and add the chicken. Add sliced fresh carrots, celery, and onion and simmer until tender. If you only need the broth, reserve the chicken meat for salad or for stuffed pasta.

4. Let the soup or broth cool slightly, then cover and refrigerate for up to 3 days. When ready to proceed, scrape the fat off the surface. The soup or broth can be frozen for up to 3 months.

MEAT BROTH: Add 2 pounds meaty beef or veal bones along with the chicken in step 1. Add more water if needed, so that the ingredients are completely covered. In step 3, add 1 large fresh tomato, chopped, or 1 cup canned Italian peeled tomatoes with their liquid, and 1 garlic clove. Cook as above for 3 hours.

Roman Easter Soup

BRODETTO PASQUALE ALLA ROMANA

Though traditional in Rome, versions of this soup can be found in many parts of Italy, under many different names. One friend told me that in his family it was called "sick soup," because his mother always served the soothing, nutritious restorative to family members who were under the weather.

Marjoram is a fragrant herb with a slightly lemony flavor. If you can't find it fresh, substitute parsley, oregano, or even thyme. Don't use a dried herb here—its flavor would overwhelm the soup.

SERVES 6

8 cups chicken or meat broth (page 42)
4 large egg yolks
½ cup freshly grated Parmigiano-Reggiano
1 tablespoon fresh lemon juice, or more to taste

Salt and freshly ground black pepper
2 teaspoons chopped marjoram or flat-leaf
  parsley
6 to 12 slices Italian bread, toasted

1. In a medium pot, heat the broth just to a simmer.

2. In a small bowl, beat the egg yolks, cheese, and lemon juice until blended. Gradually beat in 1 cup of the hot broth. Slowly pour the mixture into the remaining broth. Reheat gently. Taste for seasoning, adding salt and pepper and more lemon juice if needed. Stir in the herbs.

3. To serve, place 1 or 2 slices of the bread in each serving dish. Spoon on the soup.

VARIATION: In my home, we always had "little rag soup," *stracciatella*. Omit the lemon juice and herbs, and use 3 whole eggs. After bringing the broth to a simmer, add 4 ounces pastina or other tiny pasta and cook until tender. Whisk the eggs with the cheese, then slowly stir the mixture into the hot broth to form "rags."

Soup in a Sack

MINESTRA NEL SACCHETTO

I found versions of this soup under various names from several different regions of Italy, including Abruzzo, the Marches, and Emilia-Romagna. Rather than pasta or rice, tiny cubes of a baked omelet are added to the broth. The omelet is like a delicious sponge that soaks up the flavors of the soup.

At one time, the omelet mixture, which could be made with bread crumbs or semolina in place of the flour, was wrapped in a clean linen or cotton sack and poached in the simmering broth instead of baked.

My friend Nancy Weber told me that when her mother made this soup for holidays, family members would eat so much of it they would not be able to eat the rest of the meal. Nancy's mother added finely chopped prosciutto to the egg mixture.

SERVES 8

6 large eggs
¼ cup milk
¼ cup all-purpose flour
¼ cup freshly grated Parmigiano-Reggiano,
  plus more for serving

1 tablespoon finely chopped flat-leaf parsley
Pinch of freshly grated nutmeg
12 cups chicken or meat broth, preferably
  homemade (see page 42)

1. Preheat the oven to 350°F. Butter a 9-inch square baking dish.

2. In a large bowl, beat the eggs and milk. Whisk in the flour until smooth. Stir in the cheese, parsley, and nutmeg.

3. Pour the batter into the prepared pan. Bake for 15 to 18 minutes or until a knife inserted in the center comes out clean. Cool slightly. (The omelet can be made ahead; cover and refrigerate.)

4. When ready to serve, cut the omelet into ½-inch cubes. Heat the broth to a simmer, then turn off the heat. Put the cubes into the broth and let stand for 5 minutes.

5. Serve with freshly grated Parmigiano-Reggiano.

Bread Soup

Susan Sarao Westmoreland's grandmother used to make chicken soup with a bread, egg, and cheese topping, something like a savory French toast. Her grandmother cut the finished bread into bite-size pieces before adding them to the soup, but I like to use whole bread slices. Now Susan makes this comforting soup for her little boy, Lucio.

SERVES 6

4 large eggs
¼ cup freshly grated pecorino romano or
   Parmigiano-Reggiano, plus more for serving
Freshly ground black pepper

Six ½-inch-thick slices Italian bread
1 tablespoon unsalted butter
1 tablespoon olive oil
8 cups hot chicken broth

1. With a fork, beat the eggs with the cheese and pepper to taste in a shallow dish until well blended. Soak the bread slices in the egg mixture, turning to coat both sides.

2. In a large skillet, heat the butter and oil over medium heat. Drop a bit of egg in the skillet to see if it is hot enough: if it sizzles, add the bread slices. Cook the bread until golden brown, turning once, about 4 minutes per side.

3. Meanwhile, heat the chicken broth. Place a bread slice in each serving bowl. Carefully spoon on the broth. Sprinkle with more cheese and serve.

Souffléd Chicken Soup

SCIUSCEDDU OR SOFFIELLO

When Rose Di Dio told me about this soup, I could not imagine what it would be like. I had never heard of a cheese soufflé baked on top of soup. But once I tried it, I thought it was spectacular.

Rose makes this soup for special occasions all year round. She learned the recipe from her husband's mother, who came from Messina, in Sicily. Rose says that her mother-in-law would save the chicken for another use and put little veal meatballs in the strained broth to simmer, but she prefers to use the chicken meat. Because the cheese soufflé forms a soft airy pillow on top, the dish is called soffiello in Italian, or sciusceddu in Sicilian dialect, meaning puffy or airy. It is so substantial, especially when made with meatballs, sciusceddu is served as a main dish in Sicily.

You will need an ovenproof serving bowl or pot large enough to hold both the soup and the soufflé topping as it bakes. I use a bright red 6-quart enameled pot. Choose one that is not too shallow, or the hot soup may spill out when you lift it from the oven. Remember, too, that it will be quite heavy.

SERVES 8 TO 10

1 recipe Chicken Soup (page 42)
5 large eggs, separated
One 16-ounce container ricotta
1 cup freshly grated pecorino romano or
   Parmigiano-Reggiano

2 tablespoons finely chopped flat-leaf parsley
Freshly ground black pepper

1. Preheat the oven to 350°F.

2. Bring the soup to a simmer over low heat in a 6-quart pot.

3. Meanwhile, in a large bowl, whisk the egg yolks until blended. Stir in the ricotta, grated cheese, parsley, and pepper to taste.

4. In a large bowl, beat the egg whites until soft peaks form. With a rubber spatula, gently fold the egg whites into the cheese mixture. Scrape the cheese mixture onto the soup. Very carefully transfer the pot to the oven. Bake for 25 minutes, or until the soufflé is puffed and golden brown. (The soufflé will sink slightly when removed from the oven.)

5. To serve, cut through the soufflé with a large spoon. Place portions of the soufflé in the serving bowls and spoon the soup around it. Serve hot.

Chicken Soup with Escarole and Little Meatballs

ZUPPA DI POLLO CON SCAROLA E POLPETTINI

We always preferred pasta to soup at our house, except when the soup in question was this one. My mother usually made it for Christmas, but we welcomed it at any time of the year. Children especially love the little meatballs, and may not even notice they are eating their greens along with them. Some people call this soup minestra maritata, *and it does seem like a simplified version of the soup on page 50.*

SERVES 8

½ small head escarole (about 8 ounces)
8 cups chicken broth or mixed meat and
  chicken broth

2 large carrots, chopped

MEATBALLS
8 ounces ground veal or beef
1 large egg
¼ cup very finely minced onion
½ cup dry bread crumbs

½ cup freshly grated Parmigiano-Reggiano
½ teaspoon salt
Freshly ground black pepper to taste
Freshly grated Parmigiano-Reggiano for serving

1. Trim the escarole and discard any bruised leaves. Cut off the base. Separate the leaves and wash well in cool water, paying special attention to the center of the leaves, where soil collects. Stack the leaves and cut them into bite-size pieces. You should have about 2 cups.

2. In a large pot, combine the escarole, broth, and carrots. Bring to a simmer and cook until the escarole is almost tender, about 30 minutes.

3. Meanwhile, combine the meatball ingredients. Shape the mixture into tiny balls, less than 1 inch in diameter.

4. When the escarole is cooked, drop the meatballs into the soup. Return the soup to a simmer and cook over low heat until the meatballs are cooked through, about 20 minutes. Serve hot, with grated Parmesan.

Good Luck Lentil Soup

MINESTRA DI BUONA FORTUNA

Lentil soup is traditional for New Year's Day, a harbinger of good things to come throughout the New Year. I often have a crowd over for a buffet lunch and serve big bowls of this warming soup, followed by Roast Pork Porchetta Style (page 170). For a hearty one-dish meal, you can add cooked rice or pasta to the soup just before serving.

SERVES 8

2 tablespoons olive oil

2 ounces pancetta, chopped

1 medium onion, chopped

1 garlic clove, finely chopped

1 small dried peperoncino, crumbled, or a pinch of crushed red pepper

1 pound lentils, picked over and rinsed

1 small red bell pepper, chopped

½ cup dried tomatoes, cut into narrow strips

Salt

Extra virgin olive oil

1. In a large pot, combine the oil, pancetta, onion, garlic, and peperoncino and cook over medium heat until the onion is wilted and golden.

2. Add the lentils, then stir in the pepper and tomatoes. Add 6 cups water. Bring to a simmer over medium heat. Lower the heat and simmer, stirring occasionally, for about 45 minutes, until the lentils are almost tender.

3. Add salt to taste and simmer until the lentils are cooked.

4. Serve hot or at room temperature, with a drizzle of extra virgin olive oil.

TIP: Pancetta is unsmoked Italian bacon. Rolled into a sausage shape, pancetta is used to flavor bean dishes or sauces. When buying, have it sliced into ¼-inch-thick pieces and dice it before cooking.

Pancetta freezes well. I always buy a little more than I need and wrap 2-ounce portions in aluminum foil so I have it on hand whenever I need it. It is easier to chop when it is still partly frozen and firm.

Married Soup

MINESTRA MARITATA

A lot of people assume that this soup got its name because it was served at wedding banquets, but in fact "married soup" refers to the wedded bliss of the flavors of the various meats and vegetables.

I had the best version of minestra maritata *at Ciro a Santa Brigida, one of my favorite restaurants in Naples. When I ordered it, the waiter, who realized we were Americans, was delighted that we knew about it, and proudly told me how their chef prepared it from an old family recipe. The soup was hearty and rich and though it is often served today as the first course of a Christmas Day dinner, he said that at one time poor people would have eaten it as their entire meal. It would have been made from wild greens and the most inexpensive cuts of pork, like ears and feet. This version is based on a recipe from* La Cucina Napoletana, *the definitive book on Neapolitan cooking by Jeanne Carola Francesconi.*

Minestra maritata has a long history. Apicius, the famous Roman gourmand who wrote the earliest known cookbook, described a soup called piselli maritati, *a combination of peas and various meats.*

You can substitute other greens or meats, if necessary. Chard, chicory, kale, or regular cabbage are all good, and you can use Genoa or other Italian salami in place of the soppressata, or a ham bone for the prosciutto bone. For best flavor, make the soup a day before serving it. You will need two large pots (about 8-quart capacity) for this recipe.

SERVES 10 TO 12

1 pound meaty pork ribs
   (country-style pork ribs)
1 prosciutto bone, optional
2 medium carrots
2 celery ribs with leaves
1 medium onion
1 pound Italian-style pork sausages
4 ounces prosciutto, in one thick slice
One 4-ounce chunk of soppressata
One piece of Parmigiano-Reggiano rind,
   about 2 × 3 inches, optional

1 small dried peperoncino, crumbled, or a pinch
   of crushed red pepper
1½ pounds (1 small head) escarole, trimmed
1 pound (1 medium bunch) broccoli rabe,
   trimmed
1 pound (about ½ small head) savoy cabbage,
   cut into strips
8 ounces broccoli, cut into florets (about 2 cups)
Freshly grated Parmigiano-Reggiano

1. In a large pot, bring 5 quarts water to a boil. Add the pork ribs, prosciutto bone, if using, carrots, celery, and onion. Lower the heat to a simmer and cook for 30 minutes.

2. Skim off the foam that has risen to the surface of the broth. Add the sausages, prosciutto, soppressata, Parmigiano rind, if using, and peperoncino. Simmer for 2 hours.

3. Meanwhile, bring a large pot of water to a boil. Add half the greens. Bring to a simmer and cook for 10 minutes. Remove the greens with a slotted spoon and place them in a colander set over a large bowl to drain. Cook the remaining greens the same way and drain well. Let cool. Chop the greens into bite-size pieces.

4. Remove the meats and sausage from the broth and let the broth cool slightly. Discard the bones and cut the meats and sausage into bite-size pieces.

5. Skim the fat from the broth. Strain the broth into a large clean pot. Return the meats to the broth. Add the greens. Return to the simmer and cook for 30 minutes.

6. Serve with grated Parmigiano-Reggiano.

TIP: After you have scraped off every usable bit, save the rind of Parmigiano-Reggiano to add flavor to soups.

Sausage, Fava Bean, and Cabbage Soup

FAVATA

In Sardinia, this hearty soup, really a one-dish meal, is served for Martedì Grasso, *Fat Tuesday, the final Tuesday of* Carnevale. *It is typically made with pig's feet and skin, but I use meaty baby back ribs and pork sausages.*

Dried fava beans can have thick skins, so always buy them with the skins removed. See Sources, page 296, for stores that sell skinless favas.

SERVES 6

1 pound baby back pork ribs, trimmed and cut into individual ribs
12 ounces Italian-style pork sausage
12 cups cold water
8 ounces dried peeled fava beans
½ cup slivered dried tomatoes or 1 fresh tomato, peeled, seeded, and chopped

1 medium onion, finely chopped
1 small tender celery rib, chopped
1 small carrot, chopped
1 garlic clove, chopped
4 cups shredded cabbage
Salt and freshly ground black pepper
6 slices Italian bread, toasted

1. In a large pot, combine the meats with cold water to cover by 1 inch. Bring to a simmer and cook until foam rises to the surface. Drain the meat. Return it to the rinsed pot and add the 12 cups cold water. Bring to a simmer.

2. Add the fava beans, tomatoes, onion, celery, carrot, and garlic. Return to the simmer and cook over low heat for 1 hour.

3. Add the cabbage to the pot, along with salt and pepper to taste. Cook for 1 hour more, stirring occasionally. Add a little more water if the soup becomes too thick.

4. Remove the pork ribs and sausage from the pot. Cut the meat into bite-size pieces, discarding the rib bones. Skim the fat from the surface of the soup. Return the meats to the pot.

5. To serve, reheat the soup gently. Taste for seasoning. Place a slice of toasted bread in each bowl and pour on the soup.

The Feast of Saint Joseph

The Feast of Saint Joseph, on March 19, is a joyful holiday. It not only celebrates the life of a beloved saint, the patron of home and family, but also marks the beginning of spring. In Sicily, the almond trees bloom and the pale green shoots of the new wheat are thriving after the winter rains.

Throughout Italy, but especially in the south, there are feasts marking this special day. Many special foods are associated with it and many, though not all, are fried. In southern Italy, Saint Joseph is known as San Giuseppe Frittelaro, Saint Joseph the fryer.

When I visited Sicily, Anna Tasca Lanza, whose family owns the Regaleali Winery, showed us how Saint Joseph's Day was celebrated in the nearby towns. One common element is the Saint Joseph's tables. Families who want the saint to intercede for them or to show their appreciation for blessings received, such as the recovery of the health of a loved one or good fortune, prepare an elaborate buffet. The dining table is covered with the finest cloth, flowers, and candles, and is presided over by a picture or statue of Saint Joseph.

As many as one hundred dishes are prepared, from fried artichokes to rice balls, asparagus, little fish, and frittatas to gorgeous desserts like cream-filled cakes that resemble peaches, cassata, cannoli, and, always, *sfinci*, fried cream puffs stuffed with ricotta or pastry cream. Everything is meatless since the feast falls during Lent. Special long loaves of bread, called the *bastone di San Giuseppe*, Saint Joseph's staff, are placed on the table, along with bunches of fennel and oranges, which symbolize spring. Pitchers hold layers of wine and water separated by a thin layer of olive oil. Dried legumes are traditional at this time of year, especially fava beans. There are always a number of soups and stews made with them, the idea being to use up the remains of the last year's harvest. Seeds and beans also represent the promise of spring when they begin to sprout.

The townspeople go from house to house to view the displays, but no one is allowed to taste the food until it has been blessed by the priest and visited by the *virgineddi*, a young boy and girl chosen to represent Saint Joseph and the Virgin Mary.

At one home in Vallelunga, we were asked if we had been to visit other tables in town. When we replied enthusiastically that we had, the lady of the house cut us short, saying, "But in my house, ALL of the food is homemade." There is a lot of competition, with families vying to have the most elaborate presentation without relying on takeout.

On another day, we visited the tiny hill town of Salemi, which is known for its Saint Joseph's Day celebration. The people there decorate the village with elaborate, detailed sculptures made from bread. The town gates are covered with birds, flowers, wreaths, stars, and fantastical animal figures, and ropes of green branches are suspended over the streets and doorways decorated with more of the bread sculptures. In the churches, there are even votive offerings made from bread. These are fashioned to look like hearts, feet, hands, and other body parts, and even babies and soldiers. They represent a life saved or fervent thanks for a cure. Parades, music, entertainment, and feasting are all part of the celebration.

Saint Joseph's Day Soup

MINESTRA DI LEGUMI PER SAN GIUSEPPE

From Syracuse in Sicily, this Saint Joseph's Day soup not only honors the beloved saint but gives cooks the opportunity to clear out their larders of any small amounts of dried legumes. Adjust the amounts and varieties of legumes according to what you have on hand. Soak the beans and chickpeas overnight; the peas and lentils do not need pre-soaking, since they cook fairly quickly. In Sicily, borage, a leafy green vegetable, is added to the soup toward the end of the cooking time. It is not widely available here, but you can use escarole, Swiss chard, or spinach instead.

SERVES 10 TO 12

4 ounces chickpeas

4 ounces cannellini beans

4 ounces dried peeled fava beans

4 ounces lentils

4 ounces split peas

1 medium fennel bulb, finely chopped

1 cup chopped canned Italian peeled tomatoes

1 large onion, chopped

¼ cup olive oil

8 ounces borage, escarole, or other leafy green vegetable, trimmed, rinsed, and cut into 1-inch pieces

Salt and freshly ground black pepper

About 2 cups Italian bread cut into bite-size cubes

¼ cup olive oil

1. Place the chickpeas and both beans in a large bowl, add water to cover by several inches, and refrigerate for several hours, or overnight; drain.

2. In a large pot, combine the chickpeas and beans, add cold water to cover by 1 inch, and bring to a simmer. Cook for 1 hour, adding more water if needed. Add the lentils, split peas, fennel, tomatoes, onion, olive oil, and water to cover as necessary. Cook for 1 hour more. Add the greens and salt and pepper to taste. Cook for 30 minutes, or until the soup is thick and all of the legumes are tender. (The fava beans and split peas will break apart and thicken the soup.)

3. Just before serving, heat the oven to 400°F. Toss the bread cubes with the oil and spread them in a single layer in a roasting pan. Bake, stirring once, until toasted and crisp, about 10 minutes.

4. Spoon the soup into serving bowls. Sprinkle the croutons on top.

Sauces and Ragus

SALSE E RAGÙ

Before tomatoes arrived in Italy from the New World in the seventeenth century, pasta was eaten with lard, grated cheese, and herbs. But tomatoes grew so well in southern Italy, with its warm sun and volcanic soil, that they quickly caught on as the perfect topping for pasta as well as pizza.

Tomato sauces are not the only kind to dress pasta. Pesto, made with basil, pine nuts, and cheese, has become extremely popular in this country in recent years. *Besciamella*, a white sauce made with flour, milk, and butter, is used as is or mixed with tomato sauce or cheese. Butter and herb sauces are quick to make and always good.

Tuscan Tomato Sauce

SALSA DI POMODORO ALLA TOSCANA

We tend to think of tomato sauce as a southern Italian preparation, but this fresh-tasting sauce is actually Tuscan. I came across it in La Grande Cucina Toscana *by Giovanni Righi Parenti. The author recommends it as a sauce for Potato Tortelli (page 92), but it goes well with fresh fettuccine or potato gnocchi.*

MAKES 3 CUPS

3 tablespoons unsalted butter
1 tablespoon olive oil
1 medium onion, finely chopped
½ cup chopped carrot
¼ cup chopped celery
1 small garlic clove, minced
One 28- to 32-ounce can Italian peeled
   tomatoes, passed through a food mill, or
   3 pounds fresh plum tomatoes, peeled,
   seeded, and finely chopped

½ cup chicken or meat broth
1 tiny peperoncino, crushed, or a pinch of
   crushed red pepper
Salt
2 or 3 basil leaves, torn

1. In a medium saucepan, heat 2 tablespoons of the butter and the oil over medium heat. When the butter begins to melt, add the onion, carrot, celery, and garlic. Lower the heat and cook, stirring occasionally, until the vegetables are soft, about 7 minutes.

2. Stir in the tomatoes, broth, peperoncino, and salt to taste. Bring to a simmer, partially cover, and cook over low heat, stirring occasionally, until the sauce is thickened, 20 to 30 minutes, depending on the tomatoes. (The sauce can be made ahead up to this point. Let cool, then refrigerate in an airtight container for up to 5 days or freeze for up to 1 month. When ready to serve, bring the sauce to a simmer.)

3. To serve, remove from the heat. Stir in the remaining 1 tablespoon butter and the basil.

TIP: When making tomato sauce, remember that the acid in foods can react with certain metals. Stainless steel is okay, but avoid cooking, mixing, or storing in aluminum or cast-iron utensils. Also, do not cover such foods with aluminum foil—use plastic wrap instead.

Fake Sauce

SUGO FINTO

Sugo Finto *literally means "fake sauce," a strange name for such a delicious and useful sauce. But it is so full of flavor that even though there is no meat in it, you might be fooled into thinking there is.*

This recipe is from Lars Leicht, who learned to make it from his Aunt Rossanna, who lives in Anagni, outside of Rome. She uses it to make the timballo *on page 98, but this sauce is perfect for those times when you want something more complex than a plain tomato sauce, yet don't want to add meat. It is good on many types of pasta.*

Lars told me that in his region of Lazio, cooks sometimes add chopped sage and rosemary leaves and call it sugo bugiardo, *"liar's sauce," since sauces with game and meat usually are seasoned with those herbs.*

This recipe makes a big batch of sauce. If you need only a small amount, the rest can be frozen in small batches in plastic containers.

MAKES ABOUT 7 CUPS

¼ cup olive oil
1 medium yellow onion, finely chopped
2 garlic cloves, finely chopped
2 small carrots, finely chopped
4 fresh basil leaves, chopped
1 small dried peperoncino, crushed, or a pinch
 of crushed red pepper

1 cup dry white wine
Two 28- to 35-ounce cans Italian peeled
 tomatoes, passed through a food mill, or
 6 pounds fresh plum tomatoes, peeled,
 seeded, and chopped
Salt

1. In a large saucepan, combine the oil, onion, garlic, carrots, basil, and peperoncino. Cook over medium heat, stirring occasionally, until the vegetables are tender, about 10 minutes.

2. Add the wine and bring to a simmer. Cook for 1 minute. Add the tomatoes and bring to a simmer. Turn the heat to low and season to taste with salt. Cook for 30 minutes, or until the sauce is reduced and thickened. Use immediately, or transfer to containers and let cool, then refrigerate for up to 5 days or freeze for up to 1 month.

Vegetable Ragu

RAGÙ DE VERDURA

Not all ragu has to be made with meat. Here is a satisfying version made with vegetables that is particularly good with penne or other dried pasta. After tossing this sauce with the pasta, drizzle it with some full-bodied extra virgin olive oil, as they do with many pastas in Italy. Grated cheese is optional.

MAKES 3 CUPS

¼ cup olive oil

¼ cup finely chopped shallots or onion

4 cups chopped eggplant

½ cup chopped red bell pepper

½ cup dry white wine

2 cups peeled, seeded, and chopped fresh tomatoes or canned tomatoes, with their juice

Salt and freshly ground black pepper

1. In a large nonstick skillet, heat the oil over medium heat. Add the shallots, eggplant, and bell pepper and cook, stirring frequently, until the vegetables are soft, about 10 minutes.

2. Add the wine and cook for 1 minute. Add the tomatoes and salt and pepper to taste. Reduce the heat to low. Cook, stirring occasionally, for 40 minutes, or until the vegetables are very tender and the sauce is thick. If the sauce becomes too dry, stir in some water.

Pecorino Di Fossa

During the twelfth century, Saracen pirates who plied the Adriatic Sea frequently raided the rich farmlands of Romagna in east central Italy, stealing whatever they could from the local farmers. To protect their homemade cheese, the farmers would hide the wheels of cheese in underground caves. When the coast was clear and the cheeses were recovered, they discovered that the cheeses had aged beautifully underground, developing a unique aroma and flavor. Today, the cheese, known as *pecorino di fossa*, or sheep's milk cheese from the pit, is made annually in mid-August, then wrapped in cloth and buried in the earth inside specially dug caves. Very little air and no light reaches the closely packed cheeses, so they ferment and age very slowly. On November 25, the feast of Saint Catherine, beginning at four in the morning, the townspeople gather to watch as the cheeses are unearthed. A small amount of pecorino di fossa is imported into this country by the Sini Fulvi company. If you can find it, eat the cheese plain or grated onto soups, pasta, and vegetables.

Butter and Sage Sauce

SALSA DI BURRO E SALVIA

A simple mixture of butter and fresh sage dresses up ravioli, fettuccine, gnocchi, or any other fresh pasta. Sometimes I use other herbs, like thyme, basil, or rosemary, or a combination for a change. Always save a little of the pasta cooking water to extend the sauce if necessary. The hot water thins the sauce without diluting it too much.

Any pasta tossed with butter and sage sauce is enhanced with generous grindings of black pepper and freshly grated Parmigiano.

MAKES ½ CUP

8 tablespoons (1 stick) unsalted butter   4 to 6 sage leaves

In a small saucepan, heat the butter with the sage leaves until melted and foamy. Serve immediately over hot cooked pasta.

Béchamel Sauce

SALSA BALSAMELLA

MAKES 3 ½ CUPS

6 tablespoons unsalted butter
½ cup all-purpose flour
3 cups hot milk

Salt to taste
Pinch of freshly ground nutmeg

1. In a medium saucepan, melt the butter over medium-low heat. With a wooden spoon, stir in the flour until well blended. Cook 1 minute.

2. Gradually whisk in the milk, stirring constantly until smooth. Add the salt and nutmeg. Cook, stirring, until the mixture comes to a simmer. Cook 1 minute more. (Can be made ahead to this point. Place a sheet of plastic wrap directly on the surface of the sauce. Refrigerate up to 24 hours. The sauce will thicken as it stands. Reheat gently, stirring in a little more milk to thin the sauce if necessary.)

VARIATION: To make Salsa Rosa (Pink Sauce), combine 1 cup Béchamel Sauce with ½ cup Tuscan Tomato Sauce (page 56) or Fake Sauce (page 57).

Mother Leone's Meat Sauce

RAGÙ DI MAMA LEONE

Josie Clemente was in her eighties and living in a nursing home when she decided to compile her favorite recipes in a cookbook for her family. The neatly typed book covers everything from stuffed frankfurters to lobster Cantonese, but the real treasures are the Italian recipes that Josie learned from her mother and mother-in-law.

Josie's niece Aileen Riotto Sirey, one of the founders of the National Organization of Italian-American Women, a group of women who are committed to preserving their Italian heritage, was kind enough to share Josie's book with me. The recipe makes a lot, but the ragu freezes well. I especially like to serve this with Potato Dumplings (page 100).

MAKES ABOUT 3 QUARTS

4 ounces pancetta or salt pork, diced

¼ cup olive oil

4 tablespoons (½ stick) unsalted butter

2 medium onions, finely chopped

1 pound ground lean beef

8 ounces ground lean pork

4 chicken livers, trimmed and finely chopped

4 chicken gizzards, cut into small pieces
   (optional)

5 garlic cloves, finely chopped

1 tablespoon minced rosemary

½ teaspoon ground allspice

Salt and freshly ground black pepper

6 pounds fresh tomatoes, peeled, seeded, and
   chopped, or three 28- to 35-ounce cans Italian
   peeled tomatoes, passed through a food mill

2 carrots, finely chopped

1 celery rib, finely chopped

1. Put the pancetta, olive oil, and butter in a large saucepan over medium heat. When the butter is melted, add the onions and cook, stirring, until tender and golden, about 7 minutes.

2. Add the beef, pork, chicken livers, and gizzards, reduce the heat to low, and cook for 30 minutes, stirring frequently to break up the lumps of meat.

3. Stir in the garlic, rosemary, allspice, and salt and pepper to taste. Stir well and continue to cook for 20 minutes. (Josie recommends that you stop here and inhale the aroma deeply!)

4. Add the tomatoes, with their juice, the carrots, and celery and bring to a simmer. Cook, stirring occasionally, for 1½ hours, or until the sauce is thick. Taste for seasoning.

5. Serve with meat or cheese ravioli, gnocchi, fresh fettuccine, or dried pasta.

MARRYING PASTA AND SAUCE: To help the sauce adhere to the pasta better, many Italian cooks place the hot sauce in a large pot or skillet with the pasta and toss it well over medium heat for about 1 minute. If the pasta is a little dry, stir in some of the hot pasta cooking water. For a final touch, remove the pot from the heat and stir in a tablespoon of butter or a drizzle of extra virgin olive oil and a handful of grated cheese, if you are using it.

Pesto Genovese

Nothing says summer like freshly made pesto. The emerald green color and bright pungent flavors are especially appealing. In this version, fresh parsley blended with the basil keeps the color brilliant green and tames the sometimes overwhelming flavor of basil, which becomes stronger as the summer season progresses.

Though many recipes call for butter, this one, which I learned in Genoa, has a touch of soft creamy cheese added for smoothness and richness. In Genoa, they use a fresh sour cheese called prescinsceua, but you can use robiola, fresh goat cheese, or even cream cheese.

MAKES 1 CUP

1 cup basil leaves
½ cup parsley leaves
¼ cup pine nuts or walnuts
1 garlic clove
Pinch of salt

⅓ cup extra virgin olive oil
½ cup freshly grated Parmigiano-Reggiano
2 tablespoons soft fresh cheese, such as robiola, goat cheese, or cream cheese

1. With a mortar and pestle, or in a food processor or blender, crush or finely chop the basil, parsley, nuts, and garlic. Add the salt. Gradually blend in the olive oil and the cheeses until smooth.

2. Toss with hot cooked fettuccine, gnocchi, or linguine, adding some of the pasta cooking water if necessary to thin the sauce.

Sicilian Ragu

RAGÙ ALLA SICILIANA

This is a simple meat ragu that I learned to prepare from a Sicilian-American co-worker when I was first married. It is a good alternative to some of the more complicated ragus.

MAKES ABOUT 1½ QUARTS

2 tablespoons olive oil
1 medium onion, chopped
2 garlic cloves, finely chopped
1 pound ground veal or beef
2 tablespoons tomato paste

One 28- to 35-ounce can Italian peeled
   tomatoes, passed through a food mill
Salt and freshly ground black pepper
4 basil leaves, torn

1. In a large saucepan, combine the oil and onion and cook over medium heat for 5 minutes, or until the onion is tender. Add the garlic and cook for 1 minute more.

2. Add the meat and cook, stirring frequently to break up lumps, until the meat is lightly browned. Add the tomato paste and cook for 2 minutes. Add the tomatoes and 1 cup water and bring to a simmer. Add salt and pepper to taste and cook for 1 hour, or until the ragu is thickened, stirring occasionally.

3. Stir in the basil and remove from the heat.

Tomato Sauce

When I teach cooking classes, someone always asks about adding sugar to tomato sauce. I prefer not to and feel that if the sauce needs sweetness, the tomatoes were not what they should be. Use only ripe fresh tomatoes or a good brand of canned tomatoes.

Though flavorful ripe plum tomatoes are always the first choice, canned tomatoes are a perfectly acceptable substitute. It is important to find a brand made with tomatoes that are tender and sweet and fully ripened. That is why I buy whole canned tomatoes, because once the can is opened, it is easy to see whether the tomatoes are fully red and ripened without hard greenish ends.

Tomato paste brings out the tomato flavor and makes the sauce thicker, darker, and richer. I use an Italian brand that comes in a tube. That way I can use as much as I need and easily store the remainder.

Umbrian Ragu

RAGÙ ALL'UMBRA

The Tuscan Year is an evocative book about daily life in a valley in the Tuscan country-side. Following the seasons, author Elizabeth Romer writes about food and cooking as it is done by her neighbor, Silvana, a farmer's wife.

One day Silvana goes to a nephew's wedding in the neighboring region of Umbria and is intrigued with the delicious ragu served on the tagliatelle at the wedding banquet. Tuscans and Umbrians apparently tease each other about their food, the Tuscans claiming that the Umbrian cuisine is too rich. Though it is much more elaborate than Silvana's best ragu, she approves of its flavor served over fresh tagliatelle or fettuccine.

Since we don't have easy access to the fresh black truffles in the original ragu, you can use a jarred or canned truffle, found at most gourmet shops. You can also leave the truffle out, and the ragu will still be delicious. I have also tried it with a drop or two of truffle oil, which can be very good—it must be used sparingly, though, or the flavor will be overwhelming.

MAKES 3 CUPS

1 ounce dried porcini mushrooms (about ¾ cup)

3 tablespoons unsalted butter

8 ounces ground pork

4 ounces ground veal

2 ounces pancetta

1 celery rib, cut in half

1 medium carrot, cut in half

1 small onion, peeled

3 tablespoons dry white wine

2 medium fresh tomatoes, peeled, seeded, and chopped

1 tablespoon tomato paste

¼ cup heavy cream

1 small black truffle, thinly sliced, or a few drops of truffle oil, optional

Pinch of freshly grated nutmeg

1. Put the mushrooms in a bowl, add 2 cups hot water, and let soak for 30 minutes.

2. Drain the mushrooms, reserving the liquid. Strain the liquid through a paper coffee filter or a strainer lined with dampened cheesecloth. Rinse the mushrooms well under running water, examining each piece—pay special attention to the stems, which may have bits of soil clinging to the base. Drain well and chop.

3. In a large saucepan, melt 2 tablespoons of the butter over medium heat. Add the meats, celery, carrot, and onion and cook just until the meat loses its raw color; do not brown.

4. Add the wine and simmer for 1 minute. Stir in the tomatoes, tomato paste, and half of the mushroom liquid and cook over very low heat for 1 hour, or until thick. If the ragu becomes too dry, add more of the liquid.

5. Meanwhile, in a small skillet, melt the remaining 1 tablespoon butter. Add the chopped mushrooms and cook for 5 minutes.

6. Remove the celery, onion, and carrot from the ragu and discard. Add the mushrooms to the ragu and cook for 10 minutes. (The ragu can be prepared ahead to this point; reheat before proceeding.)

7. Just before serving, stir in the cream, truffle, and nutmeg, and remove the ragu from the heat. (To preserve the flavor of the truffle, do not cook further at this point.) Serve over fresh tagliatelle or fettuccine.

Sunday Meat and Tomato Sauce

RAGÙ DELLA DOMENICA

My mom made a batch of this sauce every Saturday. We would first eat it on Sunday, tossed with stubby pasta like rigatoni or shells. The meat was served as a second course, usually accompanied by a vinegary salad that cut the richness of the slow-cooked meats. We liked it so much, none of us minded having the same meal a second time during the week, usually Wednesday, saving Mom from having to make another dinner.

For holidays, Mom always made an extra-large batch, enriching it further with additional meats, such as a piece of pork shoulder or beef chuck. And, instead of the dried pasta we ate every Sunday, she would use the sauce with lasagne or manicotti.

Mom used her own homemade sugna, *lard, for searing the meats instead of olive oil. Chunks of* cotenna, *pork skin, seasoned and rolled up like a braciola (see step 1) were also added. The pork skin gave the sauce a wonderful flavor and slightly gelatinous texture, though I never ate the skin itself, because of its chewy texture and unctuousness.*

I have lightened and updated the recipe by using olive oil instead of lard and eliminating the pork skin. Despite that, most Italians would still consider this an old-fashioned recipe; meatless tomato sauces and quick-cooking ones are far more popular in southern Italy today. You can substitute Meatballs with Raisins and Pine Nuts (page 72) for the ones in this recipe, if desired.

At home, the finished pasta was always dusted with pecorino romano, but today I often use freshly grated Parmigiano-Reggiano.

MAKES ABOUT 2 QUARTS

FOR THE BRACIOLE

1 pound very thinly sliced boneless beef round
2 garlic cloves, finely chopped
2 tablespoons freshly grated pecorino romano
2 tablespoons chopped flat-leaf parsley
Salt and freshly ground black pepper

SAUCE

2 tablespoons olive oil
1 pound meaty country-style pork spareribs
1 pound Italian-style plain or fennel pork sausages
4 garlic cloves, peeled
¼ cup tomato paste
Three 28- to 35-ounce cans Italian peeled tomatoes
Salt and freshly ground black pepper

MEATBALLS

1 pound ground beef or a combination of beef
  and pork
½ cup dry bread crumbs, preferably homemade
2 large eggs
1 teaspoon very finely minced garlic
½ cup freshly grated pecorino romano or
  Parmigiano-Reggiano

2 tablespoons finely chopped flat-leaf parsley
1 teaspoon salt
Freshly ground black pepper
2 tablespoons olive oil

1. To make the braciole, lay the beef slices on a work surface and sprinkle with the garlic, cheese, parsley, and salt and pepper. Roll up each piece like a sausage and tie it with kitchen string. Set aside.

2. To make the sauce, heat the oil in a large heavy pot over medium heat. Pat the pork ribs dry and put them in the pot. Cook, turning occasionally, until nicely browned on all sides. Transfer the ribs to a plate.

3. Place the braciole in the pot and brown on all sides. Remove and set aside with the ribs.

4. Place the sausages in the pot and brown on all sides. Set aside.

5. Drain off most of the fat from the pot. Add the garlic and cook until lightly golden. Remove and discard the garlic. Stir in the tomato paste and cook for 1 minute.

6. With a food mill, puree the tomatoes, with their juice, into the pot. (If you prefer a chunkier sauce, just add the tomatoes and break them up with the back of a spoon.) Stir in 2 cups water and salt and pepper to taste. Add the braciole and pork ribs, bring the sauce to a simmer, and cook over low heat, stirring occasionally, for 2 hours or until thick. If the sauce becomes too thick, add a little more water.

7. Meanwhile, make the meatballs. Combine all the ingredients except the oil in a large bowl and mix together thoroughly. (Hands are best for this job.) Rinse your hands with cool water and lightly shape the mixture into 2-inch balls. (Note: If you are making the sauce for lasagne or another baked pasta, shape the meat into tiny balls the size of a small grape.)

8. Heat the oil in a large heavy skillet. Add the meatballs and brown them well on all sides (they will finish cooking in the ragu). Transfer the meatballs to a plate.

9. When the ragu has cooked for 2 hours, add the sausages and meatballs (unless you have made tiny meatballs). Cook for 30 minutes, or until the ragu is thick and dark and the meats are very tender.

10. Remove the meats from the ragu and toss the ragu with the pasta of your choice. Serve the meats as a second course, or reserve them for another day.

Please Pass the Ragu, Gravy, or Sauce

While most cooks of Italian extraction make some type of mixture of meats and tomato for pasta, not all of them call it ragu. In my family, it was always called meat sauce, or simply sauce, while other Italian Americans we knew referred to it as gravy. But the term ragu does not have an accurate English translation and neither *gravy* nor *sauce* is really correct.

Ragu is an Italianization of the French word *ragoût,* meaning a stew, though it derives from *ragoûter,* to reawaken the appetite. The term ragu probably sounded foreign to the American ear in the late nineteenth century, when Italians began to migrate here in droves, so a translation was needed. In American usage, a stew is typically chunks of meat and vegetables simmered slowly in a liquid for a long time. It would not have been served over pasta—especially since few people ate pasta at that time.

Gravy is the typically American sauce for meat, made from the drippings of a roast such as turkey or beef. It may have come to be used instead of ragu since the braised meats in the ragu give up their juices much as the juices of a roast go into a gravy. While gravy is not exactly an accurate term, it does have similarities to a ragu and its familiarity would have made pasta—an exotic dish at that time—more acceptable to non-Italians by association.

Since a sauce is defined as a liquid that is served with food to add flavor or to enhance its appeal, a ragu cannot accurately be called a sauce. The meat in the ragu, however, makes it too substantial.

In short, although it has characteristics of both, a ragu is neither a sauce nor a gravy. Its proper name is ragu.

Meat Sauce Bologna Style

RAGÙ BOLOGNESE

Ragu in the style of Bologna transcends regional differences and is eaten in one form or another all over Italy. The ragu is thick and dark and the flavor is very rich. A little goes a long way.

This is best served on ribbons of fresh fettuccine, with a sprinkling of grated Parmigiano-Reggiano.

MAKES ABOUT 5 CUPS

2 tablespoons unsalted butter

2 tablespoons olive oil

2 ounces pancetta, finely chopped

1 small onion, finely chopped

2 small carrots, finely chopped

1 tender celery rib, finely chopped

8 ounces ground veal

8 ounces ground pork

8 ounces ground beef

½ cup dry red wine

¼ cup tomato paste

2 cups meat or chicken broth

Salt and freshly ground black pepper

½ cup milk

1. In a large pot, melt the butter with the oil over medium-low heat. Add the pancetta, onion, carrots, and celery and cook slowly, stirring occasionally, for 30 minutes, or until the vegetables are very tender and golden.

2. Add the meats and stir well. Cook, stirring often to break up the lumps, until the meats are lightly browned.

3. Add the wine and simmer until the liquid evaporates, about 2 minutes. Stir in the tomato paste, broth, and salt and pepper to taste. Bring to a simmer. Partially cover the pan, reduce the heat to low, and cook, stirring occasionally, until the ragu is thick, 2½ to 3 hours. If the ragu becomes too dry, add a little more broth or water.

4. The ragu can be made ahead to this point. Store in the refrigerator up to 5 days or in the freezer up to one month. Stir in the milk and cook 15 minutes more.

Meatballs with Raisins and Pine Nuts

POLPETTE CON UVA PASSA E PINOLI

Kevin Benvenuto, who owns Benvenuti Pizzeria and Trattoria on Staten Island, gave me his beloved grandmother Carolina's meatball recipe. He serves her meatballs at the restaurant, along with pasta fagioli, seafood, and pizza.

These are just as traditional as those in Sunday Meat and Tomato Sauce, but they are made with three kinds of ground meat, and bread rather than crumbs, and are flavored with pine nuts and raisins. The bread gives them a light, almost fluffy texture. These meatballs would also be wonderful cooked in the ragu with other meats rather than on their own in a simple tomato sauce.

The biggest mistake cooks make when preparing meatballs is to leave out the bread or bread crumbs. While you might think they would make the meatballs heavy, they actually give the meatballs a lighter texture, because they hold in the meat juices and prevent them from becoming too dense.

MAKES 16

4 slices Italian bread, torn into small pieces
    (about 2 cups)
½ cup milk
1 pound ground chuck
8 ounces ground veal
8 ounces ground pork
4 large eggs, lightly beaten
3 garlic cloves, very finely chopped
3 tablespoons finely chopped flat-leaf parsley
½ cup raisins

½ cup pine nuts
¼ cup grated pecorino romano
1½ teaspoons salt
¼ teaspoon freshly grated nutmeg
Freshly ground black pepper
1 cup fine dry bread crumbs
Olive oil for frying
1 recipe Sunday Meat and Tomato Sauce
    (page 68)

1. Soak the bread in the milk for a few minutes. Drain and squeeze out the excess liquid.

2. In a large bowl, combine the meats, bread, eggs, garlic, parsley, raisins, pine nuts, cheese, salt, nutmeg, and pepper to taste, mixing very well. (Hands are best for this.) Rinse your hands to prevent the meat mixture from sticking and shape the mixture into 2½-inch balls. Roll the meatballs lightly in the bread crumbs.

3. Heat about ¼ inch oil in a large heavy skillet over medium heat. Add the meatballs and fry about 15 minutes or until browned on all sides, turning them carefully with tongs.

4. Place the meatballs in the ragu and simmer until cooked through, about 30 minutes.

Sausage and Mushroom Ragu

RAGÙ DI SALSICCIA E FUNGHI

We ate this ragu in Puglia, the heel of Italy's "boot," served over homemade cavatelli (see page 104), but it is also good on potato gnocchi (see page 100).

MAKES 3½ CUPS

1 ounce dried porcini mushrooms
1 large onion, chopped
2 medium carrots, chopped
1 celery rib, chopped
¼ cup olive oil
1 pound Italian-style pork sausages (without fennel seeds)

½ cup dry white wine
8 ounces white mushrooms, finely chopped
One 28- to 35-ounce can Italian peeled tomatoes, passed through a food mill or 2 pounds fresh plum tomatoes, peeled, seeded and chopped

1. Put the mushrooms in a bowl, add 2 cups hot water, and let soak for 30 minutes.

2. Drain the mushrooms, reserving the liquid. Strain the liquid through a paper coffee filter or a strainer lined with dampened cheesecloth. Rinse the mushrooms well under running water, examining each piece—pay special attention to the stem pieces, which may have bits of soil clinging to the base. Drain well and chop.

3. In a large skillet, cook the onion, carrots, and celery in the oil over medium heat, stirring occasionally, until tender, about 5 minutes.

4. Meanwhile, remove the sausage from the casings and chop it fine.

5. Add the meat to the skillet and cook, stirring often to break up the lumps, until lightly browned.

6. Add the wine and bring to a simmer. Cook until most of the wine is evaporated.

7. Add the dried and fresh mushrooms, reserved soaking liquid, and add the tomato puree. Bring to a simmer over low heat. Cook, stirring occasionally, until the ragu has thickened, about 1 hour. Add a little water if the ragu becomes too thick.

Pasta, Risotto, and Polenta

The old story about pasta being a Chinese invention that was introduced to Italy by Marco Polo is not true. Drawings found in Etruscan tombs show people making and drying ribbons of a pasta-like dough five centuries before Christ. Later, still long before Marco Polo, the Romans cooked noodles called *lagane*, which they ate with chickpeas.

Italians eat pasta every day, from simple, inexpensive dried pasta to fresh pasta made with eggs. For special occasions, stuffed pastas are a treat, whether served in broth or tossed with a sauce or ragu. Meat sauces or those based on cream or cheese are typical for winter meals, while lighter tomato- or vegetable-based sauces prevail in summer.

Rice was probably introduced to Italy from the the Middle East. Since it was difficult to cultivate, supplies were scarce and expensive. Even today, rice is eaten near where it is grown, in Piedmont, Lombardy, the Veneto, and Emilia-Romagna, usually as risotto. One exception is *arancini*, the fried rice balls of Sicily, though I can't think of another rice dish typical of that region.

Polenta is a staple of northern Italy. Though it is not very interesting served plain, it is the perfect foil for all kinds of sauces and stews. Polenta is usually made from yellow cornmeal, but Venetians prefer white, because its milder flavor is a better complement to the many fish dishes of the region. Polenta can also be fried or grilled, or layered with cheese and/or sauce and baked in a casserole.

Fresh Egg Pasta

PASTA ALL'UOVO

Many students ask me why they should bother to make pasta from scratch when fresh pasta is so readily available today. The answer is that even the best store-bought pasta doesn't have the texture and freshness of homemade. Besides, a lot of pasta that is sold as fresh just isn't. You would be better off substituting a high-quality Italian dried pasta.

It takes patience and practice to become adept at making pasta. I have worked to make these instructions as clear as possible, but there is nothing like getting your hands into the dough. If you are making pasta for the first time, don't even think of trying it on a day when you are having guests and have a dozen other things to do.

The dough can be made on a board or in a food processor or heavy-duty electric mixer. The rolling out can be done with a hand-cranked or electric pasta machine or a rolling pin. The best kind of rolling pin to use is a long, straight, narrow pin. The heavy kind with handles and ball bearings will press the dough rather than stretch it.

If you are buying a pasta rolling machine, choose a model that is heavy for its size and has wide rollers. Avoid flimsy machines with a lot of attachments. All you really need, though even it is not essential, is a fettuccine-cutting attachment. Also avoid those pasta extrusion machines, where you put the ingredients in and press a button, and pasta comes out. The machines are expensive and the resulting pasta has the wrong texture.

MAKES ABOUT 1 ¼ POUNDS; ENOUGH TO SERVE 6 TO 8

About 3 cups unbleached all-purpose flour
4 large eggs, beaten

1 teaspoon olive oil (optional, but a good idea, especially for stuffed pastas)

TO MAKE THE DOUGH BY HAND

Pour 3 cups flour into a mound on a countertop or large pasta board: a rough surface such as wood or plastic is better than a smooth one such as marble. With a fork, make a wide crater in the center of the mound. Pour in the eggs and olive oil, if using, into the crater and begin stirring with the fork, gradually incorporating some of the flour from the inside of the crater. Use your other hand to support the wall of flour surrounding the eggs.

When the dough forms a ball and becomes too firm to stir, sweep the remaining flour to one side. Lightly flour your hands and begin kneading: push the dough away with the heels of your hands and pull it back toward you with your fingertips. Continue kneading, gradually incorporating some of the remaining flour, until the ball becomes somewhat smooth, feels moist, and is only slightly sticky. Do not add more flour than is necessary to create a firm ball of dough, or it may become too dry.

Put the dough aside and cover it with an overturned bowl. Wash and dry your hands to remove scraps of dough. Scrape the kneading surface clean with a plastic or metal dough scraper or spatula to remove any hardened pieces of dough and excess flour that could later cause lumps in the dough. Put the scrapings and remaining flour in a sieve and shake the sieve over the work surface and your hands to coat them lightly with flour.

Knead the dough again until it is smooth and elastic, and moist but not sticky, about 8 to 10 minutes, adding more flour if necessary. There should be no streaks of flour in the dough, and the color should be evenly yellow. The more the dough is kneaded, the lighter and better the pasta will be, so do not skimp on it. But work quickly, so that the dough does not dry out.

TO MAKE THE DOUGH IN A FOOD PROCESSOR OR HEAVY-DUTY MIXER

Pour the eggs and olive oil into a food processor fitted with the steel blade or a heavy-duty electric mixer with the flat beater in place. With the machine running, begin adding the flour a tablespoon at a time. Stop when the dough forms a ball and cleans the sides of the bowl. Pinch the dough. It should feel moist but not sticky and should be fairly smooth. If not, gradually add more flour as needed.

Place the dough on a lightly floured surface and knead for 1 minute, adding more flour if necessary, until it is firm and smooth, without any streaks of flour, and moist but not sticky.

LET THE DOUGH REST

Cover the dough with an inverted bowl and let it rest for 30 minutes at room temperature. This will allow the dough to soften so it is easy to work with.

Cut the dough into 4 to 6 pieces (it may feel moister after its rest). While you work with one piece, keep the remainder covered.

TO ROLL OUT THE DOUGH BY HAND

Lightly dust a countertop or large pasta board with flour. Be sure that the surface is perfectly flat and not warped.

Shape the piece of dough into a disk. Choose a wooden rolling pin at least 24 inches long and 1½ to 2 inches in diameter and dust it lightly with flour. Place the pin in the center of the dough and push it away from you toward the edge. Rotate the dough a quarter turn, center the pin on it, and push it toward the edge once more. Repeat rotating the dough and rolling it out from the center, keeping the shape round and the thickness even. Flip the dough over from time to time to be sure it is not sticking; if necessary, dust lightly with flour. Work quickly so that the dough does not dry out. If it should tear, pinch it together or patch it with a small piece of dough from the edge. The dough is ready when it is very thin and you can easily see your hand through it when it is held up to the light.

TO ROLL OUT THE DOUGH WITH A PASTA MACHINE

Following the manufacturer's instructions, clamp the pasta machine to a large countertop or sturdy table. Set the rollers at the widest opening and dust them lightly with flour.

Flatten the dough into an oval disk. Turn the handle of the pasta machine with one hand and guide the piece of dough through the rollers with your other hand. If the dough sticks or tears, dust it lightly with flour. Fold the dough lengthwise into thirds. Pass the dough through the machine again, flouring it if necessary. Repeat folding and passing the dough through the widest setting 5 or 6 times.

Move the dial to the next notch, closing the rollers slightly, and pass the dough through the rollers. As the dough emerges, lift it straight out so that it stays flat without wrinkling. (Do not fold it.) Continue to pass the dough through the machine, moving the dial up one notch each time, until the desired thinness is reached. This will vary according to the machine, but I usually stop at the second-to-the-last setting for fettuccine and flat pasta and the last setting for stuffed pasta. The pasta should be thin enough to see your hand through it without tearing. Don't be tempted to reroll scraps of dough; hardened bits can stick in the machine and tear the pasta.

Lay the strip of dough on a lightly floured kitchen towel. Repeat with the remaining dough, being sure to make all of the strips of equal thickness. Turn the pieces often so that they do not stick. If the dough will be used to make stuffed pasta such as ravioli, it should be kept covered so that it remains pliable. Use it as soon as possible.

FETTUCCINE

Let the dough strips dry until they are slightly leathery but still pliable, about 20 minutes. If using your pasta machine's cutting attachment, follow the manufacturer's instructions.

To cut by hand, cut the dough strips into 10-inch lengths. Starting from a short end, loosely roll up a strip of dough. With a large heavy chef's knife, cut the rolled-up pasta crosswise into ¼-inch strips. Separate the strips and lay them on a floured surface to dry for about 1 hour.

The pasta can be used immediately, frozen, or allowed to dry completely.

To freeze the pasta, arrange the strips, without touching one another, on baking sheets in the freezer. When the pasta is firm, gather it into a bundle and wrap it well in layers of plastic wrap or foil. Freeze for up to 1 month.

To dry, place the pasta strips, without touching one another, on baking sheets. Cover with lightweight kitchen towels. (Do not cover them with plastic or foil, or they will become moldy.) Leave the strips at room temperature for several days, until the strips are completely dry and snap when broken, then put in plastic bags.

Make the Fountain

When Italians make bread, pasta, or even cakes or pastry, they *fare la fontana*, make the fountain. Instead of putting the ingredients in a mixing bowl, they first pile the flour on a board, then push the flour in the center to the sides to make a hole or crater—like a fountain. Into the fountain go the liquid ingredients and seasonings. Then, very carefully, the cook begins to stir the liquid with her fingers, gradually incorporating the flour from the inside walls of the crater. This method is espe-

cially good for bread and pasta, because any unnecessary flour can be pushed aside when the dough reaches the right consistency.

If you want to "make the fountain," use a cutting board or surface that has not been used for chopping, so that it is smooth—and odor-free. Try to keep one hand dry while you stir with the other. Use the dry hand to support the wall of flour so the liquid does not escape. Work slowly and carefully until all of the liquid is incorporated.

Fettuccine and Chickpeas for the Day of the Dead

FETTUCCINE E CECI

Pasta with legumes of one kind or another is traditionally eaten on November 2, the Italian day to remember the dead. Many families leave a plate of food for the restless souls who are out and about on that night. The next morning, the children find the plate empty and believe that spirits have visited their home in the night.

SERVES 4

¼ cup olive oil

2 garlic cloves, finely chopped

1 small dried peperoncino, crumbled, or a pinch of crushed red pepper

One 15-ounce can chickpeas, rinsed and drained, or 2 cups cooked chickpeas

1 small bay leaf

Salt

½ recipe Fresh Egg Pasta (page 76), cut into fettuccine (see page 78)

1. In a saucepan large enough to hold all of the ingredients, including the cooked pasta, combine the oil, garlic, and hot pepper. Cook over medium-low heat for 1 minute, or until the garlic is fragrant. Add the chickpeas, 1 cup water, and the bay leaf. Simmer for 15 minutes, stirring occasionally and crushing half of the chickpeas with the back of the spoon. Add salt to taste.

2. Meanwhile, cook the fettuccine in a large pot of boiling salted water until al dente, tender yet firm to the bite. Drain, reserving some of the cooking water.

3. Add the fettuccine to the saucepan with the chickpeas. Toss well over medium heat, adding a little of the cooking water if the pasta seems dry. Serve hot.

WINE MATCH: Marzemino, Battistotti

The Herring Group

For Ash Wednesday, in the town of San Ippolitto, the members of the Compagnia dell'Aringa, "the Herring Group," put on silly masks and go through the streets of the town carrying long canes with a herring suspended on a string at the end of each one. They knock on doors and ask for offerings to help finance their annual festival and various charitable endeavors. In the afternoon, they gather in the town piazza and everyone is served their special dish, a plate of pasta with a secret herring sauce. The festival continues with singing and dancing.

Cannelloni

Unlike most stuffed pastas, cannelloni is cooked before it is filled. You can assemble the pasta up to twenty-four hours ahead of time, then bake it just before serving. Substitute Salsa Rosa for the Béchamel Sauce, if you prefer.

SERVES 8

FILLING

1 tablespoon olive oil

1½ pounds boneless veal shoulder, cut into 1-inch cubes

2 medium carrots, chopped

1 tender celery rib, chopped

1 medium onion, chopped

1 garlic clove, finely chopped

Pinch of freshly ground nutmeg

Salt and freshly ground black pepper

1 recipe Béchamel Sauce (page 61)

1½ cups freshly grated Parmigiano-Reggiano

1 recipe Fresh Egg Pasta (page 76)

1. To make the filling, heat the oil in a large skillet over low heat. Add the veal, carrots, celery, onion, garlic, nutmeg, and salt and pepper to taste. Cover and cook, stirring occasionally, for 1 hour, or until the meat is very tender. If the meat becomes dry, add a little water. Let cool.

2. Chop the mixture very fine. Scrape into a bowl. With a rubber spatula, stir in 1 cup of the Béchamel and ½ cup of the Parmigiano. Taste for seasoning. Cover and refrigerate until ready to use. (The filling can be made up to 24 hours ahead of time.)

3. Cut the pasta sheets into 4-inch squares.

4. Meanwhile, in a large pot, bring about 4 quarts water to a boil. Add the pasta pieces a few at a time, and cook, stirring occasionally, until tender, 2 to 3 minutes. Remove the pasta with a slotted spoon and lay flat on towels to drain.

5. Preheat the oven to 375°F.

6. Butter a large baking pan. Spoon a heaping tablespoon of the filling to one side of a piece of pasta, and roll up the pasta. Repeat with the remaining pasta and filling,

arranging the pieces close together in the pan. Spoon on the remaining sauce and sprinkle with the Parmigiano. (The cannelloni can be assembled ahead. Cover with plastic wrap and refrigerate for up to 24 hours.) Bake for 30 to 40 minutes, or until heated through and lightly golden.

WINE MATCH: Rubesco, Lungarotti

Meat Ravioli

AGNOLOTTI

Chicken and beef are my favorite combination for filling these ravioli, but veal or pork can be substituted. Leftover cooked meats from a stew, soup, or roast could also be used, and you can substitute chard, escarole, or another mild-tasting leafy green for the spinach if you like. I usually serve the ravioli with Sugo Finto or Bolognese Sauce, but Butter and Sage Sauce is also good.

I have numerous gadgets for making ravioli that I have bought or been given over the years. Among them are beautifully crafted brass and wood stamps for making round or square ravioli in different sizes, a special wooden rolling pin that cuts out ravioli squares, and a two-piece metal and plastic device that looks like an egg carton cuts them perfectly. My pasta maker even has a ravioli-making attachment.

Despite all this equipment, I always make my ravioli the same uncomplicated way: I roll out strips of dough with the pasta machine, dot one long side of each with filling, fold the dough over the filling, seal, and cut the ravioli. The technique is described in detail in the recipe for Ravioli for the Feast of Saint John the Baptist (page 88). To me it is the simplest method, and if every raviolo is not perfectly shaped, no matter. The pasta has a handcrafted appearance that pleases me.

I recommend freezing the ravioli once they are shaped. This is a restaurant technique, certainly not one that your grandmother used. But freezing them allows you to make the ravioli well in advance, then store them easily in plastic bags and serve them a few at a time—or all once—without a lot of last-minute effort. Also, freezing eliminates the possibility of the moisture in the filling soaking through the pasta dough and making the ravioli stick to the drying surface, a problem that can occur when you to keep uncooked ravioli overnight in the refrigerator.

MAKES ABOUT 80, ENOUGH TO SERVE 8 TO 10

FILLING

2 tablespoons olive oil

12 ounces lean ground beef

1 boneless, skinless chicken breast

2 ounces pancetta, chopped

1 medium onion, chopped

1 medium carrot, chopped

1 small celery rib, chopped

1 garlic clove, minced

Salt and freshly ground black pepper

½ cup dry white wine

One 10-ounce package fresh spinach, rinsed and
  stemmed

½ cup freshly grated Parmigiano-Reggiano

2 large egg yolks

1 recipe Fresh Egg Pasta (page 76)

1 recipe Sugo Finto (page 57), Meat Sauce
  Bologna Style (page 71), or Butter and Sage
  Sauce (page 60)

Salt

½ cup freshly grated Parmigiano-Reggiano

1. To make the filling, heat the oil in a large skillet over medium heat. Add the beef and chicken and cook, until the meat loses its pink color, breaking up the lumps of beef with a wooden spoon.

2. Add the pancetta, onion, carrot, celery, and garlic and cook for 10 minutes, or until the vegetables are softened. Sprinkle with salt and pepper, add the wine, and simmer for 1 minute. Cover the pan, reduce the heat to low, and cook for 1½ hours, or until the meat is very tender. Add a little water to the pan if the mixture becomes too dry and begins to stick. Remove from the heat and let cool.

3. In a large pot, combine the spinach, ½ cup water, and salt to taste. Cover and cook over medium-low heat until the spinach is wilted and tender, about 5 minutes. Drain and let cool.

4. Scrape the meat mixture into a food processor or a food grinder. Chop or grind the meat until it is coarsely ground, but not pasty. Transfer to a bowl.

5. Wrap the spinach in a towel or a piece of cheesecloth and squeeze it to extract all of the liquid. Finely chop the spinach or pass it through the grinder. Add to the meat mixture, along with the cheese, and mix well. Taste for seasoning. Stir in the egg yolks. Cover and refrigerate until ready to use. (The filling can be made up to 24 hours ahead of time.)

6. Have ready several baking sheets lined with lint-free towels. Cut the pasta into long strips about 4 inches wide.

7. Keeping the remaining pasta covered with a kitchen towel, lay one strip on a lightly floured surface. Fold it lengthwise in half to mark the center, then unfold. Beginning about 1 inch from one of the short ends, place teaspoonfuls of the filling about 2 inches apart in a straight row down one side of the fold. Lightly brush around the filling with cool water. Fold the dough over the filling. Press firmly to eliminate air bubbles and seal the dough. Use a fluted pastry wheel or a sharp knife to cut between the mounds of filling. Separate the ravioli and press the edges together firmly with a fork to seal. Place the pieces in a single layer on a prepared baking sheet. Repeat with the remaining dough and filling. Cover with a towel and refrigerate until ready to cook, or up to 3 hours, turning the ravioli several times so that they do not stick to the towels. (For longer storage, place the baking sheets in the freezer and freeze until the ravioli are firm, about 30 minutes. Transfer the ravioli to a heavy-duty plastic bag, press out the air, and seal the bag tightly. Freeze for up to 1 month. Do not thaw before cooking.)

8. When ready to cook the ravioli, bring 4 quarts water to a boil in a large pot. Reheat the sauce over low heat. Pour half into a heated serving bowl.

9. Lower the heat under the pasta pot so that the water boils gently, add half the pasta and 1 tablespoon salt, and cook until tender, 2 to 5 minutes, depending on the thickness and freshness of the pasta. Using a slotted spoon, remove the pasta from the pot, draining well.

10. Add the cooked ravioli to the serving bowl. Cover and keep warm. Cook the remaining ravioli, drain, and add it to the bowl, along with the remaining sauce. Sprinkle with the cheese and serve immediately.

TIP: Cook ravioli and other stuffed pasta in simmering water. Rapidly boiling water agitates the pasta too much, causing the pieces to break open as they cook.

WINE MATCH: Ramitello, Di Majo Norante

Fresh Pasta Ribbons in a Hot Garlic Bath

TAGLIERINI IN BAGNA CAODA

The Piemontese are Italy's garlic lovers, using it lavishly in dishes like Angel of Death Cheese, soft cheese mashed with garlic and herbs, and the sauce known as bagna caoda, *meaning warm bath. Bagna caoda is traditionally served as a dip for cut-up raw vegetables like peppers, carrots, and celery, cooked cauliflower or potatoes, and chunks of bread. In the fall, newly made Barbera wine is part of the feast.*

The Piemontese also use the sauce to dress narrow pasta ribbons and serve on Good Friday and other days when meat is not eaten. I make this quick and easy sauce often, since I always have the ingredients on hand.

SERVES 6

SAUCE

⅓ cup extra virgin olive oil

4 (or more) garlic cloves, very finely chopped

One 3-ounce jar anchovy fillets, drained

2 tablespoons unsalted butter

1 recipe Fresh Egg Pasta (page 76)

Salt

1. In a small saucepan, combine the oil, garlic, and anchovy fillets. Cook over low heat, mashing the anchovies with the back of a wooden spoon, until the sauce is smooth, about 5 minutes. Remove from the heat and stir in the butter until melted.

2. One at a time, loosely roll up the pasta sheets, and with a large heavy chef's knife, cut into narrow strips about ⅛ inch wide.

3. Meanwhile in a large pot, bring at least 4 quarts water to a boil over high heat. Add the pasta and salt to taste. Cook until al dente, tender yet firm to the bite. Drain, reserving a cup or so of cooking water.

4. Toss the pasta with the sauce. Add some of the cooking water if the pasta seems dry. Serve hot. This pasta is not served with cheese.

WINE MATCH: Barbera Tre Vigni, Vietti

Ravioli for the Feast of Saint John the Baptist

RAVIOLI DI SAN GIOVANNI

The summer solstice, in late June, marks the turning point in the solar cycle, when the sun begins its long descent. Medieval people considered Midsummer's Night, as the eve of the solstice was called, a magical time when witches roamed the earth and created mischief, transferring their powers and initiating new members into their group. Since the feast day of Saint John the Baptist falls on June 24, so close to the solstice, people who are born on his day are believed to be very fortunate.

Romans eat snails on the eve of Saint John's Day. The tradition derives from the belief that since snails have horns, they are related to devils. Eating the snails meant the number of devils was reduced, and everyone would be better off.

At this time of year, certain herbs and nuts are believed to be at their peak with health-restoring properties. In Sicily, green walnuts are gathered and used to make nocino, a delicious bittersweet liqueur that is given as a medication for illnesses of the lungs. After maturing, the liqueur is ready on All Souls' Day, November 2, to drink a toast to the departed.

In Parma, herbs like verbena, mint, and rue are gathered at dawn, when the leaves are wet with dew—said to be the blood of Saint John—to make these ravioli. It is an old wives' tale that eating the ravioli on Saint John's Day is guaranteed to keep the witches away. Fresh spinach or Swiss chard are good stand-ins for the herbs.

MAKES ABOUT 80, ENOUGH TO SERVE 8 TO 10

FILLING

10 ounces fresh spinach or Swiss chard, rinsed and stems removed

Salt

One 16-ounce container whole-milk or part-skim ricotta, drained (see page 219)

1 large egg, beaten

½ cup freshly grated Parmigiano-Reggiano

Freshly ground black pepper to taste

Pinch of freshly grated nutmeg

1 recipe Fresh Egg Pasta (page 76)

Salt

½ cup freshly grated Parmigiano-Reggiano

1 recipe Butter and Sage Sauce (page 60) or Meat Sauce Bologna Style (page 71)

1. To make the filling, place the greens in a large pot with ½ cup water and salt to taste, cover, and cook over medium-low heat until wilted and tender, about 5 minutes. Drain and let cool.

2. Wrap the greens in a kitchen towel or a piece of cheesecloth and squeeze to extract all of the liquid. Place the greens on a cutting board and chop them fine.

3. In a large bowl, stir together all the filling ingredients with a wooden spoon. Cover and refrigerate until ready to use.

4. Have ready several baking sheets lined with lint-free towels and sprinkled with flour. Cut the pasta into long strips about 4 inches wide.

5. Keeping the remaining pasta covered with a kitchen towel, place one strip on a lightly floured surface. Fold it lengthwise in half to mark the center, then unfold. Beginning about 1 inch from one of the short ends, place teaspoonfuls of the filling about 2 inches apart in a straight row down one side of the fold. Lightly brush around the filling with cool water. Fold the dough over the filling. Press the edges firmly to eliminate air bubbles and seal the dough. Use a fluted pastry wheel or a sharp knife to cut between the mounds of filling. Separate the ravioli and press the edges together firmly with a fork to seal. Place the ravioli in a single layer on a prepared baking sheet. Repeat with the remaining dough and filling. Cover with a towel and refrigerate until ready to cook, or up to 3 hours, turning the pieces several times so that they do not stick to the towels. (For longer storage, place the baking sheets in the freezer and freeze until the ravioli are firm, about 30 minutes. Transfer the ravioli to a heavy-duty plastic bag, press out the air, and seal the bag tightly. Freeze for up to 1 month. Do not thaw before cooking.)

6. When ready to cook the ravioli, bring 4 quarts water to a boil in a large pot. Reheat the sauce over low heat. Have ready a heated large shallow serving bowl or platter.

7. Lower the heat under the pasta pot so that the water boils gently, add half the pasta and 1 tablespoon salt, and cook, stirring gently, until the pasta is tender, 2 to 5 minutes, depending on the thickness and freshness of the pasta, and whether it has been refrigerated or frozen.

8. Pour half of the sauce into the bowl. Using a slotted spoon, remove the pasta from the pot, draining well. Add the ravioli and keep warm. Cook the remaining ravioli, drain, and add it to the bowl, with the remaining sauce. Sprinkle with the cheese and serve immediately.

TIP: Here are three ways to heat up the pasta serving bowl.
1. Set the bowl over the pasta pot (but watch it carefully, or the water will boil over).
2. Place the bowl in the sink and set the colander or strainer in it. Drain the pasta into the colander and lift the colander out of the bowl. Tip the bowl to discard the water.
3. While the pasta cooks, place the bowl (and serving dishes too) in a 250°F oven. Wear oven mitts when handling the hot plates.

WINE MATCH: Rosso Conero, Umani Ronchi

RICOTTA FILLING FOR RAVIOLI

When my grandmother made ravioli, she did not use any fancy gadgets. Her only tool was a big rolling pin, made from a broom handle, and a whiskey shot glass. She rolled out two big sheets of gossamer dough on her enormous kitchen table with the extra-long pin. She dotted one sheet with the filling, usually this classic one with ricotta cheese, then covered it with the second sheet of dough. She used a shot glass to cut out individual round ravioli. She spread clean, sun-dried bedsheets over every available surface, including the bed, and placed the ravioli on them to dry.

By three o'clock on a Sunday or holiday, all the ravioli would be gone. No matter how many Grandma made, they would all be quickly eaten.

MAKES ENOUGH TO FILL 80 RAVIOLI, TO SERVE 8

One 16-ounce container whole-milk or
  part-skim ricotta
1 large egg, beaten

½ cup freshly grated Parmigiano-Reggiano
2 tablespoons chopped flat-leaf parsley
Freshly ground black pepper

In a large bowl, stir together all of the ingredients with a wooden spoon. Use to fill the ravioli as described in the previous recipe.

WINE MATCH: Pinot Grigio, Organi

Good Friday Pasta

PASTASCIUTTA DELLA VIGILIA

Since animal products are not eaten during Holy Week, this Sardinian pasta is always made with eggless pasta and served without cheese. Note its similarity to Pasta for Saint Joseph's Day (page 106).

SERVES 6

1 cup finely chopped walnuts
¼ cup dry bread crumbs, preferably homemade
¼ cup olive oil
2 garlic cloves, finely chopped

½ cup chopped flat-leaf parsley
Salt
1 pound linguine or spaghetti

1. In a food processor or blender, combine the walnuts and bread crumbs and process until very finely chopped.

2. In a large skillet, heat the oil over medium heat. Add the garlic and cook for 1 minute. Stir in the nut mixture, parsley, and salt to taste. Cook, stirring, for 5 minutes.

3. Meanwhile, bring at least 4 quarts of water to a boil in a large pot. Add salt to taste. Add the pasta and cook until al dente, tender yet firm to the bite. Drain, reserving about a cup of the cooking water.

4. Immediately toss the pasta with the nut mixture. Add a little of the reserved cooking water if it seems dry. Serve immediately.

WINE MATCH: Vermentino La Cala, Sella and Mosca

Potato Tortelli

TORTELLI DI SAN LORENZO, O TORTELLI DI PATATE

Tortelli are similar to tortellini, but they are made from little circles of pasta dough rather than squares. The circles are topped with a bit of filling, folded in half, and then the two ends are pinched together (the word tortelli *means refolded). The finished pasta looks like little collars.*

Potato tortelli are eaten all year in Tuscany, but at Borgo San Lorenzo, near Florence, they are traditional on the Day of San Lorenzo, August 10, followed by roast duck. I like them dressed with Tuscan Tomato Sauce, but they are also good with a meat ragu or Butter and Sage Sauce.

SERVES 6

FILLING

3 medium all-purpose potatoes (about 12 ounces)

2 tablespoons unsalted butter, softened

¼ cup freshly grated Parmigiano-Reggiano

Big pinch of freshly grated nutmeg

Salt and freshly ground black pepper

1 recipe Fresh Egg Pasta (page 76)

Flour

1 recipe Tuscan Tomato Sauce (page 56) or Butter and Sage Sauce (page 60)

Salt

½ cup freshly grated Parmigiano-Reggiano for serving

1. Scrub the potatoes, but do not peel them. Place in a pot with cold water to cover, bring to a simmer, and cook until tender when pierced with a fork, about 20 minutes. Drain and let cool slightly.

2. Peel the potatoes. Place them in a bowl and mash them with a potato masher or fork until smooth. Stir in the butter, cheese, nutmeg, and salt and pepper to taste. Set aside.

3. Cut the pasta into 2½-inch-wide strips. Keeping the remaining pasta covered with a kitchen towel, lay one piece on a lightly floured surface. With a 2-inch round cookie or biscuit cutter, or a small glass, cut out circles of dough.

4. Place a teaspoonful of the filling in the center of each circle. Do not use more filling, or the tortelli may burst open when they cook. Lightly brush halfway around the

edge of each circle with cool water. Fold the other half of the dough over the filling. Press firmly to eliminate air bubbles and seal the edges of the dough. Moisten the corners, bring the two corners of each half-circle together, and pinch them to seal. Place the tortelli in a single layer on a towel-lined baking sheet. Repeat with the remaining dough and filling. Cover with a towel and refrigerate until ready to cook, or up to 3 hours, turning the pieces several times so that they do not stick to the towels. (For longer storage, place the baking sheets in the freezer. Once the tortelli are firm, after about 1 hour, transfer to a heavy-duty plastic bag, press out the air, and seal tightly. Freeze for up to 1 month. Do not thaw before cooking.)

5. When ready to cook the tortelli, bring 4 quarts water to a boil in a large pot. Reheat the sauce over low heat. Heat a large shallow serving bowl.

6. Add half the pasta and 1 tablespoon salt to the boiling water and cook until the pasta is tender, 2 to 5 minutes, according to the thickness and freshness of the pasta. Using a slotted spoon, remove the pasta from the pot, draining well.

7. Pour some of the sauce into the serving bowl. Add the cooked tortelli and spoon on a little more sauce. Keep warm. Cook the remaining tortelli, drain, and add to the bowl, along with the remaining sauce. Sprinkle with cheese and serve immediately.

WINE MATCH: Chianti Classico, Banfi

Christmas Beet Ravioli

CASONSEI

From the Veneto and Lombardia regions of Italy, these ravioli stuffed with beets are the prettiest you will ever see. The beet-red filling shows through the dough and gives the ravioli a beautiful rosy color. They are typically served at Christmastime.

SERVES 4 TO 8

4 medium beets, trimmed
½ cup ricotta
½ cup freshly grated Parmigiano-Reggiano
2 tablespoons dry bread crumbs

Salt and freshly ground black pepper

1 recipe Fresh Egg Pasta (page 76)

SAUCE

8 tablespoons (1 stick) unsalted butter, melted
   and still warm
1 tablespoon poppy seeds

Salt
½ cup freshly grated Parmigiano-Reggiano

1. In a large pot, combine the beets with cold water to cover and bring to a simmer. Cover, reduce the heat to low, and cook until the beets are tender when pierced with a knife, 20 to 30 minutes. Drain the beets and let cool.

2. Slip the skins off the beets and cut them into chunks. Transfer to a food processor and chop the beets. Add the cheeses and bread crumbs and pulse just to blend. The mixture should be slightly coarse. Add salt and pepper to taste.

3. Line two large baking sheets with lint-free kitchen towels and sprinkle the towels with flour. Cut the pasta into long strips about 4 inches wide.

4. Keeping the remaining strips covered with a kitchen towel, lay one strip on a lightly floured surface. Fold the strip lengthwise in half to mark the center, then unfold. Beginning about 1 inch from one of the short ends, place teaspoonfuls of the filling about 2 inches apart in a straight row down one side of the fold. Lightly brush around the filling with cool water. Fold the dough over the filling. Press firmly to eliminate air bubbles and seal the dough. Use a fluted pastry wheel or a sharp knife to cut between the mounds of filling. Separate the ravioli and press the edges together

firmly with a fork to seal. Place the ravioli in a single layer on a prepared baking sheet. Repeat with the remaining dough and filling. Cover with a towel and refrigerate until ready to cook, or up to 3 hours, turning the pieces several times so that they do not stick to the towels.

5. When ready to cook the ravioli, bring 4 quarts water to a boil in a large pot over high heat. Have ready a heated large shallow bowl. Melt the butter with the poppy seeds in small saucepan; keep warm.

6. Lower the heat under the pasta pot so that the water is just simmering. Add half the pasta and 1 tablespoon salt and cook, stirring occasionally until the pasta is tender, 2 to 5 minutes, depending on the thickness and freshness of the pasta. Using a slotted spoon, remove the pasta from the pot, draining well.

7. Pour half of the sauce into the heated bowl. Add the cooked ravioli and keep warm. Cook the remaining ravioli, drain, and add to the bowl, along with the remaining sauce. Sprinkle with the cheese and serve immediately.

TIP: Poppy seeds tend to turn rancid quickly. Like nuts or sesame seeds, they are best stored in the refrigerator or freezer. Smell them before using; if they do not smell fresh, discard them.

WINE MATCH: Soave Classico Superiore, Pieropan

Carnival Lasagne

LASAGNE DI CARNEVALE

Lent begins a forty-day period of fasting and abstinence from eating meat and, in some cases, dairy products. In anticipation, Carnevale, the days that precede the start of Lent, is a time of parties and feasting. In the old days, the parties got pretty wild, and the revelers wore face masks and costumes to protect their identities.

A proper Neapolitan-style lasagne di carnevale *is the perfect dish for the occasion— fresh pasta layered with ragu, meats, eggs, and cheeses, all unavailable during the long, solemn Lenten season. Lasagne is a production to make, but it is always a big hit. It can, and should, be made in stages. Make the sauce up to three days ahead of time, and assemble the lasagne the day before you plan to serve it. Dried lasagne can be substituted for the fresh, though it will make the dish heavier. If you can find it, mozzarella that is freshly made and has never been refrigerated has the best texture. Leave it at cool room temperature and use it the same day. Since the pasta tends to drink up the sauce, especially when the lasagne is made ahead of time, I reserve some to reheat and spoon over the baked lasagne.*

SERVES 8 TO 10

1 recipe Sunday Meat and Tomato Sauce
  (page 68), made with tiny meatballs
1½ recipes Fresh Egg Pasta (page 76)
Salt

One 32-ounce container whole-milk or part-
  skim ricotta
1 pound fresh mozzarella, diced
1¼ cups freshly grated Parmigiano-Reggiano
  or pecorino romano, or a combination

1. Remove the meats from the sauce. Refrigerate the pork and braciole for another use. Cut the sausages into thin slices and set them aside with the meatballs for the lasagne.

2. Cut the pasta into 12 strips 14 by 6 inches. Lay out some lint-free kitchen towels on a work surface. Have ready a large bowl of cold water.

3. Bring a large pot of water to a boil. Add salt to taste. Add a few strips of the lasagne and cook until tender yet firm to the bite, 1 to 2 minutes for fresh pasta. Scoop the pasta sheets out of the water with a small sieve and a slotted spoon. Place them in the bowl of cold water to cool, then, lay the pasta out flat on the towels. Repeat cooking and cooling the remaining pasta in the same way; the towels can be stacked one on top of the other.

4. Preheat the oven to 350°F.

5. Spread a thin layer of the sauce in a 13 × 10 × 3-inch baking pan. Set aside the 2 best-looking pasta strips for the top layer. Make a layer of pasta, overlapping the pieces slightly. Spread about one-fourth of the ricotta on top of the pasta, then scatter on about one-quarter of the meatballs and sliced sausages and one-quarter of the mozzarella. Spoon on about 1 cup more of the sauce and sprinkle with ¼ cup of the grated cheese. Repeat the layers three more times and top with a final layer of pasta. (The lasagne can be prepared ahead of time to this point. Cover tightly with plastic wrap and refrigerate up to overnight. Remove from the refrigerator at least an hour before baking.) Make a final layer of 1 cup sauce and the remaining grated cheese.

6. Bake the lasagne for 1 hour and 10 to 30 minutes, or until the top is browned and the sauce is bubbling around the edges. If it starts to get too brown on top before it is heated through, cover the pan loosely with aluminum foil. Remove from the oven and let cool for 15 minutes.

7. Cut the lasagne into squares and serve.

WINE MATCH: Lacryma Christi Rosso, Mastroberardino

Carnevale

Once the Christmas season ends with the Epiphany, the month-long Carnevale season begins. Carnevale is the merriest time of the entire year, but it all comes to an end when Lent begins, on Ash Wednesday. *Carnevale* in Latin means farewell to flesh, and once *Martedì Grasso*, literally Fat Tuesday, is over, the Lenten season brings forty days of fasting and abstinence from meat.

Lasagne is the classic Carnevale dish. Stuffed with meats, cheeses, and eggs, all things that must be avoided during Lent, it satisfies the craving for something rich and hearty. There are a number of sweets that are typical of Carnevale too, including cannoli, cassata, and *migliaccio*, a cheesecake made with semolina. In Liguria, doughnuts flavored with orange flower water and lemon zest are served on *Giovedì Grasso*, Fat Thursday, during the week that precedes Ash Wednesday. *Dita di apostoli*, literally, the fingers of the Apostles, are crepes filled with almonds, cinnamon, and ricotta, eaten in Puglia.

Timbale of Boniface VIII

TIMBALLO DI BONIFACIO VIII

Anagni, a sleepy town sixty kilometers southeast of Rome, is the last stop on the Rome subway line. In the center of the town's medieval quarter, a fruttivendolo, fruit and vegetable store, is operated by Rossanna Gatti. Her nephew, my friend Lars Leicht, tells me that his Aunt Rossanna is a marvelous cook who can work all morning, close her shop at one o'clock, and whip up an incredible feast by two o'clock. This elaborate layered pasta is a specialty of the region.

In Anagni, the dish, which is similar to lasagne, is said to have been a favorite of Pope Boniface VIII. Centuries ago, the popes were more than spiritual leaders. They were often involved with politics, and Boniface VIII was one of the most powerful and famous leaders of his time. When the situation in Rome got too hot—politically or physically—the pope would come to Anagni, just a day's carriage ride away.

From what he thought was the safety of the tenth-century Cathedral of Santa Maria in Anagni, Boniface excommunicated both Frederick I, king of Germany and emperor of the Holy Roman Empire, and France's King Philip the Fair. In retaliation, the French invaded Anagni. They captured the pope and, according to a legend that became infamous as lo schiaffo di Anagni, slapped the elderly pope as he sat on his throne in full papal vestments. After three days, the enraged citizens rose up and liberated the pope.

Lars's Aunt Rossanna gave him the recipe for the timballo, which he taught me how to make at a luncheon he hosted at the magnificent Long Island estate of Villa Banfi, the wine company for which he works.

Lars says some cooks layer the pasta and filling with a meat ragu, but his aunt uses Sugo Finto instead and feels that it is rich enough this way. A round baking pan is typical in Anagni for this dish, but a roasting pan is more convenient.

SERVES 8 TO 10

PASTA
About 2½ cups all-purpose flour
3 large eggs

1 teaspoon olive oil
Pinch of salt

FILLING
8 ounces boiled ham, cut into 1-inch chunks
3 hard-cooked eggs, peeled
1 pound fresh mozzarella, cut into 1-inch chunks

Salt and freshly ground black pepper
1 cup freshly grated Parmigiano-Reggiano
1 cup freshly grated pecorino romano
1 recipe Sugo Finto (page 57)

1. To make the pasta, follow the directions on page 76, using the ingredients listed above. Add a few drops of water if the dough seems dry. Set the dough aside on a lightly floured surface, covered with an inverted bowl, and drape a dish towel over it. Let rest for at least 1 hour (Aunt Rossanna recommends leaving it overnight, though it is not necessary).

2. Lay out some lint-free kitchen towels on a work surface. Have ready a large bowl of cold water. Roll out the dough with a rolling pin or a pasta machine, following the directions on page 77. You will need a total of 12 strips of pasta about 16 by 4 inches. Bring a large pot of water to a boil. Add salt to taste. Add a few strips of the lasagne and cook until tender yet firm to the bite. Scoop the pasta sheets out of the water with a small sieve and a slotted spoon. Place them in the bowl of cold water to cool, then lay out flat on the towels. Cook the remaining pasta in the same way. The towels can be stacked one on top of the other. Combine the grated cheeses and set aside.

3. Preheat the oven to 375°F. Oil a $13 \times 10 \times 3$-inch baking dish.

4. To make the filling, pass the ham, eggs, and mozzarella chunks through the medium holes of a meat grinder. Or place them in a food processor and chop fine. Taste for seasoning, adding salt and pepper as needed.

5. To assemble the timballo spread a thin layer of sauce in the bottom of the baking dish. Add a layer of pasta, overlapping the strips slightly and going up the sides of the pan. Coat the pasta with more sauce. Sprinkle with one-third of the filling and ¼ cup of the grated cheeses. Repeat to make two more layers of pasta, sauce, filling, and cheeses. Finish with another layer of pasta and sprinkle with the remaining grated cheese. Reserve the leftover sauce to serve with the pasta, if desired.

6. Bake the timballo for about 1 hour or until puffed and golden brown, covering it loosely with foil halfway through the baking time if it begins to brown too much on top. Remove from the oven and let cool on a rack for 15 minutes.

7. Cut the timballo into squares to serve.

WINE MATCH: Brunello, Villa Banfi

Potato Dumplings

GNOCCHI DI PATATE

In Rome, gnocchi are traditionally eaten on Thursday, but no one is quite sure why. In many regions of southern Italy, potato gnocchi are called strangolapreti, *meaning priest chokers, because in the face of such a delicious treat, a greedy priest could easily eat too many and not live to regret it.*

This version is another recipe from Josie Clemente's cookbook (see page 62). Be sure to use long white baking potatoes, which make tender gnocchi. Boiling potatoes result in a slick, waxy texture. How you mash the potatoes is important too. For best results, use a food mill, ricer, or potato masher. If you use an electric mixer, beat them just until smooth, or they may turn gummy.

To shape the gnocchi, use a table fork, a large plastic comb, or a riga gnocchi, *a special small grooved wooden block. I bought my* riga gnocchi *in Italy, but you can find them at Italian specialty stores that sell cooking equipment. Any of these tools will make grooves in the gnocchi, which helps them to catch and hold the sauce. Some cooks roll the gnocchi over the holes of a cheese grater, which gives them a pebbly rather than ridged surface.*

SERVES 6

1¼ pounds baking potatoes (about 3 medium), scrubbed
1 tablespoon unsalted butter, softened
1 teaspoon salt
About 2 cups all-purpose flour
1 large egg, beaten

1 recipe Tuscan Tomato Sauce (page 56), Mother Leone's Meat Sauce (page 62), or Sunday Meat and Tomato Sauce (page 68)
½ cup freshly grated Parmigiano-Reggiano or Pecorino Romano

1. Place the potatoes in a large pot with cold water to cover. Cover the pot and bring to a simmer. Cook about 20 minutes or until the potatoes are tender when pierced with a knife. Drain and let cool slightly.

2. While the potatoes are still warm, peel them and cut into chunks. Mash the potatoes, using the smallest holes of a ricer or food mill or a potato masher. Blend the butter and salt into the warm potatoes. Stir in 1 cup of the flour. The dough will be stiff. Add the egg and stir until blended.

3. Scrape the potato mixture onto a floured surface. Knead briefly, adding just as much of the remaining flour as necessary to make a soft dough; it should be slightly

sticky. The trick is to add just enough flour so that the gnocchi hold their shape when cooked but not so much that they become heavy. Set the dough aside for a moment.

4. Scrape the work surface to remove any bits of dough. Wash and dry your hands. Set out one or two large baking pans and dust them with flour. Dust your hands with flour.

5. Cut the dough into 8 pieces. Keeping the remaining dough covered, roll one piece under your palms into a long rope about ¾ inch thick. Cut it into ½-inch-long nuggets. To shape the dough, hold a fork in one hand with the tines pointed down (or use a wide-toothed comb or *riga gnocchi*). With the thumb of the other hand, roll each piece of dough over the back of the tines, pressing lightly to make ridges on one side and an indentation on the other, and let the gnocchi drop onto one of the prepared pans, leaving space between them. Repeat with the remaining dough. Cover and refrigerate the gnocchi up to 3 hours until ready to cook. (The gnocchi can also be frozen and, in fact, keep their shape better if they are. Place the baking sheets in the freezer for 1 hour, or until firm. Transfer the gnocchi to a large heavy-duty plastic bag. Freeze for up to 1 month. Do not thaw before cooking.)

6. When ready to cook the gnocchi, bring a large pot of water to a boil and add salt to taste. Heat the sauce over low heat. Have ready a heated shallow serving bowl.

7. Drop half the gnocchi into the boiling water, a few at a time, and cook for about 30 seconds after the gnocchi have rise to the surface. Skim the gnocchi from the pot with a slotted spoon, draining them well, and briefly put them in a colander set over a bowl to be sure they are well drained before adding them to the sauce.

8. Pour a thin layer of the sauce into the serving bowl. Spoon the first batch of gnocchi on top. Sprinkle with cheese. Cook the remaining gnocchi, drain, and add to the bowl, along with the remaining sauce and cheese. Serve hot.

WINE MATCH: Falerno Rosso, Villa Matilde

Manicotti

My mother made the lightest, most delicate manicotti for Christmas, Easter, and other occasions throughout the year. Strangely, though, I have never seen manicotti in Italy, nor has anyone I have asked about them. The name means cooked hands—possibly a reference to what happens when you turn the crepes with your fingertips. Whatever their origin, they are delicious and enjoyed by many Italian-American families.

Once you get the knack, the crepes are easy to make. You can even make them using two pans at one time.

SERVES 6 TO 8

CREPES

1 cup all-purpose flour
3 large eggs

½ teaspoon salt
Vegetable oil

FILLING

One 32-ounce container whole or part-skim
  milk ricotta
4 ounces fresh mozzarella, chopped or shredded
½ cup freshly grated Parmigiano-Reggiano or
  pecorino-romano
1 large egg
2 tablespoons chopped flat-leaf parsley

Pinch of salt
Freshly ground black pepper to taste
3 cups Sugo Finto (page 57), Tuscan Tomato
  Sauce (page 56), or Sunday Meat and Tomato
  Sauce (page 68)
Freshly grated Parmigiano-Reggiano or
  pecorino romano

1. To make the crepes, whisk together the flour, 1 cup water, the eggs, and salt in a large bowl until smooth. Cover and refrigerate for at least 30 minutes.

2. Heat a 6-inch omelet or crepe pan or a nonstick skillet over medium heat. Brush the pan lightly with olive oil. Holding the pan in one hand, spoon in about ⅓ cup of the crepe batter and rotate the pan to completely cover the bottom. Pour off any excess batter. Cook for 1 minute, or until the edges of the crepe turn brown and begin to lift away from the pan. Flip the crepe over and brown lightly on the other side. Transfer the cooked crepe to a dinner plate. Repeat with the remaining batter, stacking the cooked crepes, separating them with strips of wax paper. When all of the

crepes are cooked, cover with plastic wrap and refrigerate until ready to use. (The crepes can be made up to 2 days ahead.)

3. To make the filling, stir together all of the ingredients in a large bowl.

4. Preheat the oven to 350°F.

5. Spoon a thin layer of the sauce over the bottom of a 13 × 9 × 2-inch baking dish. Place about ¼ cup of the filling across the center of a crepe, roll up, and place it in the dish. Continue with the remaining crepes and filling, placing them close together. Spoon on the remaining sauce. Sprinkle with cheese.

6. Bake for 30 to 45 minutes, or until the sauce is bubbling and the manicotti are heated through. Let rest 10 minutes before serving.

WINE MATCH: Regaleali Rosso

Cavatelli

Dora Marzovilla prepares mounds of these pasta nuggets by hand every day for her family's New York restaurant, I Trulli, where my husband is the wine director.

I love to watch Dora at work. With just a flick of the wrist, she cuts and shapes a batch of the dough in practically no time. Dora learned to make cavatelli and other regional pastas such as orecchiette and minchiareddi while growing up in her hometown of Rutigliano in Puglia. If you visit that region, especially on a Sunday morning, you can still see women making fresh pasta on makeshift tables set up outside their kitchen doors.

Chewy cavatelli are excellent with meat ragus or chunky vegetable sauces. In Puglia, where fresh pasta made without eggs is traditional, one typical sauce is made with broccoli rabe, turnip tops, or other bitter greens braised with anchovies, another with cauliflower and pancetta.

MAKES ABOUT 1¼ POUNDS, ENOUGH TO SERVE 6 TO 8

2 cups fine semolina flour
1 cup all-purpose flour, plus more for dusting
1 teaspoon salt

1 recipe Sausage and Mushroom Ragu
  (page 74) or Mother Leone's Meat Sauce
  (page 62)
Freshly grated Parmigiano-Reggiano or
  pecorino romano

1. In a bowl, mix together the two flours and the salt. Gradually add enough warm water—about 1 cup—to make a stiff dough.

2. Turn the dough out onto a lightly floured surface and knead until smooth, about 2 minutes.

3. Dust two baking sheets lightly with flour. Cut the dough into 8 pieces. Work with one piece at a time, keeping the remainder covered with an overturned bowl. On the lightly floured surface, roll one piece of dough under your palms into a long rope about ½ inch thick. Cut into ½-inch lengths.

4. Holding a small knife with a dull blade and rounded tip with your index finger pressed against the blade, flatten each piece of dough, pressing and dragging it slightly so that it curls around the tip of the knife to form a shell shape. Arrange

cavatelli, not touching, on one of the prepared pans. Repeat with the remaining dough. (If you are not using the cavatelli within an hour, place the pans in the freezer. When the pieces are firm, scoop them into a heavy-duty plastic bag and seal tightly. Freeze until ready to use. Do not thaw before cooking.)

5. When ready to cook the cavatelli, bring a large pot of water to a boil over high heat. Heat the sauce over low heat.

6. Add the cavatelli and salt to taste to the boiling water. Cook, stirring occasionally, until the pasta is tender yet still slightly chewy. Drain. In a heated serving bowl, toss the pasta with the sauce and sprinkle with cheese.

WINE MATCH: Barbera, Bruno Giacosa

Dried Pasta

Dried pasta in boxes or cellophane bags has no equal for ease, adaptability, reliability, and convenience. You can find it everywhere, it is inexpensive, and with it and just a handful of other ingredients, you can create a great meal in practically no time. I could eat it every day and never get tired of it.

Since dried pasta is so readily available, some people think that it is not special enough for feast-day meals. But nothing could be further from the truth. Dried pasta goes well with many types of sauces. It was our favorite pasta on Christmas Eve, served with one of the seafood sauces. And we ate it every Sunday and many holidays with a hearty meat ragu. Dried pasta is delicious in baked dishes such as Grandma Amico's Sicilian Baked Pasta (page 108) or tossed with vegetables in a tomato sauce as in Summer Spaghetti with Green Beans (page 111). Never underestimate how good it can be, and do not compare it with fresh pasta—they simply are not the same.

Pasta for Saint Joseph's Day

PASTA DI SAN GIUSEPPE

Dora Marzovilla taught me how to make this pasta, which is traditional in Puglia for Saint Joseph's Day. Dora always uses tripolini *or* mafalde, *long dried pasta ribbons with wavy edges.*

Bread crumbs are the principal ingredient in this dry sauce, and the pasta is said to resemble the saint's beard.

There are many variations on this pasta throughout southern Italy, some with anchovies, others with onions. A similar pasta made with sautéed bread crumbs, raisins, and almonds is traditional in Calabria for Saint Joseph's Day. Another version, without the almonds and raisins but with parsley added, is served on Christmas Eve. It constitutes one of the thirteen dishes of the cenone, *the Christmas Eve feast. It is eaten on other days of abstinence as well, when no meat is permitted.*

SERVES 6

¼ cup plus 2 tablespoons olive oil
2 cups dry bread crumbs, preferably homemade
½ cup almonds, very finely chopped
8 anchovy fillets packed in olive oil, with their oil

1 pound tripolini, mafalde, or other ribbon
 pasta
Salt

1. Heat 2 tablespoons of the oil in a medium skillet over medium heat. Add the bread crumbs and almonds and cook, stirring constantly, until toasted, about 5 minutes. Transfer the crumb mixture to a plate.

2. Rinse out the skillet and dry well. Add the remaining ¼ cup olive oil and the anchovy fillets, reserving the anchovy oil. Cook, stirring and mashing the anchovies with a wooden spoon, until they are dissolved, about 5 minutes. Remove from the heat and set aside.

3. Meanwhile bring a large pot of water to a boil over high heat. Add the pasta and salt to taste and cook until the pasta is al dente, tender yet still firm to the bite. Drain.

4. Toss the pasta with the crumbs. Drizzle with the anchovy mixture and reserved anchovy oil. Serve immediately.

TIP: Buy anchovies in glass jars rather than cans so that you can see if they are plump and meaty; avoid any that look old and crumbly.

WINE MATCH: Gravina Bianco, Botromagno

Grandma Amico's Sicilian Baked Pasta

PASTA AL FORNO

My husband's maternal grandmother, Adele Amico, came from Palermo. Her family says she was a wonderful cook, though no one ever thought to write down her recipes. Charles had spoken so often of this baked pasta timbale and how his grandmother used to prepare it for all of the important winter holidays that I had to try to re-create it. With the help of Charles, his mom, Margaret, and sister Sara, I came up with this formula. After several tries they pronounced it perfect, "just like Grandma's."

It is quite a presentation. Two layers of tomato-sauced pasta surround a rich meat and cheese filling. After it is baked in a crumb-lined pan, the pasta is allowed to cool. It is unmolded like a great big cake, with the crumbs forming a crusty brown coating. Grandma always served the pasta warm, not hot, and accompanied each portion with a big spoonful of tomato sauce. The sauce not only moistens the pasta, which is purposely somewhat dry in order to hold it together, but also helps to warm it up a bit.

Making this dish is something of a production, but you can do a lot of the work ahead of time, then just assemble and bake it when you are ready to serve it.

SERVES 8 TO 12

SAUCE

1 onion, finely chopped

¼ cup olive oil

2 garlic cloves, finely chopped

¼ cup tomato paste

Four 28- to 35-ounce cans Italian peeled
   tomatoes, passed through a food mill

Salt and freshly ground black pepper

6 basil leaves

MEAT FILLING

1 pound ground beef

1 garlic clove, finely chopped

4 chicken livers, cleaned and diced

Salt and freshly ground black pepper

1 cup fresh or frozen peas

2 tablespoons butter, softened

1 cup fine dry bread crumbs, preferably
   homemade

2 pounds perciatelli or bucatini

Salt

½ cup freshly grated Parmigiano-Reggiano

½ cup freshly grated pecorino romano

1 cup cubed fresh pecorino, caciocavallo, or
   provolone

3 hard-cooked eggs, sliced

1. To make the sauce, in a large saucepan, cook the onion in the oil over medium heat for 5 minutes, or until tender. Add the garlic and cook for 1 minute more. Add the tomato paste and cook for 2 minutes.

2. Add the tomatoes and bring to a simmer. Add salt and pepper to taste and cook for 1 hour, or until the sauce is thickened, stirring occasionally. Stir in the basil and turn off the heat.

3. To make the filling, cook the beef in a large nonstick skillet over medium heat, stirring frequently, until it loses its pink color, about 10 minutes. Tip the pan and spoon off any excess fat.

4. Add the garlic, chicken livers, and salt and pepper to taste. Cook, stirring, until the chicken livers lose their pink color. Add 2 cups of the prepared tomato sauce, bring to a simmer, and cook until thickened, about 20 minutes. Stir in the peas. (The sauce and filling can be made ahead. Cool, cover, and refrigerate for up to 3 days.)

5. Generously grease a 13 × 9 × 3-inch nonreactive baking pan with the butter. Sprinkle with ¾ cup of the bread crumbs, being sure the entire surface of the pan is generously coated.

6. Bring a large pot of water to a boil. Add the pasta and 2 tablespoons salt. Cook until the pasta is almost tender yet still firm to the bite, about 8 minutes. Drain the pasta and return it to the pot. Combine the grated cheeses and toss the pasta with 3 cups of the plain tomato sauce and the cheeses.

7. Preheat the oven to 350°F.

8. Spoon half the pasta into the prepared pan, being careful not to disturb the bread crumbs. Spoon the meat filling evenly over the pasta. Scatter the cheese cubes and egg slices on top. Arrange the remaining pasta over all. Flatten the pasta with the back of a spoon. Sprinkle with the remaining ¼ cup bread crumbs. (The dish can be assembled up to 1 day ahead and refrigerated. Remove from the refrigerator 1 hour before baking.)

9. Bake the pasta for 1 to 1½ hours, or until heated through and crusty on top. Let the pasta rest on a rack for at least 15 minutes.

10. Meanwhile, reheat the remaining tomato sauce.

11. Slide a thin metal spatula around the edges of the pan. Invert the pasta onto a large tray or cutting board. Cut into squares. Top each portion with some tomato sauce and serve.

WINE MATCH: Nero d'Avola, Morgante

Summer Spaghetti with Green Beans

SPAGHETTI CON FAGIOLINI

Ricotta salata, a salted and pressed form of ricotta, adds a creamy texture to this fresh-tasting summer spaghetti. If you can't find it, substitute a mild, unsalty feta, or use Parmigiano. This is the perfect pasta for summer dinner parties.

SERVES 6

12 ounces green beans, trimmed
Salt
½ medium onion, finely chopped
¼ cup olive oil
5 medium ripe tomatoes, peeled, seeded, and chopped

Freshly ground black pepper
½ cup finely chopped basil
1 pound spaghetti
1 cup grated ricotta salata
Extra virgin olive oil

1. Bring about 4 quarts water to a boil in a large pot. Add the green beans and salt to taste. Cook for 5 minutes, or until crisp-tender. Turn off the heat. Scoop out the green beans with a slotted spoon or strainer, reserving the cooking water. Drain and pat dry. Cut the beans into 1-inch lengths.

2. Meanwhile in a large nonreactive skillet, cook the onion in the olive oil over medium-low heat until tender and golden, about 10 minutes.

3. Add the tomatoes and salt and pepper to taste. Cook, stirring occasionally, until the tomatoes thicken and the juices evaporate. Stir in the beans and season to taste if needed. Simmer for 5 minutes more. Stir in the basil.

4. Meanwhile, bring the pot of water back to a boil. Add the spaghetti and cook until almost tender. Drain well.

5. Toss the spaghetti with the sauce in the skillet. Add the cheese and toss over medium heat until the cheese is melted and creamy. Remove from the heat and add a drizzle of extra virgin olive oil. Serve immediately.

WINE MATCH: Sauvignon Blanc, Rivera

Selvapiana Seven P Pasta

SETTE P PENNE DI SELVAPIANA

The Rufina zone of Chianti in Tuscany is known for its elegant and subtle red wines, especially those from the Selvapiana winery owned by the Giuntini family. When my husband, Charles, and I visited there one recent December, I asked about the traditional local dishes, especially those that would be prepared for the coming holidays.

To my surprise, I was told that everybody is too busy working these days and few people bother to make traditional recipes anymore. For the holidays or for any occasion, they probably roast a chicken and make this quick, modern pasta, which everyone loves. The "seven P's" are porro *(leek),* pancetta, peperoncino, pomodori *(tomatoes),* panna *(cream),* Parmigiano-Reggiano, *and* penne.

Though it is not a traditional recipe, the Giuntini family enjoys it so much they request it for holidays and special occasions. It is indeed festive, and I like that it is so quick and easy.

SERVES 4 TO 6

1 medium tender leek
2 tablespoons extra virgin olive oil
3 ounces sliced pancetta, chopped
1 small dried peperoncino, crumbled, or a pinch of crushed red pepper
2 cups peeled, seeded, and chopped fresh tomatoes or drained canned Italian peeled tomatoes

Salt
1 pound penne rigati or another short ridged pasta
½ cup heavy cream
½ cup freshly grated Parmigiano-Reggiano

1. Trim the leek and cut it lengthwise in half. Rinse well under cool running water, separating the layers to remove any grit. Cut crosswise into narrow slices.

2. In a nonreactive skillet large enough to hold all of the ingredients—including the cooked pasta—combine the olive oil, pancetta, leek, and peperoncino. Cook, stirring occasionally, until the leek is tender, about 10 minutes.

3. Stir in the tomatoes and a pinch of salt. Simmer for 10 minutes more.

4. Meanwhile, bring at least 4 quarts of water to a boil in a large pot over high heat. Add the pasta and salt to taste and cook until the pasta is al dente, tender yet firm to the bite. Drain.

5. Meanwhile, stir the cream into the tomato mixture and bring to a simmer over medium-low heat. Add the pasta and cheese. Toss well. Serve immediately.

WINE MATCH: Chianti Rufina, Selvapiana

Christmas Eve

LA VIGILIA DI NATALE

The big Christmas Eve dinner traditional in many parts of Italy is called *il cenone*. In the south, the holiday is celebrated with an enormous seafood feast, a reminder of the time when meals eaten on the vigil of the holiday were completely meatless.

Jeanne Carola Francesconi, author of *La Cucina Napoletana*, suggests for a "modern" Christmas Eve dinner: smothered broccoli rabe (also called Christmas broccoli), then vermicelli with garlic and oil, or with anchovy, or with clams. This is followed by fried or roasted *capitone* (a large eel) and other fish that could be anything "according to the purse, from the humble baccalà to the luxurious lobster." *La caponata* (also known as *insalata di rinforzo*, see page 196), not to be confused with the Sicilian eggplant dish of the same name, closes the series of savory dishes. They are followed by the sweets of Christmas: marzipan, various kinds of cookies, and *croccante* (page 266). To finish, *sciosciole*: dried fruits and nuts, stuffed figs, chestnuts on a string, etc. To that, I would add *struffoli*, which at least one Italian I know said was as essential for Christmas in Italy as turkey on Thanksgiving in this country.

In Calabria, the dishes of the *cenone* include pasta ammuddicata (with bread crumbs) and *la ghiotta di Natale*, stockfish with cauliflower, raisins, pine nuts, olives, and tomatoes. Eel is popular in many different regions. In Puglia, people eat spaghetti dressed with eel or some other fish in tomato sauce, grilled or roasted eel, and fried baccalà.

In Naples, Christmas Eve is a family holiday. After a frenzied day of shopping and visiting, by nightfall the dark streets are empty except for a few latecomers bearing flowers or a bottle of wine as they rush to join the other revelers at Mamma's house. With the exception of a few hotel dining rooms, stores and restaurants are shut tight, and woe betide the poor tourist who has not made plans to dine with a Neapolitan family.

Owing to a glitch in our travel plans, my husband and I once spent an unplanned Christmas Eve in Naples. We dined on several courses of pastries and cookies in the only place we could find open—a café and pastry shop. Since I would much rather eat savory dishes than sweets, all I could think about were the steaming bowls of hot pasta and platters of grilled fish being consumed within the brightly lit houses we passed as we forlornly made our way back to our hotel.

In my home, Christmas Eve dinner always began with a huge seafood salad. Then there was linguine with lobster or crab sauce, followed by shrimp aragonate or stuffed lobster, baccalà, stuffed calamari, a big green salad, and broccoli rabe. The next course was fresh fruit, including exotics like pomegranates, clementines, and blood oranges, plus wedges of fresh fennel, all kinds of roasted nuts, including of course chestnuts, and dried fruits like apricots, dates, and figs. Finally the desserts would arrive: mounds of *struffoli*, homemade cookies, and store-bought pastries, accompanied by chilled glasses of Asti Spumante.

Many Italians in this country speak fondly of the Christmas Eve dinner of the seven fishes—but some say the fishes should number thirteen, while others say nine. The seven fishes represent the sacraments of baptism, marriage, communion, confirmation, holy orders, absolution, and extreme unction, while the thirteen represent Christ and his disciples at the Last Supper. Nine represents the Holy Trinity times three. The number is always an odd one because odd numbers are believed to bring good luck.

When I asked my friends in Italy how many types of fish they served for Christmas Eve dinner, they looked at me blankly. They all ate fish dinners, but no one counted the number of fish. To my surprise, none of them had even heard of this tradition. How could it be that an Italian custom that is held so dear in this country was unheard of in Italy?

I did some research and found the seven-fishes dinner mentioned as an old tradition in several of my Italian cookbooks with regard to some, but not all, of the southern regions of Italy. The custom seems to be unknown in Italy now, though it is faithfully kept up by the families of Italian immigrants abroad. I suspect that it may be even more common here now than it ever was in Italy. Here, when a man from southern Italy married a woman whose family originated in Sicily or another region where the seven-fishes dinner seems to be unknown, she might take up the custom from her husband's family to please him. In this way, the custom grew.

Italian Americans cherish traditions as a way to hold on to their heritage, which becomes more and more diluted with each generation, as people intermarry, move away from the old Italian neighborhoods, and become more Americanized. In Italy, on the other hand, people consider customs such as these old-fashioned and let go of them much more readily.

Linguine with Lobster

LINGUINE CON ARAGOSTA

Christmas Eve at our house meant a platter of linguine with lobster sauce. The aroma filled the entire house and we could hardly wait until it was time to eat.

My mom bought whole lobsters. The claws and body cavities were used to make the sauce; the meaty tails were reserved to serve as a second course, lightly stuffed with seasoned bread crumbs and baked.

Since fresh tomatoes are hard to come by in December, the sauce was made with the best canned tomatoes she could find. If good fresh tomatoes are available, by all means substitute them for the canned.

Hard-shell blue crabs can be substituted for the lobster. They have a special flavor all their own. Instructions on how to prepare them follow. Though the sauce won't be as tasty as when made with whole crustaceans, you can also use frozen or shelled lobster or crab. See the variation at the end of the recipe.

This dish is deliciously messy to eat. Be sure to provide a bowl for the shells, crackers, and picks or cocktail forks to help remove all of the meat.

SERVES 4 TO 6

2 live lobsters (about 1½ pounds each) or
    4 frozen lobster tails, thawed
⅓ cup olive oil
2 large garlic cloves, lightly crushed
1 small dried peperoncino, crushed, or a pinch
    of crushed red pepper

One 28- to 35-ounce can Italian peeled
    tomatoes, chopped or passed through a
    food mill
2 tablespoons chopped flat-leaf parsley
Salt
1 pound linguine

1. If using whole lobsters, place them upside down on a cutting board with their cavities facing up. Do not remove the bands that keep the lobster claws shut. Protecting your hand with a heavy towel or pot holder, hold each lobster above the tail and plunge the tip of a heavy chef's knife into the lobster where the tail joins the body. Remove the dark vein in the tail, but leave the dark green tomalley and the coral, if any. You can use the tails in the sauce, or reserve them to make Baked Stuffed Lobster Tails (page 151). Cut the lobsters at the joints into 1- to 2-inch chunks. Cut off the claws. Do not remove the shells.

2. In a large nonreactive Dutch oven or heavy pot, heat the oil with the garlic and peperoncino over medium heat. Add the lobster pieces and cook, stirring often, for 10 minutes.

3. Add the tomatoes, parsley, and a pinch of salt. Bring to a simmer. Cook, stirring occasionally, until the sauce is thickened, about 30 minutes.

4. Meanwhile, bring 4 to 6 quarts water to a boil in a large pot. Add 1 tablespoon salt and the linguine and cook, stirring frequently, until the linguine is al dente, tender yet firm to the bite. Drain well. Toss the pasta with the sauce and lobster pieces. Serve immediately.

LINGUINE WITH BLUE CRAB SAUCE: Substitute 6 live blue crabs for the lobsters. To clean the crabs, protecting your hand with a thick towel or pot holder, hold each crab against the work surface and pry off the flat central portion of the shell (called the apron) with a dull knife. Rinse the crabs under cold water. Cut crosswise in half. Scrape out the spongy fibers inside.

VARIATION: To make the sauce with lobster or crab meat only, make the sauce as above, leaving out the lobster in step 2. About 5 minutes before the sauce is ready, stir in 8 to 12 ounces of lobster or crab meat.

TIP: Peperoncini are small red devilishly hot chiles that are sold dried. I like to stock up on them when I am in Italy, but I have also found the same dried chiles, no more than half an inch long, in Asian markets in this country. Substitute crushed red pepper if necessary.

WINE MATCH: Fiano di Avellino, Terredora

Linguine with Red Mussel Sauce

LINGUINE CON LE COZZE

Small clams can also be prepared this way. Linguine with mussels is often served on Christmas Eve.

SERVES 4 TO 6

3 pounds mussels
⅓ cup olive oil
3 large garlic cloves
1 small dried peperoncino or a pinch of crushed
   red pepper
2 pounds fresh tomatoes, peeled, seeded, and
   chopped, or one 28- to 35-ounce can Italian
   peeled tomatoes, drained and chopped

2 tablespoons chopped flat-leaf parsley
Salt
1 pound linguine

1. Place the mussels in cool water to cover and let stand for 30 minutes.

2. Scrub the mussels with a stiff brush and scrape off any barnacles or seaweed. Discard any mussels with cracked shells or that do not shut tightly when tapped. Remove the beards by pulling them toward the narrow end of the shells.

3. Put the mussels and ½ cup water in a large pot over medium-high heat, cover, and cook until the mussels begin to open, about 4 minutes. Transfer the opened mussels to a bowl. Cook the unopened mussels a few minutes longer, then discard any that refuse to open.

4. Working over a bowl to catch the juices, shell the mussels, placing them in another bowl. If the mussels are sandy, rinse them in the mussel juices and lift them out. Strain the juices through a sieve lined with dampened cheesecloth or a paper coffee filter.

5. In a large saucepan, heat the oil with the garlic and peperoncino over medium heat until the garlic is fragrant, about 1 minute. Stir in the tomatoes, mussel juices, parsley, and a pinch of salt. Cook, stirring occasionally, until the sauce is thickened, about 20 minutes. Stir in the mussels and remove from the heat.

6. Meanwhile, bring a large pot of water to a boil and add salt to taste. Add the linguine and cook until al dente, tender yet still firm to the bite. Drain and place in a heated bowl.

7. Toss the pasta with the mussel sauce and serve immediately.

TIP: Crushed peperoncini or red pepper should be used sparingly in Italian cooking. It is not meant to make the food fiery hot and is never sprinkled on top of foods. In cooked dishes, it is first heated with olive oil, so that its flavor is disbursed. In salads, it is mixed with the dressing for the same result.

WINE MATCH: Bianco Marino Selezione Oro, Colle Picchione

Linguine with White Clam Sauce

LINGUINE ALLE VONGOLE

In Naples and Rome, tiny vongole verace, *little clams the size of your thumbnail with beautiful markings, are tossed in their shells into the pan with garlic, oil, and other seasonings. That way, all of the sweet clam juices are captured in the sauce to flavor the pasta. You can cook Manila clams or cockles this way, but since most clams here are much larger, and the shells can carry a lot of grit, it is usually better to remove the seafood from the shells before adding them to the sauce.*

Throughout Italy, linguine or spaghetti is the pasta shape of choice for this type of oil-and-garlic-based sauce. Remember, too, that Italians would never toss this pasta, or any pasta with seafood, with grated cheese. The flavor of the cheese would overwhelm the delicacy of the clams.

In Puglia, the same pasta is made with tiny black mussels. On May 31, in the town of Porto Cesareo, there is an annual fish festival. The markets all feature special displays and in the piazza, an enormous cauldron of oil is set up to fry fish. Everyone stops to have some. The restaurants all prepare special sauces made with fish and shellfish. Among the most popular preparations are clams or mussels in red or white sauce.

SERVES 6

2 pounds littleneck or other small hard-shell
   clams
⅓ cup extra virgin olive oil
6 garlic cloves, lightly crushed
2 tablespoons chopped flat-leaf parsley

1 small dried peperoncino, crumbled, or a pinch
   of crushed red pepper
1 pound linguine
Salt

1. With a stiff brush, scrub the clams well under cold running water. Discard any that have broken shells or that don't close up tightly when handled.

2. Place the clams in a large pot with ¼ cup cold water. Cover the pot, heat to medium-high, and let the clams steam just until they begin to open. When you start to hear them pop, transfer the opened clams to a bowl (do not overcook clams, or they will get chewy). Cook the remaining clams until they open. Discard any that refuse to open.

FROM LEFT TO RIGHT: Baked Clams *(page 18)*; Chickpea-Flour Fritters *(page 10)*; and Asparagus and Prosciutto Frittata *(page 16)*

Carnival Lasagne *(page 96)*

RIGHT: Linguine with White Clam Sauce *(page 120)*

Cold Stuffed Breast of Veal *(page 162)*

RIGHT: Christmas Eve Seafood Salad *(page 134)*

Crispy Lamb Chops *(page 180)*

Chocolate Cake for Passover *(page 222)*

FOLLOWING PAGE: Saint Joseph's Fritters *(page 280)*

3. Working over a small bowl to catch the juices, scrape the meat from the clam shells, placing it in another bowl. Pour all of the liquid from the pot into the bowl with the juices. If the clams are sandy, rinse them one at a time in the clam juices and lift them out. Strain the liquid through a sieve lined with cheesecloth or a paper coffee filter into a bowl. Put the clams into the strained liquid.

4. In a skillet large enough to hold the cooked pasta, heat the oil with the garlic, parsley, and peperoncino over medium-low heat. When the garlic just begins to turn golden, add about two-thirds of the clam juices and cook until reduced by half. Stir in the remaining juices and the clams and cook for 1 minute more. Turn off the heat.

5. Meanwhile, bring a large pot of water to a boil. Add the linguine and salt to taste. Cook, stirring frequently, until the linguine is almost tender. Drain the pasta.

6. Add the pasta to the clam sauce and toss over high heat for 1 minute. Serve immediately.

TIP: Long thin pasta like spaghetti and linguine are best with seafood sauces and plain tomato sauces.

WINE MATCH: Greco di Tufo, Mastroberardino

Venetian Risotto with Peas for San Marco

In Venice, visitors are greeted by the Lion of San Marco, the symbol of Saint Mark the Evangelist, the patron saint of the city. The lion stands on a tall column that flanks the entrance to Saint Mark's Square, often called the living room of Venice.

Mark was the author of the second book of the New Testament and later founded the Christian Church in Alexandria. On one of his travels, a great storm came up and blew his ship toward a cluster of islands. An angel appeared and told Mark that a great city would be built there one day in his honor. It was not until several centuries later that people fleeing the onslaught of Attila the Hun and his army did just that, establishing Venice.

At one time, risi e bisi—*rice and peas in Venetian dialect—was the official dish for Saint Mark's Day, April 25. It symbolized the coming of spring and the wealth of the Republic of Venice, since rice was an expensive commodity. It was served ceremoniously from a steaming tureen to the doge, the chief magistrate. Made with fresh spring peas and rice,* risi e bisi *is served* all'onda, *meaning wavy, because it is wetter than a typical risotto and ripples and flows when spooned out.*

Freshly picked sweet peas are magnificent in this dish, but tiny frozen sweet peas are an acceptable substitute.

SERVES 6

3 tablespoons olive oil
2 ounces pancetta (1 thick slice) chopped
1 medium yellow onion, finely chopped
2 cups medium-grain rice, such as Carnaroli or Vialone Nano
6 cups hot chicken broth

Salt and freshly ground black pepper
2 cups shelled tender peas or thawed frozen peas
2 tablespoons finely chopped flat-leaf parsley
½ cup freshly grated Parmigiano-Reggiano
2 tablespoons unsalted butter

1. In a large saucepan, heat the oil with the pancetta over medium heat. Stir in the onion with a wooden spoon and cook for 10 minutes, or until tender and golden.

2. Stir in the rice and cook for 1 minute. Add about ½ cup of the hot broth and stir well, until the liquid is absorbed. Continue adding broth ½ cup at a time in the same way. After about 10 minutes, stir in salt and pepper to taste and add the peas and pars-

ley. Continue adding the liquid and stirring until the rice is tender yet still firm. The risotto should have a loose, somewhat soupy consistency. Use hot water if you run out of broth. Remove the pan from the heat.

3. Add the cheese and butter and stir well. Serve immediately.

WINE MATCH: Terre Alta, Livio Felluga

Artichoke Risotto

RISOTTO DI CARCIOFI

Although they are available all year round, the peak season for artichokes is from March to May. In Italy, they are eaten in every way imaginable, from the famous Roman carciofi alla giudea, *Jewish-style artichokes, which are deep-fried until the leaves are as crisp as potato chips, to stuffed—with anything from meat to cheese or bread crumbs. They are stewed with lamb or goat, braised in wine for a pasta sauce, or roasted with fish and potatoes.*

Artichoke risotto is a favorite starter for a Passover dinner for Sephardic and Levantine Jews (not for Ashkenazi Jews, who do not eat beans or rice at Passover). If you are making this as a main dish, use chicken or vegetable broth in place of the water.

SERVES 4 TO 6

3 medium artichokes
1 medium onion, chopped
3 tablespoons olive oil
1 garlic clove, minced
½ cup dry white wine

2 tablespoons chopped flat-leaf parsley
Salt and freshly ground black pepper
2 cups medium-grain rice, such as Vialone
    Nano or Carnaroli

1. Cut off the top ½ to ¾ inch of each artichoke and discard. Rinse the artichokes under cold water, spreading the leaves open. Carefully bend back the outer dark green leaves of each artichoke and snap them off close to the base. Continue removing leaves in the same manner until you reach the pale yellowish cone of tender leaves at the center. With a vegetable peeler or paring knife, peel off the tough outer skin from the base of the artichoke and the stem. Trim the end of each stem. Cut the artichokes lengthwise in half and scoop out the fuzzy chokes. Cut the halves lengthwise into thin slices.

2. In a medium saucepan, cook the onion in the olive oil over medium heat until very tender, 10 minutes. Add the garlic and cook for 1 minute. Add the artichoke slices, wine, parsley, and salt and pepper to taste. Cook, stirring occasionally, for 5 minutes.

3. Meanwhile, heat 5 cups water.

4. Add the rice to the artichoke mixture and stir for 2 minutes, or until the rice is hot. Add ½ cup of the water and cook, stirring occasionally, until the liquid is absorbed.

Continue adding water about ½ cup at a time, stirring and simmering until it is absorbed. The rice is done when it is tender yet firm to the bite. Taste for seasoning.

5. Stir in one more spoonful of liquid to keep the risotto moist and creamy. Serve immediately.

TIP: Just before removing risotto from the heat, always stir in an extra spoonful of liquid. The rice will continue to absorb the liquid, so that by the time it is served, the consistency will be just right.

WINE MATCH: Sauvignon Blanc, Puiatti

Red Risotto

RISO ROSSO

A Milanese chef told me the secret to a flavorful risotto is to cook the onion long and slowly, for as much as an hour. I cook it over low heat for 20 minutes, until the onion turns a golden amber color and has a deep, rich flavor.

This brilliantly colored risotto is not just a novelty dish but is traditional in the fall for Rosh Hashanah, when beets have just come into season and are full of sweetness. It is also lovely for Valentine's Day. If you are kosher, substitute vegetable broth for the chicken broth.

SERVES 6

4 medium beets (about 1¼ pounds), trimmed
3 tablespoons unsalted butter
1 tablespoon olive oil
1 medium onion, finely chopped
2 cups medium-grain rice, such as Vialone
  Nano or Carnaroli

½ cup dry white wine
About 5 cups hot chicken broth
Salt and freshly ground black pepper
½ cup freshly grated Parmigiano-Reggiano

1. Preheat the oven to 450°F.

2. Scrub the beets and place them on a sheet of aluminum foil. Fold up the edges of the foil to seal in the beets. Place the package on a baking sheet. Bake for 45 to 60 minutes, or until the beets are tender when pierced with a knife. Let cool.

3. Peel the beets and chop them. You should have about 2 cups. (The beets can be prepared a day or two ahead and refrigerated.)

4. In a wide saucepan, melt 2 tablespoons of the butter with the olive oil over very low heat. Add the onion and cook until tender and golden, 10 to 20 minutes. Do not let it brown.

5. Add the rice to the onion and stir for 2 minutes, or until hot. Add the wine and cook and stir until the liquid is absorbed. Add the beets and cook for 1 minute. Add about ½ cup of the hot broth and cook, stirring constantly, until the broth is absorbed. Continue adding broth ½ cup at a time, stirring after each addition.

After about 10 minutes, stir in salt and pepper to taste. Continue to add broth and stir until the rice is tender but still firm to the bite. If you run out of broth, use hot water.

6. Remove the pan from the heat and stir in one more ½ cup of broth. The risotto should be creamy and moist, not dry. Stir in the remaining 1 tablespoon butter until melted. Serve immediately.

TIP: If you have leftover risotto, mix it with an egg and shape it into little pancakes. Fry the cakes in olive oil or butter until they are crusty and serve them as a side dish or starter.

WINE MATCH: Breganze de Breganze, Maculan

Quick Lobster or Crab Linguine

LINGUINE CON ARAGOSTA O GRANCHIO

In Naples today, seafood sauces are often made with little pacchino *tomatoes, similar to the sweet tiny cherry or grape tomatoes available here. They make a quick, delicious sauce with any kind of seafood, especially lobster or crab.*

SERVES 6

⅓ cup extra virgin olive oil

2 large garlic cloves, lightly crushed

1 small dried peperoncino, crumbled, or a pinch of crushed red pepper

2 pints grape or cherry tomatoes, halved, or quartered if large

Salt

8 ounces fresh crab or lobster meat, picked over to remove shells

2 tablespoons flat-leaf parsley

1 pound linguine or spaghetti

1. In a large nonreactive skillet, heat the oil with the garlic and peperoncino over medium heat until the garlic is golden. Add the tomatoes and salt to taste. Cook, stirring frequently, until the tomatoes are softened and the juices thicken slightly, about 5 minutes.

2. Stir in the crab meat and parsley. Cook for 5 minutes, until heated through.

3. Meanwhile, bring at least 4 quarts water to a boil in a large pot. Add the linguine and salt to taste. Cook, stirring frequently, until the pasta is al dente, tender yet firm to the bite. Drain.

4. Toss the pasta with the sauce. Serve immediately.

TIP: To cook long strands of pasta like linguine or spaghetti evenly, push the pieces down into the boiling water as soon as they are soft enough to bend, and stir them frequently.

WINE MATCH: La Segreta Bianco, Planeta

Polenta

On Fat Tuesday, the last day of Carnevale, the people of Tossignano in Emilia-Romagna celebrate with a grand feast known as a polentata. It was initiated in the seventeenth century when war shortages had left people with little to eat and certainly not enough for a Carnevale celebration. The local rulers opened up the government storehouse, giving the people access to the wine and polenta stored there, and the occasion has been celebrated ever since.

In the town square, enormous pots of soft golden polenta are cooked and cut into slices. Layered with a rich meat and tomato ragu and sprinkled with cheese, the polenta is baked and then served to the vast crowd that assembles in the piazza. Everyone gets a portion of the delicious polenta pasticiatta.

Mixing the cornmeal first with cold water ensures that the polenta will come out lump-free. Serve it hot with a sprinkling of cheese or cream, or topped with a meat or fish ragu or stew. Or let it cool, so it becomes firm and easy to slice. Fry or grill the slices and use them as a base for crostini or to accompany grilled sausages, quail, or other meats.

SERVES 6

1½ cups coarse-grain yellow cornmeal, preferably stone-ground	Salt 4 tablespoons (½ stick) unsalted butter

1. In a bowl, stir together the cornmeal and 2 cups cold water.

2. In a large heavy saucepan, bring 2 cups water to a boil. Stir in the cornmeal and 2 teaspoons salt. With a wooden spoon, cook the mixture, stirring constantly, until it comes back to the boil and begins to thicken. Reduce the heat to very low (use a Flame-Tamer if necessary to keep the polenta from scorching on the bottom). Cook the polenta, stirring occasionally, for 30 to 40 minutes, until very thick and creamy. Add a little water if the mixture becomes too thick.

3. Remove from the heat and stir in the butter. Taste for seasoning. Pour the polenta onto a large platter. Serve hot.

Polenta with Soft Cheese and Browned Butter

TOC'N BRAIDE

This version of polenta, topped with soft cheese and browned butter, is from the Friuli–Venezia Giulia region of northeastern Italy. Made with milk, it is softer and creamier than other polentas. Though it is very simple, it is also very rich and should stand alone as a first course, not a side dish.

SERVES 4

1 cup fine yellow cornmeal, preferably stone-ground
1 cup milk

Salt

TOPPING

¾ cup ricotta
2 tablespoons soft fresh goat cheese
3 tablespoons unsalted butter

1 tablespoon fine yellow cornmeal
Pinch of salt

1. In a bowl, stir together the cornmeal and 2 cups cold water.

2. In a large heavy saucepan, bring the milk to a simmer. Add the cornmeal. Cook, stirring until the mixture comes to a gentle simmer. Lower the heat (place the pan over a Flame Tamer if necessary to keep the polenta from scorching). Cook, stirring occasionally, for 30 to 40 minutes, until the polenta has thickened and lost its raw taste. It should be pourable; if it is too thick, add a little water. Add salt to taste.

3. While the polenta is cooking, make the topping: whisk the cheeses in a bowl until smooth. Just before the polenta is done, melt the butter in a small skillet. Add the 1 tablespoon cornmeal and the salt and cook, swirling the pan, until the cornmeal is toasted and lightly browned.

4. Spoon the polenta into four soup plates. Top with the cheese mixture and drizzle with the melted butter. Serve immediately.

TIP: To clean the pot after cooking polenta, fill it with cold water and 2 tablespoons of powdered dishwasher soap. Let soak for 30 minutes to 1 hour. Any residue comes off right away.

WINE MATCH: Pinot Bianco, Castello di Spessa

Fish and Seafood

PESCE E FRUTTI DI MARE

Though Italy is a peninsula surrounded by water, fish has always been expensive. With transportation hampered by mountains and poor roads, only people who lived near the shore had easy access to fresh fish and seafood. As a result, preparations are never too elaborate. When you are fortunate enough to get really good, fresh seafood, why mask its quality with heavy sauces or seasonings?

Whole fish and fish steaks are grilled or roasted and sprinkled with parsley, olive oil, and lemon. The same seasonings are used on poached shellfish, or they may be cooked in tomato sauce or baked under a light coating of seasoned bread crumbs.

Preserved fish such as baccalà and stockfish are widely used in Italy, since at one time they were inexpensive (though no more) and always available. Sicilians came up with a way to can tuna in olive oil, and many recipes call for this staple.

Christmas Eve Seafood Salad

INSALATA DI FRUTTI DI MARE

When I was growing up, this Neapolitan-style salad was so special we ate it just once a year, on Christmas Eve. Now I make it all the time, especially in summer, when its lightness and freshness are really appreciated.

In *Southern Italian Cooking, Family Recipes from the Kingdom of the Two Sicilies*, author Jo Bettoja recommends serving a salad like this one as an antipasto for the Feast of the Three Saints, which is held in the beginning of August in the town of Bisceglie in Puglia. Because the town has three patron saints, the celebration lasts for three days. The saints, Mauro, Sergio, and Pantaleone, were all martyred for their faith in ancient times and have been invoked for protection against plague, war, disease, and earthquakes.

The octopus is my favorite part, but octopus can be tough if it is not cooked properly. There are a lot of opinions on how to tenderize it. Some say that it should be pounded before cooking, to break up the fibers. Others assert adding a cork to the pot of boiling water will somehow make the meat soft. My mother claimed that the octopus should be dipped three times—for the Holy Trinity—in the boiling water before allowing it to cook. But in my experience, these tricks are not necessary; it is merely a matter of timing.

You can make this salad ahead of time, but don't add the lemon juice until just before serving. If it is added too soon, the acid in the juice will "cook" the seafood by breaking down the protein, resulting in a mushy texture. Also, the sprightly lemon flavor fades if the salad sits too long.

Clams, mussels, or scallops are also good in this recipe. Other good additions are pitted black or green olives and thin strips of roasted peppers.

SERVES 12

1 fresh or frozen octopus (about 2 pounds)
Salt
1 pound small to medium shrimp, shelled and
 deveined
1 pound cleaned squid, cut into ½-inch rings,
 tentacles left whole
2 cups thinly sliced celery
½ cup extra virgin olive oil

3 tablespoons fresh lemon juice, or to taste
2 tablespoons chopped flat-leaf parsley
2 garlic cloves, finely chopped
½ teaspoon lemon zest
½ small peperoncino, crumbled, or a pinch of
 crushed red pepper

Lettuce and radicchio leaves   Lemon slices
Flat-leaf parsley

1. If the octopus is frozen, thaw it in a large bowl of cold water, changing the water frequently; drain. Remove the hard beak from the base of the tentacles.

2. Fill a large saucepan with water and bring to a simmer. Add 1 teaspoon salt and the octopus, partially cover the pan, and cook until the octopus is tender when pierced with a fork, 45 minutes to 1 hour according to size.

3. Meanwhile, bring a second pan of water to a boil. Add 1 teaspoon salt and the shrimp and cook for 2 or 3 minutes, according to size. Remove the shrimp with a slotted spoon, transfer to a colander, and cool under cold running water. (Leave the water at a boil.) Drain the shrimp well.

4. Drop the squid rings into the boiling water and cook for 1 minute, or until opaque. Drain thoroughly.

5. Drain the octopus and scrape away any loose skin with a small knife. Cut the octopus tentacles into bite-size pieces.

6. Pat all the seafood dry. Cut the shrimp into bite-size pieces. Combine the seafood and celery in a large bowl. (The salad can be made ahead to this point, covered and refrigerated for up to 2 hours.)

7. In a small bowl, whisk the olive oil, lemon zest, lemon juice, parsley, garlic, and salt and pepper to taste. Pour the dressing over the seafood mixture and toss well. Taste and adjust the seasoning.

8. Arrange the lettuce and radicchio leaves on a large platter. Spoon the salad into the center. Garnish with parsley and lemon slices. Serve immediately.

WINE MATCH: Falanghina, Feudi di San Gregorio

Cleaning Clams and Mussels

To *clean clams,* soak them in cold water for 30 minutes. Drain. With a stiff brush, scrub the clams under cold running water.

To *clean mussels,* soak them in cold water for 30 minutes. Drain. Scrub the mussels with a stiff brush under cold running water. To remove the "beards" (fine threads the mussels use to attach themselves to solid objects), grasp them and tug them toward the hinged end of the mussel. If they refuse to budge, trim them off with scissors.

Discard any clams or mussels with broken shells or that do not close tightly when handled.

Ligurian Seafood Salad

CAPPON MAGRO

A spectacular platter of poached seafood and vegetables glistening with a luscious green sauce, this is the typical centerpiece of a Christmas Eve dinner in Liguria. I also serve it at other times of the year when I want a dramatic presentation. Smaller portions make a fine appetizer and it is also a perfect one-dish meal.

This version is inspired by the one at restaurant Puny in Portofino. The name cappon magro *means "lean cappone," a variety of Mediterranean fish. The name is ironic, since this is one of the most lavish salads imaginable. I adapted it using the seafood that I find in my area, but vary it as you wish. Firm-fleshed fish are essential, since tender fillets like sole or flounder break apart too easily. Some cooks add steamed mussels or clams in their shells; scallops work well too. I have seen other versions garnished with raw oysters, hard-cooked eggs, or* mosciame, *a type of salted and preserved fish.*

Cappon magro can be made in stages, but avoid cooking the vegetables more than 2 hours ahead of time, or they will need refrigeration, which would rob them of their fresh, delicate flavor and texture. Just wrap them in paper towels and keep them at room temperature.*

The seafood and sauce can be prepared ahead, covered, and refrigerated for up to 24 hours before serving. Remove them from the refrigerator about 30 minutes before serving.

SERVES 8

BROTH

1 carrot
1 celery rib
1 small onion
1 cup dry white wine
Salt
5 peppercorns

1 medium live lobster
16 large shrimp, shelled and deveined
1½ pounds firm-fleshed fish, such as tuna or
   halibut, cut into chunks

SAUCE

1 or 2 slices Italian or French bread, crusts
   removed, cut into ½-inch cubes
2 to 3 tablespoons white wine vinegar
2 cups flat-leaf parsley leaves
1 garlic clove
½ cup coarsely chopped green olives
¼ cup capers, rinsed and drained

¼ cup pine nuts
6 anchovy fillets
2 hard-cooked egg yolks (whites reserved for
   another use)
1 cup extra virgin olive oil
Salt and freshly ground black pepper

VEGETABLES

Salt

8 ounces green beans, trimmed

1 small cauliflower, trimmed and cut into small
 florets

4 medium potatoes

1 loaf Italian or French bread, cut into 1½-inch
 slices

1 garlic clove, halved

Extra virgin olive oil

1. To make the broth, in a large pot, combine 2 quarts water with the carrot, celery, onion, wine, salt to taste, and peppercorns, and bring to a simmer. Cook for 30 minutes.

2. Cook each variety of seafood separately: Place the lobster in the pot, cover, and cook for 14 minutes. Remove the lobster to a plate.

3. Add the shrimp to the pot. When the water returns to the boil, cook for 1 minute, or until the shrimp are pink and firm. Remove the shrimp with a slotted spoon.

4. Reduce the heat so that the liquid is barely simmering. Add the fish chunks and cook until barely opaque in the center: Timing will depend on the thickness of the fish—figure on about 4 minutes per ½ inch of thickness. Remove the fish with a slotted spoon. Let cool, then cover all the seafood and refrigerate. (The seafood can be prepared up to 24 hours ahead.)

5. Strain the broth and discard the solids. Let the broth cool.

6. To make the sauce, sprinkle the bread cubes with the vinegar and let soak until it has been absorbed. In a food processor, combine the parsley and garlic and pulse until finely chopped. Add the olives, capers, and pine nuts. Process to chop fine. Add the soaked bread, anchovies, and egg yolks and coarsely chop. With the machine running, gradually add the olive oil and process until creamy. Season to taste with salt and pepper. The sauce should flow like thick cream. Add some of the cooled fish broth if needed to loosen it. Cover and refrigerate. (The sauce can be made up to 24 hours ahead.)

7. No more than 2 hours before you plan to serve the salad, cook the vegetables: Bring about 2 quarts water to a boil in a medium pot. Add 2 teaspoons salt. Add the cauliflower and cook for 5 to 6 minutes, or until tender when pierced with a fork.

Remove the cauliflower with a slotted spoon, transfer to a colander, and cool under running water. Drain and blot dry.

8. Drop the green beans into the pot and cook until tender, 7 to 8 minutes. Transfer to a colander, and rinse until cool. Drain and blot dry.

9. Place the potatoes in the pot and cook until tender when pierced with a knife, about 20 minutes. Drain and let cool slightly, then peel and slice thick.

10. To assemble the dish, toast the bread slices. Rub them lightly with the garlic. Drizzle with oil.

11. Arrange the cauliflower, beans, and potato slices on a large serving platter. Drizzle the vegetables with some of the sauce. Separate the lobster tail from the body, leaving the claws intact. Remove the tail meat and cut it into slices. Arrange the lobster meat, shrimp, and fish chunks over the vegetables. Drizzle with the remaining sauce. Place the lobster body in the center of the platter. Arrange the toasted bread around the edges. Serve immediately.

WINE MATCH: Pigato, A Maccia

Scungilli Salad

INSALATA DI SCUNGILLI

My father once volunteered to make this salad for a party at the local Knights of Colum-bus chapter where he was the Commander, and we all pitched in to help him boil and slice scungilli for two hundred people! There must have been twenty-five pounds of it in our refrigerator and our house smelled fishy for a week afterward, but Dad was happy and everybody raved about his salad.

Scungilli are sea snails known in this country as whelks. They are similar to conch, which are common in Florida and the Caribbean. Either conch or whelks can be used in this recipe, though the flavor of whelks is stronger. Depending upon where you live, you might be able to buy fresh conch in the shell, but usually it appears partially cooked and frozen. Not very beautiful to look at, whelk meat is pleasantly chewy, with a deep briny flavor reminiscent of clams. Scungilli are usually sold frozen and partially cooked. Ask your fish provider to order them for you if you can't find them.

SERVES 4

1 pound frozen partially cooked scungilli
Salt
¼ cup olive oil
2 tablespoons chopped flat-leaf parsley
1 small garlic clove, finely chopped

1 small dried peperoncino, crumbled, or a
    pinch of crushed red pepper
2 to 3 tablespoons fresh lemon juice
Lettuce leaves for serving
Lemon wedges for garnish

1. Place the frozen scungilli in a bowl with cold water to cover, place the bowl in the refrigerator, and let thaw for several hours, or overnight, changing the water occa-sionally.

2. Bring a medium saucepan of water to a boil. Add the scungilli and 1 teaspoon salt. When the water returns to the simmer, cook the scungilli for 20 minutes, or until tender when pierced with a fork. Drain and pat dry.

3. Slice the scungilli into ⅛-inch-thick slices: when you come to a dark tube inside the body of the scungilli, filled with a spongy matter, pull or cut it out and discard, as it may be gritty. There is another tube on the outside of the body that does not need to be removed. Rinse the slices well and drain.

4. In a medium bowl, toss the scungilli with the oil, parsley, garlic, salt to taste, and peperoncino. Add lemon juice to taste. Chill briefly or serve immediately, on a bed of lettuce with lemon wedges.

WINE MATCH: Furore Bianco, Marisa Cuomo

Scungilli in Spicy Tomato Sauce

SCUNGILLI IN SALSA PICCANTE

Joe's Clam Bar in Little Italy used to be a great place to go for clams, fried calamari, seafood salad, and these scungilli. The place was decorated with fishing nets, buoys, and starfish to resemble an old beach house at the shore, even though it was in the heart of one of New York's busiest neighborhoods.

One day many years ago, my husband got the voglia (pronounced in Brooklyn Italian as "woo-lee"), or urge, for scungilli in hot sauce, a special treat. We took our friend Glenn, who had never been to Joe's and had never even tasted scungilli. Since Charles and I ordered it, Glenn decided to try it too, only he wanted his extra hot. The scungilli were served awash in a fiery red sauce on a bed of friselle, thick slices of dried bread generously seasoned with black pepper. Glenn liked it so much, he even ordered seconds.

No matter how you serve it, this spicy dish is delicious. Friselle are available at many Italian bakeries and food shops, or you can mail-order them (see Sources, page 296). The friselle should be dipped in a little water to dampen and soften them before being topped by the scungilli and sauce. They are also good as a base for seafood or tomato salads. Substitute toasted Italian bread if you can't find friselle.

SERVES 4

1 pound frozen partially cooked scungilli
¼ cup olive oil
1 large garlic clove, lightly crushed
1 small dried peperoncino, crumbled, or a pinch of crushed red pepper, or to taste
2 pounds fresh tomatoes (about 5), peeled, seeded, and chopped, or 2½ cups chopped Italian peeled canned tomatoes, with their juice

½ cup dry white wine
Salt
Friselle biscuits, moistened, or sliced Italian bread, toasted

1. If the scungilli are frozen, place them in a bowl with cold water to cover. Place the bowl in the refrigerator and let thaw for several hours, or overnight, changing the water occasionally.

2. Slice the scungilli into ¼-inch-thick slices: when you come to a dark tube inside the body of the scungilli, filled with a spongy matter, pull or cut it out and discard, as it

can be gritty. There is another tube on the outside of the body that does not need to be removed. Rinse the slices well and pat dry.

3. In a large saucepan, heat the oil with the garlic and peperoncino over medium-low heat until the garlic is golden. Add the tomatoes, wine, and salt to taste. Bring to a simmer, reduce the heat to low, and cook for 10 minutes, stirring occasionally. Remove and discard the garlic.

4. Add the scungilli and bring to a simmer. Cook for 30 minutes, stirring occasionally, or until the scungilli are chewy but tender and the sauce has thickened. If the sauce becomes too thick, stir in a little water. Taste for seasoning.

5. Serve hot over moistened friselle.

WINE MATCH: Salina Bianco, Hauner

Shrimp with Garlic and Toasted Bread Crumbs

GAMBERI ARAGONATI

Big shrimp crusted with garlic and crunchy bread crumbs were always a part of our family's Christmas Eve celebration. My father would peel and stuff pans full of fresh sweet shrimp, which would disappear faster than you can say Buon Natale! *Easy to do, they are a pleasure to enjoy any time of the year. Don't forget the last squeeze of fresh lemon juice; it really brings out the flavor of the shrimp.*

Aragonati appears to be a dialect word for gratinati, *meaning food that is baked under a browned crust. It has nothing to due with the herb oregano, though it is often misspelled* oreganati.

SERVES 6

1 cup fresh bread crumbs, made from Italian or French bread
⅓ cup very finely chopped flat-leaf parsley
1 large garlic clove, finely chopped

Salt and freshly ground black pepper
About ¼ cup olive oil
1½ pounds large shrimp, peeled and deveined
Lemon wedges

1. Preheat the oven to 450°F. Lightly oil a large baking pan.

2. In a bowl, combine the bread crumbs, parsley, garlic, and salt and pepper to taste. Add 3 tablespoons oil, or enough to moisten the crumbs.

3. Arrange the shrimp in the pan in a single layer, curling each one into a circle. Spoon a little of the crumb mixture onto each shrimp. Drizzle with a little more oil.

4. Bake for 10 to 15 minutes, depending on the size of the shrimp, or until the shrimp turn pink and the crumbs are lightly browned. Serve with lemon wedges.

WINE MATCH: Pinot Grigio, Organi

On Shrimp

When buying shrimp, make sure they are fresh and sweet-smelling, though farm-raised shrimp have a milder smell than those that are caught in the wild. The flesh should be firm and not mushy. Shrimp come in different colors, depending on where they grow and the variety, but there should not be any black spots on the shells, which indicate a lack of freshness.

To shell them, start at the underside of the shrimp. Separate the tiny feelers and pull off the shell. It will come off easily in segments. The last segment covering the tails can be left on as a "handle" or removed. It is up to you.

Shrimp have a long dark vein that should be removed, since it is often sandy. With a small knife, make a shallow cut next to the vein down the back of the shrimp and either pull the vein out with your fingers or rinse it away under cold water. The fine lighter vein along the inner curve does not need to be removed.

The Capo's Tuna

TONNO DEL CAPO

Every May, dozens of fishermen in Favignana, Sicily, gather to fish for giant tuna. The methods they use are highly ritualized and date back at least to the Arab occupation of the island. The capo, *or chief of the hunt, is called the* rais, *an Arabic word for leader. The men begin preparations weeks ahead of time, constructing an elaborate system of enormous net traps that are laid in the water.*

On the day of the hunt, the fishermen encircle the school of migrating tuna with their boats. As the men work, they sing an ancient ritualistic chant in Arabic led by the rais. They drive the giant fish into the chambers of the nets until they become trapped and have nowhere else to go. The fish fight desperately to escape. Finally, using long grappling hooks, the fishermen haul the exhausted fish into their small boats.

The tonnara, as the hunt is called, is a fascinating remnant of an earlier time. Once there were many of these hunts, all around Sicily, but overfishing and pollution have decreased the fishermen's yield every year. Now only one or two towns still have an annual hunt.

Most of the tuna that is caught is sold outside of Italy. Here is a simple preparation, popular in Sicily, that can be served hot or at room temperature. Sicilians cook the tuna to very well done, but I like it medium to rare.

SERVES 4

½ lemon, thinly sliced
Salt

1 thick tuna steak or several large chunks tuna
  (about 1½ pounds)

SAUCE
½ cup extra virgin olive oil
2 to 3 teaspoons fresh lemon juice
2 tablespoons chopped flat-leaf parsley
2 tablespoon chopped rinsed capers

½ teaspoon dried oregano
½ teaspoon grated lemon zest
Salt and freshly ground black pepper

1. In a large skillet or shallow saucepan, combine 3 inches water, the lemon slices, and 1 teaspoon salt and bring to a simmer over medium heat. Add the tuna. The water should just cover the fish. Simmer for 5 to 8 minutes, until the tuna is cooked medium to rare; it should be pink inside.

2. Remove the tuna with a slotted spatula, draining it well, and blot with paper towels.

3. To make the sauce, whisk the ingredients in a small bowl. (The dish can be made ahead to this point. Cover the tuna and sauce separately and let stand at room temperature for 1 hour before serving.)

4. Cut the tuna into ¼-inch-thick slices and arrange them on a platter. Whisk the sauce again and pour it over the tuna. Serve immediately.

WINE MATCH: Nozze d'Oro, Regaleali

Marinated Eel Skewers

SPIEDINI DI ANGUILLA

Eels are popular all over Italy for the cenone *on Christmas Eve. Their meat is sweet and tender. In Naples, they are deep-fried, while in northern Italy they are roasted. The only other fish that rivals eel in popularity at the holiday season is baccalà or stockfish.*

Many Italians can recall coming home the week before Christmas Eve and finding the bathtub filled with live eels. Since eels should be eaten very fresh, some cooks prefer to buy them live and kill them when it is time to cook them. The only problem is that killing and skinning an eel is quite a chore, and definitely not for the squeamish. Eels have powerful jaws and the skin is so tough it is necessary to use a pair of pliers to grasp and remove it. The eels continue to move for a while after they are killed.

Though eels are usually associated with the great Christmas Eve feasts, I have read that Sicilians also would eat eels for Saint Vitus's Feast Day in July because the movements of the freshly killed eel reminded them of people who suffer from nervous disorders of whom San Vitu is the protector. The movement is thought to symbolize life after death.

Many Asian fish markets carry eels.

SERVES 6

1½ pounds eel, skinned and cut into 2-inch chunks

12 bay leaves

1 garlic clove, thinly sliced

2 tablespoons chopped flat-leaf parsley

¼ cup olive oil

2 tablespoons white wine vinegar

Salt and freshly ground black pepper

1. In a large bowl, toss the eel with the bay leaves, garlic, parsley, oil, vinegar, and salt and pepper to taste. Cover and refrigerate for up to 3 hours.

2. Preheat a broiler or barbecue grill. Drain the eel. Thread the pieces on wooden or metal skewers, alternating the pieces with the bay leaves.

3. Broil or grill the eel, turning occasionally, until just cooked through, about 8 minutes. Serve hot.

WINE MATCH: Vignis, Venica

In Puglia, in the town of Presicce, it is traditional on Good Friday to eat the so-called "seven things" to recall the seven sufferings of Mary: dried figs, onions, salted anchovies, mint, capers, pickled peppers, and olives, accompanied by whole wheat bread.

Snails for the Feast of Saint Rosalie

BABBALUCI DEL FESTINO DI SANTA ROSALIA

When I asked my friend Bartolo Cocco about his Sicilian family's holiday recipes, he immediately replied, "Babbaluci! We always have babbaluci for the feast of Santa Rosalia."

Saint Rosalie is the patron saint of Palermo, and her feast day, July 13, is a time for celebration, with processions, music, dancing, and fireworks. Everybody eats tiny snails, called chiocciole or lumache in Italian, depending on the variety, but babbaluci in Sicilian. These aren't just any snails, though—they have been fed on the leaves of lemon and orange trees and have a very special flavor and are very tender.

You can buy snails at many Italian or Asian groceries, especially around the holidays. Before using, the snails should be kept in a large basket or pot in a dark place covered with a screen for a few days so that they can purge themselves. When we were children, we were more interested in playing with snails than eating them, organizing snail races when the adults were not looking or, better still, casually pushing the screen covering the basket askew to see what would happen when the snails crept up and over the sides.

When serving snails, supply sturdy toothpicks to remove them from their shells and lots of bread to absorb the juices. Or do as the Sicilians do and merely suck them out. A Sicilian adage says that there can never be too many women to kiss or snails to suck.

SERVES 4

1½ pounds live snails (purged as described above)
½ cup olive oil

2 garlic cloves, finely chopped
¼ cup chopped flat-leaf parsley
Salt and freshly ground black pepper

1. Wash the snails well under cold running water. Place in a large pot with cold water to cover, bring to a boil, and cook for 5 minutes.

2. Drain the snails and rinse them again. Shake well to remove the water.

3. In a large skillet, heat the oil with the garlic and parsley until the garlic is fragrant. Add the snails and salt and pepper to taste. Cook, turning frequently, for 20 minutes. Serve hot.

WINE MATCH: Pigato, Colle dei Bardellini

Baked Stuffed Lobster Tails

CODE DI ARAGOSTE AMOLLICATE

When my mother made Linguine with Lobster (page 116) for Christmas Eve, she set the lobster tails aside to serve as a second course, and prepared them in the following way.

SERVES 4

4 fresh or thawed frozen lobster tails
½ cup fresh bread crumbs, preferably homemade
2 tablespoons chopped flat-leaf parsley
1 small garlic clove, minced

½ teaspoon salt
Freshly ground black pepper
Olive oil
Lemon wedges

1. Preheat the oven to 450°F.

2. With kitchen shears, trim off the small flippers on the underside of the lobster tails. Cut off the thin translucent shell that covers the bottom of the tail meat. Bend the tails back slightly so that they lie flat. Arrange the lobster tails shell side down in a small baking pan.

3. Mix the bread crumbs, parsley, garlic, salt, and pepper together in a small bowl. Add enough oil to moisten the crumbs. Spoon the crumb mixture onto the lobster tails. Drizzle with a little more oil.

4. Bake the lobster tails for 12 to 15 minutes, or until the meat is firm and opaque. Serve hot with lemon wedges.

Baccalà Stew

GHIOTTA DI NATALE

Phil Cicconi remembers his family enjoying this stew on meatless winter Fridays, but it is also popular for Christmas Eve. Phil learned the recipe from his mother, Anna Maria, who was born in West Philadelphia of parents from Campobasso in Abruzzi. When Anna Maria married Guido Cicconi, who came from Ascoli Piceno in the Marches region of Italy, he asked her to learn to cook as they did in his region. He called it usanza Marchegiana, *the customary Marche way, and Anna Maria turned to her sister-in-law and other Marchegiane immigrants for help. Grandma Cicconi apparently learned her lessons well. Phil remembers with great fondness her white pizza, stuffed olives, and pizza Marchegiana, a high round cheese bread she served at Easter.*

Baccalà (see page 155) is so popular in Italy an entire book could be written about its many uses. In Puglia, it is cooked with tomatoes and chickpeas and tossed with fresh pasta for Christmas Eve. Eaten frequently during Holy Week preceding Easter, the fish is fried in batter, poached and served with parsley, garlic, and lemon juice; tossed in a salad with roasted peppers and boiled potatoes; whipped with olive oil and spread on toasted bread or polenta crostini; roasted; stuffed in a pizza; and so on.

I found almost the same recipe as Anna Maria's, named ghiotta di Natale, *meaning a Christmas delicacy, in a cookbook called* II Libro d'Oro della Cucina e dei Vini di Calabria e Basilicata *by Ottavio Cavalcanti. The same dish with the addition of capers and pine nuts is served for Christmas Eve in the Reggio Calabria area.*

SERVES 4

1 pound baccalà

¼ cup olive oil

1 medium onion, cut into 1-inch chunks

2 tender celery ribs, cut into 1-inch pieces

1 garlic clove, finely chopped

One 28- to 35-ounce can Italian peeled tomatoes, drained and finely chopped

Salt

1 small dried peperoncino, crumbled, or a pinch of crushed red pepper

1 pound red potatoes, scrubbed and cut into bite-size pieces

3 cups cauliflower florets (about ½ small head)

Freshly ground black pepper

6 large pitted green olives, sliced

6 prunes or ⅓ cup raisins

1. Place the baccalà in a bowl of cold water, place the bowl in the refrigerator, and soak the fish for 24 to 48 hours, depending on how salty it is. Change the water every 4

hours or so. (If you substitute *stoccafisso*, stockfish, the soaking time will be much longer, as much as a week.)

2. In a large saucepan, heat the oil over medium heat. Add the onion, celery, and garlic and cook, stirring frequently until softened, about 7 minutes.

3. Add the tomatoes, salt to taste, and peperoncino. Bring to a simmer and cook for 10 minutes. Add the potatoes and cauliflower and simmer for 10 minutes more.

4. Meanwhile, drain the fish and pull out any bones. Blot the fish dry and cut it into 2-inch chunks.

5. Add the fish to the saucepan, along with the olives and prunes. Cook for 5 to 10 minutes more, or until the fish is tender and cooked through. Serve immediately.

WINE MATCH: Mastro Bianco d'Irpinia, Mastroberardino

Fried Baccalà

BACCALÀ FRITTA

For Christmas Eve dinner, artist and sculptor Italo Scanga carries on an unusual tradition he learned in his native Calabria. Italo prepares a menu of all white foods, which in his region symbolizes the purity and holiness of the Christ child.

The menu is a meatless one, served on an all-white table. Even the flowers that decorate the dining table are white. Pasta with a sauce of cauliflower, onions, and garlic begins the meal and there is sometimes a dish of white beans. Next comes the baccalà, cooked either with potatoes and leeks or fried with a light, thin flour crust in olive oil spiked with garlic and fresh chiles. Italo, who lives in southern California, prefers a certain type of baccalà that his daughter in Rhode Island buys and ships to him every year. The flesh is thick and it has bones. He soaks it carefully before cooking, until it is just right. Italo's companion, Su-Mei Yu, contributes a salad she learned to make in Ravenna of thin sliced fennel, ripe pears, and shavings of Parmigiano-Reggiano to end the savory part of the menu. Struffoli and other typical Christmas desserts follow.

SERVES 4

Flour
Salt and freshly ground black pepper
1 pound baccalà or stockfish, soaked according
   to the directions on page 155

¼ cup olive oil
2 large garlic cloves, lightly crushed
1 or 2 fresh chiles, such as jalapeño, or
   substitute a small dried peperoncino

1. On a piece of wax paper, combine the flour with a little salt and freshly ground pepper to taste.

2. Pat the fish dry and cut it into serving pieces.

3. In a large skillet, heat the oil over medium-low heat with the garlic and chile. Cook until the garlic is golden on both sides, about 5 minutes.

4. Quickly dip the fish into the flour mixture, coating it well on all sides. Carefully place the fish in the oil. Fry the fish until golden brown, turning once, 5 to 8 minutes. The exact cooking time depends on the thickness of the fish.

5. Remove the fish with a slotted spoon and serve hot.

Salt Cod and Dried Cod

BACCALÀ E STOCCOFISSO

Though dishes in Italy remain specific to each region, *baccalà*, salted fish, and *stoccofisso*, or *pesce stocco*, dried fish, are eaten everywhere. For centuries before canning and refrigeration existed, Catholics did not eat meat on Fridays and the eve of holy days. Fresh fish was very expensive and often hard to find, so people came to rely on salted and dried fish.

Stockfish originated in Scandinavia, where it was air-dried on wood frames until it was hard as wood. (The name means stick fish.) It keeps a very long time.

Baccalà is salted fish fillets of either cod, perch, or another variety. The best-quality baccalà is skinless and made of cod. Much of what I find today comes from Canada, though it is also made in Portugal, Spain, and Scandinavia.

In Italy, Italians use the terms *baccalà* and *stoccofisso* interchangeably, although they require different handling. This is probably because in most Italian fish markets, you can buy either fish soaked and ready to use.

Because they need soaking to eliminate the salt, and to rehydrate the fish, cooking baccalà and stockfish requires advance planning and some attention. A number of people told me they had heard of someone who put the fish in the toilet tank to soak. The fresh water coming into the tank whenever the toilet was flushed ensured a frequent change of water. Let's hope this is just an old wives' tale.

Baccalà is much easier to work with than stockfish. It requires 24 to 48 hours of soaking to remove most of the salt. Just place the fish in a bowl of cold water to cover and refrigerate, changing the water four or five times. Taste the water after 24 hours. If it still tastes salty, soak the fish another three hours and taste it again.

Stockfish requires close to a week of soaking before it can be used. Look for thick, white pieces at the market. Place them in a bowl of cold water to soak and change the water two or three times a day, or as often as you think of it. As the fish begins to absorb the water, bend or flex the pieces to help them absorb it better. The color will lighten and the fish will become puffy as it is reconstituted. Stockfish is extremely smelly. If you can, keep it isolated in a cool place.

The Monzù's Swordfish Pie

IMPANATA DI PESCE SPADA

In The Leopard, *author Giuseppe di Lampedusa writes about a great feast held in one of the grand aristocratic homes of Palermo where all kinds of elaborate dishes were served, including timbales or savory pies filled with pasta, meats, and fish.*

Here is how he described one such pie: "The burnished gold of the crusts, the fragrance of sugar and cinnamon they exuded, were but preludes to the delights released from the interior when the knife broke the crust; first came a smoke laden with aromas, then chicken livers, hard-boiled eggs, sliced ham, chicken, and truffles in masses of piping hot, glistening macaroni, to which the meat juice gave an exquisite hue of suede."

In the era that Lampedusa was describing, the food would have been prepared by a French-trained chef known as a monzù, *a Sicilian term of respect that is a corruption of the word* monsieur. *Having a French-trained* monzù *to cook for you was a major status symbol in Sicily.*

I can imagine this dish being served at a party such as the one in Lampedusa's account. The luscious filling of swordfish and eggplant accented with tangy capers and sweet raisins seems exotic in the orange-accented crust. It makes a magnificent presentation and would be the star of any feast day table.

Like many preparations of this type, it can and really should be made in stages, so that it requires little last-minute effort on the part of the cook. It is delicious hot or cold.

SERVES 8 TO 10

DOUGH

4 cups unbleached all-purpose flour

2 tablespoons sugar

1 teaspoon grated orange zest

1 teaspoon salt

8 tablespoons (1 stick) cold unsalted butter,
  cut into ¼-inch-thick slices

½ cup (4 ounces) vegetable shortening

3 large eggs, beaten

3 to 4 tablespoons cold white wine

FILLING

½ cup olive oil

1 medium eggplant, cut into ¼-inch-thick slices

Salt

1 medium onion, chopped

1 tender celery rib, finely chopped

5 fresh tomatoes, peeled, seeded, and chopped or 2½ cups chopped drained canned Italian peeled tomatoes

½ cup pitted green olives, chopped

2 tablespoons chopped capers

2 tablespoons raisins

2 tablespoons pine nuts

1½ pounds thin-sliced swordfish, skinned

Freshly ground black pepper

1. To make the dough, put the flour, sugar, orange zest, and salt in a large bowl. Cut in the butter and shortening with a pastry blender or two knives until the mixture resembles coarse crumbs. Stir in the eggs and just enough wine so that the ingredients begin to come together and form a dough. Squeeze the dough between your palms and shape it into a ball. Do not overwork the dough, or it will become tough.

2. Divide the dough into two pieces, one two times as large as the other, and shape each one into a disk. Wrap each piece in plastic wrap. Refrigerate for at least 1 hour, or overnight.

3. To make the filling, heat ¼ cup of the oil in a large skillet. Blot the eggplant slices dry. Fry them, in batches, a single layer at a time until browned on both sides. Drain on paper towels. Sprinkle with salt.

4. In another large skillet, combine the remaining ¼ cup oil, the onion, and celery and cook over medium heat, stirring frequently, until the vegetables are tender, about 10 minutes. Stir in the tomatoes, olives, capers, raisins, and pine nuts. Cook until the juices evaporate and the sauce is thick, about 15 minutes. Add the swordfish and salt and pepper to taste. Baste the fish with the sauce, cover, and cook for 5 to 8 minutes, until the fish is just done. If there is too much liquid in the pan, remove the fish to a plate and reduce the liquid over medium heat. Let cool slightly.

5. Preheat the oven to 375°F.

6. On a floured surface, roll out the larger piece of dough to an 18-inch circle. Loosely wrap the dough around the rolling pin and fit it into a 9-inch springform pan. Spoon

half of the swordfish mixture into the pan. Cover with the eggplant. Top with the remaining swordfish and sauce.

7. Roll out the smaller piece of dough to a 12-inch circle. Center the dough on top of the pie. Trim off all but a 1-inch border of dough. Fold the dough over itself, pinching the edges to seal. With a small knife, cut several slits in the top of the dough to allow steam to escape.

8. Bake for 50 to 60 minutes, or until the top of the pie is golden brown and the juices visible in the slits are bubbling. Cool for 10 minutes on a wire rack.

9. Remove the sides of the pan. Let cool for 15 minutes more and serve hot, or cool and serve at room temperature.

WINE MATCH: Chardonnay, Regaleali

Handling Seafood

Since seafood spoils easily, it needs to be refrigerated and used within 24 hours of purchase. Fill a bowl with ice, then place the fish or seafood, wrapped in plastic, on top. For clams, mussels, or oysters, which must be kept alive until they are cooked, place them in a shallow pan and cover them loosely with a towel. Keep crabs and lobsters, which could escape from a pan, in a paper bag with holes poked in it for air in the refrigerator.

The third Sunday of July, Venice celebrates the Feast of the Redeemer. Everyone eats fish *in saor,* meaning fish cooked with onions, vinegar, and raisins.

Meat and Poultry

CARNE E POLLAME

Although Italians love to eat, you won't find them digging into big steaks, double-thick veal or pork chops, or half a roast chicken. Italian meals are balanced, with the components eaten in proportion: sometimes a small appetizer or antipasto to start, a moderate helping of pasta, risotto, or soup, and then a small amount of meat or poultry, with one or two generous helpings of vegetables. For most of its history, meat was always too expensive in Italy for it to be the center of a meal. In fact, it wasn't until the postwar years that people could afford to eat it on a regular basis, rather than only on holidays and feast days.

Pork, lamb, and veal are probably the most popular meats. Italian pork is especially tasty, bred to be moist and full of flavor. It is eaten cured or fresh as roasts, stews, sausages, prosciutto, or salami.

Lamb and goat are especially popular in southern Italy. The small animals thrive even though the land is rocky and the soil is poor. Roman lamb, *abbacchio*, is so young that the animals have never fed on grass. The meat is tender and delicate. Tiny rib chops can be eaten in one or two bites.

Beef is rare in Italy because there is little grazing land available. Instead, Italians eat a lot of *vitellone*, veal from older calves. It is less flavorful and drier than beef because it has a lower fat content.

Chickens are widely available, as are turkeys. The best are farm-raised and full of flavor because they are allowed to roam freely and are fed organic feed. Capons are essential for holiday meals in many areas, though turkey, either roasted whole or in parts, is becoming increasingly popular. A wide range of other birds are eaten, depending on the region, including guinea fowl, pheasant, duck, goose, and quail.

Veal Roll-Ups

PULPETTE AVVOLTE

La Confratèrnita Della Misericordia, The Confraternity of Mercy, is a lay association founded in Montalcino in Tuscany in 1846 to help the sick and others in need. Its good works are celebrated every year on the last Sunday of August, which is called the Feast of the Whites for the color of the robes worn by the members. The day begins with a special Mass, followed by a band concert, sack races, and games like the pentolaccia. *The "bad pot" works something like a Mexican piñata, but instead of a papier-mâché donkey or rooster, clay pots are suspended overhead, some filled with gifts and others with water or cinders. Participants try to guess which pot is which before hitting the pots with clubs to win the prizes, but they are sometimes disappointed by a shower or a pile of ash.*

Everyone drinks the local wine and eats these delicious veal roll-ups, tucked into some crusty bread. The bread is a perfect foil for the winy tomato sauce, but if you prefer, you can serve the veal and sauce over polenta. Great for parties and entertaining, pulpette reheat well. Serve them with a green salad tossed with a good Tuscan extra virgin olive oil and a bit of wine vinegar.

SERVES 4 TO 6

1 pound thin slices veal cutlet

FILLING

4 ounces ground veal

2 ounces pancetta, finely chopped

¼ cup chopped flat-leaf parsley

1 small garlic clove, minced

¼ cup dry bread crumbs, made from Italian or French bread

Salt and freshly ground black pepper

2 tablespoons olive oil

½ cup dry red wine

2 cups peeled, seeded, and chopped fresh tomatoes or chopped drained Italian peeled canned tomatoes

1 teaspoon tomato paste, optional

1 small dried peperoncino, crumbled, or a pinch of crushed red pepper

1. Lay a piece of plastic wrap on a work surface and place 1 slice of veal on top. Cover with another sheet of plastic wrap. Gently and evenly pound the veal with a meat mallet, rolling pin, or other heavy object, being careful not to break it up, to about ⅛ inch thick. Cut it into pieces about 3 inches square. Repeat with the remaining veal. You should have 12 pieces. Set aside.

2. To make the filling, combine the ground veal, pancetta, parsley, garlic, and bread crumbs in a large bowl. Add salt and pepper to taste. Shape the mixture into 12 small sausage shapes about 3 inches long.

3. Place one "sausage" at one end of a piece of veal. Roll up the meat to enclose the sausage. Close the roll with a wooden toothpick. Repeat with the remaining veal and filling.

4. In a medium skillet, heat the olive oil over medium heat. Add the rolls and brown on all sides. Add the wine and bring to a simmer. Cook for 1 minute, turning the rolls. Add the tomatoes, salt to taste, and peperoncino. If using fresh tomatoes, you may want to stir in the tomato paste for added richness. Reduce the heat to low, partially cover the pan, and cook, adding a little warm water as needed to prevent the sauce from becoming too thick, for 1 hour, or until the meat is tender when pierced with a fork.

5. Remove the toothpicks. Serve hot, with bread or polenta.

WINE MATCH: Chianti Classico, Viticcio

Cold Stuffed Breast of Veal

CIMA ALLA GENOVESE

A great party dish, this boneless veal breast typically is eaten cold. Have the butcher trim off the fat and bone out a breast of veal, leaving a pocket for the stuffing. Preparing the stuffed veal breast is a bit of a production, but it can be cooked completely a day ahead of time. The next day, just slice and serve it. In Liguria, the slices were arranged overlapping on a bed of colorful salad greens on a large platter and drizzled with bright green pesto sauce, a presentation given here.

There are many different versions of cima. *Other typical stuffing ingredients include hard-cooked eggs, brains, sweetbreads, and vegetables like artichokes or greens. In Genoa and throughout the region of Liguria,* cima *is served for Christmas, often with a salad of thin-sliced celery, mashed anchovies, and as much black truffle as the cook can afford.*

SERVES 10 TO 12

BROTH
1 carrot
1 celery rib
1 medium onion

A few sprigs flat-leaf parsley
1 tablespoon salt

FILLING
1 ounce dried porcini mushrooms (about ¾ cup)
2 to 3 slices Italian bread
¼ cup milk
1 pound ground veal
4 large eggs, beaten
1 cup freshly grated Parmigiano-Reggiano
2 garlic cloves, finely chopped
2 teaspoons finely chopped fresh marjoram or
   1 teaspoon dried

Salt and freshly ground black pepper
1 cup diced carrots
1 cup fresh or frozen peas
4 ounces prosciutto, in one piece, cut into
   narrow strips
¼ cup pine nuts
1 boneless breast of veal with a pocket, well
   trimmed (about 5 pounds)

PESTO
1 cup basil leaves, washed and dried
1 cup flat-leaf parsley leaves, washed and dried
1 garlic clove
Salt

1 cup extra virgin olive oil

Mixed baby greens

1. To make the broth, choose a pot large enough to hold the breast or veal. Add about 4 quarts of cold water, the carrot, celery, onion, parsley, and salt. Bring to a simmer.

2. Meanwhile, to make the filling, place the mushrooms in a small bowl with 1 cup warm water. Let stand for 30 minutes. When the mushrooms are soft, drain off the liquid. (Strain the liquid and store it in the refrigerator or freezer, to use to flavor soups or sauces.) Rinse the mushrooms in cold water, giving extra attention to the base of the stems, where grit may collect. Drain and chop fine.

3. Remove the crust from the bread. Tear the bread into small pieces. You should have about ½ cup. In a small bowl, combine the bread and milk. Let stand for 5 minutes, then squeeze out the milk.

4. In a large bowl, combine the mushrooms, bread, ground veal, eggs, cheese, garlic, marjoram, and salt and pepper to taste. Mix well. Gently stir in the carrots, peas, prosciutto strips, and pine nuts.

5. Stuff the mixture into the veal pocket, packing it in well to eliminate air bubbles, but do not fill the pocket more than two-thirds full, or the filling may burst out as it cooks. Sew up the opening, using a large needle and dental floss for thread.

6. Lay the veal breast on a large piece of cheesecloth. Roll the meat up like a sausage, using the cloth to help you shape it. Wrap the cloth around the meat and tie up the meat roll with kitchen twine. (An extra pair of hands is useful here.)

7. Carefully lower the veal into the simmering liquid. Place a heavy pot lid or other object on top of the veal to keep it submerged. Add more water if needed so that it is completely covered. Bring the liquid back to a simmer. Cover and cook for 1 hour, regulating the heat so that the water maintains the simmer.

8. Uncover the pot and cook for 1 to 1½ hours more, or until the veal is tender when pierced with a metal skewer or a thin knife.

9. Remove the meat from the pot. Place it in a large roasting pan and place a baking pan or cookie sheet on top of the meat. Top with a heavy weight, such as a few large cans or a heavy pot. (Make sure it will fit in the refrigerator.) Cover and chill overnight or for up to 2 days.

10. With a mortar and pestle or in a food processor or blender, crush or finely chop the basil, parsley, and garlic. Add salt to taste. Gradually blend in the oil. Cover and store at room temperature up to one hour or refrigerate up to 2 days. Let come to room temperature before using. When ready to serve, unwrap the veal and cut it into thin slices. Serve at cool room temperature, with the pesto sauce.

TIP: *Cima* can be an appetizer or a main course. It is usually served cold, but leftover slices can be coated with bread crumbs, lightly browned in olive oil, and served hot.

WINE MATCH: Cinque Terre, De Batte

Feast Day Meat Loaf

POLPETTONE

Although you may not think of meat loaf as a special-occasion dish, Neapolitans do. My mother told me that her mother, who came from Afragola in the province of Avellino, used to make this meat loaf for Christmas dinner. When the loaf is cut, the eggs give the slices a bull's-eye effect. Serve polpettone with potatoes roasted with rosemary and olive oil and boiled green beans dressed with olive oil, vinegar, sweet onions, and basil.

SERVES 8

MEAT LOAF MIXTURE

1½ pounds mixed ground pork, veal, and beef

1 cup torn day-old Italian bread
  (crusts removed)

½ cup milk

3 large eggs, lightly beaten

½ cup freshly grated Parmigiano-Reggiano

¼ cup chopped flat-leaf parsley

1 garlic clove, minced

1 teaspoon salt

Freshly ground black pepper

4 ounces thin-sliced prosciutto or mortadella

4 ounces thin-sliced provolone

3 to 4 hard-cooked eggs, peeled, optional

2 tablespoons plain dry bread crumbs

1. Preheat the oven to 350°F. Oil a 12 × 9 × 2-inch baking pan.

2. In a large bowl, mix all of the meat loaf ingredients. (The best way is with your hands.)

3. On a large sheet of wax paper, pat out the meat mixture to a 12 × 8 × ¾-inch-thick rectangle. Layer the prosciutto and cheese on top. If using the eggs, place them lengthwise in a row down the center. Grasp one long side of the paper. Pushing the filling ingredients in as necessary, lift the paper and roll up the meat to completely enclose the filling. Pinch the seam and ends together to seal in the filling. Using the paper to lift it, place the loaf seam side down in the baking pan. Sprinkle the top with the bread crumbs.

4. Bake for 1 hour, or until the internal temperature of the meat registers 160°F on an instant-read thermometer. Let stand for 10 minutes.

5. Using two metal spatulas, slide the loaf onto a serving platter. Cut into slices to serve.

WINE MATCH: Lacryma Christi, Sorrentino

Osso Buco with Red Wine

OSSO BUCO AL VINO ROSSO

Thick chunks of veal shank, called osso buco, *meaning bone with a hole, always seem festive to me. Everybody loves them, and their dramatic shape and size look great on the plate. I developed this version for an article that appeared in* Food & Wine *magazine on a holiday dinner for eight that could be made in three hours. While the veal shanks simmer, you can prepare the side dish: Buttered Polenta (page 129), a white wine or saffron risotto, or mashed potatoes with Parmigiano-Reggiano cheese would be my choice.*

I like to tie the slices of veal shank around the middle, like a belt, so that the pieces keep their shape as they cook. You can have the butcher do this for you, or you can do it yourself with kitchen twine. Serve the veal with small spoons so that diners can scoop out the rich marrow inside the bones.

SERVES 6

2 tablespoons olive oil
Six 2-inch-thick meaty slices veal shank, tied
2 carrots, chopped
1 medium onion, chopped
1 celery rib, chopped
2 garlic cloves, chopped

1 cup dry red wine, such as Italian Barbera or Chianti
1 cup chopped canned Italian peeled tomatoes
1 cup chicken broth
Salt and freshly ground black pepper

1. Preheat the oven to 325°F.

2. In a large Dutch oven with a tight-fitting lid, heat the oil over medium heat. Pat the meat dry with paper towels. Add the veal, in batches if necessary, and brown it well on both sides. Transfer the veal to a plate.

3. Lower the heat slightly and add the carrots, onion, celery, and garlic. Cook until tender and golden, about 7 minutes.

4. Add the wine and cook, scraping the bottom of the pot with a wooden spoon to release the browned bits. Stir in the tomatoes and broth and bring to a simmer. Return the meat and any juices that have collected on the plate to the pot and sprinkle with salt and pepper. When the liquid returns to the simmer, cover the pot and place it in the oven. Bake for 1 hour.

5. Baste the meat with the sauce. If the sauce seems dry, add a little water to the pot. Cover and cook for 1 hour more, or until the meat is very tender and coming away from the bone. Transfer the veal to a serving platter.

6. If the sauce seems thin, remove the veal, set it aside, and place the pot over high heat. Cook, stirring frequently, until the sauce is reduced and slightly syrupy. Spoon the sauce over the meat and serve immediately.

WINE MATCH: Sassoaloro, Biondi-Santi

New Year's Eve and Day

On New Year's Eve, also known as San Silvestro, in honor of the pope whose feast day falls on that day, Italians sweep their homes clean, both literally and figuratively, of all the old year's troubles, problems, and disappointments. At midnight, the doors and windows are thrown open and people toss out their damaged crockery, used furniture, and broken household items. Use caution when walking under an open window, especially in Rome.

Children are given gifts of *strenne*, small sums of money. The word comes from the name of the Roman goddess Strenia, who was honored on the first day of the year with a procession through Rome.

The New Year brings hope for a fresh start and a bright future. It is a time to look ahead and try to guess and even influence what the coming year will bring. Small rounded foods like lentils, beans, and even grapes suggest coins, and many people eat them as symbols of prosperity and abundance, hoping that they will bring them good luck. The same legumes are served with thick slices of sausages such as *zampone*, a pig's foot stuffed with spiced pork sausage meat, or *cotechino*, a similarly flavored pork sausage wrapped in pig's skin. In the Veneto, *musetto*, another type of sausage, is served with borlotti, cranberry beans cooked with onion and olive oil. Sicilians enjoy thick, hearty lentil soup.

Grapes harvested in the fall have been carefully preserved on straw mats to eat on the holiday. Traditionally, being able to preserve the grapes for several months from the fall harvest to New Year's Day was considered a favorable sign that money would last all of the year to come.

According to an old saying, "If we laugh at the first of the year, we will laugh all year; if we cry at the first of the year, we will cry all year." Families get together for parties, feasting, and fun to ensure that the good times will continue in the year ahead.

Zampone with Lentils

ZAMPONE CON LENTICCHIE

Zampone *is a large spiced sausage whose name means a pig's trotter (foot). It is tradi-tional in Emilia-Romagna, where it is part of a* bollito misto, *a boiled dinner made with cuts of veal, beef, and chicken. Zampone is hard to find in this country, but you can order it from some specialty butchers in Italian neighborhoods or by mail-order from Bal-ducci's and other sources (see page 296).*

Alternatives to zampone are cotechino and cappello da preto, *which have a similar fla-vor and tender, moist texture. Cotechino, named for its pork skin covering, has the typi-cal sausage shape, while* cappello da preto *is shaped like a priest's tricornered hat. Cotechino is sometimes available here around the holidays, but if you cannot find any of these, substitute another large unsmoked sausage, such as a French* saucisson à l'ail. *If all else fails, use good-quality Italian pork sausages, but grill or fry them rather than boil them.*

In many parts of Italy, the typical New Year's Day menu includes zampone with lentils, mashed potatoes or polenta, and spinach braised with butter and Parmigiano-Reggiano. Italians like to serve Lambrusco, a sometimes sparkling red wine, with the zampone and lentils, but it is not easy to find a good one in this country.

SERVES 8

1 onion, finely chopped
1 carrot, finely chopped
1 celery rib, finely chopped
3 tablespoons olive oil
1 garlic clove, finely chopped
1 small dried peperoncino, crumbled, or a pinch
  of crushed red pepper

1 pound lentils, picked over and rinsed
1 cup chopped fresh or canned Italian peeled
  tomatoes
6 cups chicken or meat broth
Salt
2 zamponi or cotechini (about 1 pound total)

1. In a large pot, cook the onion, carrot, and celery in the olive oil over medium heat until wilted, about 5 minutes. Stir in the garlic and peperoncino and cook for 2 min-utes more.

2. Stir in the lentils. Add the tomatoes and broth and bring to a simmer. Lower the heat, cover, and cook for 30 minutes.

3. Add salt to taste and cook until the lentils are tender, about 15 minutes more. Add a little water if the lentils seem dry.

4. While the lentils are cooking, put the sausages into a large pot with water to cover, partially cover the pot, and bring to a simmer. Cook for 45 minutes (or as recommended by the manufacturer).

5. To serve, transfer the sausage to a board. (The sausage can be kept warm in the hot water for up to 1 hour.) Cut it into thick slices. Spoon the lentils onto a warm serving platter. Arrange the sausage on top. Serve immediately.

WINE MATCH: Barbarossa Cru del Dosso, Fattoria Paradiso

Roast Pork Porchetta Style

PORCHETTA

The porchetta truck is a ubiquitous sight in Rome and the surrounding countryside. Porchetta is a whole pig stuffed with fennel and seasoned with rosemary and black pepper. Wherever there is a market or fair, you will find a truck with its glassed-in rotisserie and meltingly tender roasted pork. Order it stuffed into a panino to eat on the spot, or buy some slices to take home to the family for a snack later on. Ask for some sale—not salt in this case, but the crackling pork skin that is full of flavor.

Though I have heard of people who host pig roasts in their backyards, it isn't feasible for most of us. I have applied the same flavorings and slow-cooking technique to a pork shoulder roast with delicious results. This makes a lot, so prepare it when you are having a big party. It is the perfect roast for a New Year's Eve or Day gathering. Serve it one day hot, preceded by Good Luck Lentil Soup (page 49), or serve it cold with a pot of warm beans or lentils.

The marinated roast takes about 1 hour out of the refrigerator to come to room temperature, 4 to 4½ hours to roast, and 20 to 30 minutes to rest, so plan accordingly. The good news is that once you put it in the oven, there is little else to do, except smell the wonderful aromas it sends out as it cooks. Leftovers make great sandwiches, or you can toss strips into a stir-fry or pasta sauce.

SERVES 12

8 garlic cloves, peeled
1 tablespoon chopped rosemary
1 tablespoon fennel seeds
1 tablespoon kosher or coarse sea salt

1 teaspoon coarsely ground black pepper
¼ cup olive oil
One 7-pound pork shoulder roast

1. In a food processor, combine the garlic, rosemary, fennel, salt, pepper, and olive oil. Process to a smooth paste.

2. Poke deep pockets into the surface of the pork with a small knife. Rub the paste into the pockets. Place the pork in a roasting pan, cover tightly with plastic wrap, and refrigerate for up to 24 hours.

3. About 1 hour before cooking, remove the meat from the refrigerator.

4. Preheat the oven to 350°F.

5. Uncover the pork. Roast for 3 hours.

6. Tip the pan and carefully remove the excess fat. Roast the meat for 1 to 1½ hours longer, or until the temperature reaches 170°F on an instant-read thermometer. The skin should be crisp and a deep nutty brown. Let the meat stand for 20 minutes.

7. Remove the skin from the pork and cut it into small pieces. Carve the roast. Serve hot or at room temperature.

TIP: A boneless fresh ham can be substituted for the pork shoulder. Rub half the paste over the boned side of the meat. Make pockets through the skin and surface of the pork and spread half the paste there. Roll up the meat and tie with kitchen twine. Marinate and roast as above.

WINE MATCH: I Quattro Mori, Castel di Paolis

In the Val di Bisenzio, in the Veneto, the custom is to throw an old slipper down the stairs on New Year's Day. If it lands right side up, the year will be favorable for business and for the family.

BOLLITO MISTO

In Piedmont, New Year's Day means *bollito misto*. At least five different kinds of meat, including cuts of beef, veal, chicken or capon, and sausage are simmered together in a huge pot with flavoring vegetables. The broth is eaten first with pasta, then the meats are served as a *secondo* with a variety of different sauces, typically honey and walnut, tomato, and green sauces and *mostarda*, fruits in a sweet and tangy mustard syrup.

Roast Leg of Lamb with Garlic, Rosemary, and Little Potatoes

AGNELLO AL FORNO

In Puglia, baby lamb is slow-roasted on a spit until it is moist and tender, seasoned only with fresh rosemary, garlic, and olive oil. These same seasonings are perfect on our more mature lamb. The meat cooks in a medium oven in a little more than an hour's time. Tiny new potatoes roasted alongside pick up the flavors of the meat and seasonings. Lamb tastes best when cooked to medium-rare, on the pink side in the thickest part.

For a Palm Sunday or other spring menu, serve the lamb and potatoes with stuffed artichokes. For a first course, serve fettucine with Ragù Bolognese (page 71). Finish the meal with Cannoli (page 292).

SERVES 8 TO 10

1 shank-end leg of lamb, trimmed (about 4½ pounds)

6 garlic cloves, cut into slivers

1 branch rosemary, stems removed

16 tiny new potatoes or 6 to 8 larger potatoes, cut into 1-inch chunks

¼ cup olive oil

Salt and freshly ground black pepper

1. Preheat the oven to 350°F.

2. Make shallow slits all over the lamb with a small knife. Poke the garlic and rosemary into the slits, reserving a little for the potatoes.

3. Place the lamb fat side up in a large roasting pan. Scatter the potatoes around the lamb and sprinkle them with the remaining garlic and rosemary. Drizzle the lamb and potatoes with the olive oil and sprinkle with salt and pepper. Toss the potatoes well to coat.

4. Roast for 30 minutes.

5. Turn the potatoes and roast for 30 to 45 minutes longer, until the meat feels slightly springy to the touch and the internal temperature registers 130°F on an instant-read thermometer. Transfer the lamb to a cutting board. Cover with foil. Let rest for at least 15 minutes before slicing.

6. Test the largest of the potatoes by piercing it with a sharp knife. If they need further cooking, return them to the oven and cook until tender.

7. Slice the lamb and serve it with the potatoes.

WINE MATCH: Venegazzu, Gasparini

Easter

PASQUA

Easter Sunday is a joyous day in Italy, after the long, somber Lenten season. Though Italians say *"Natale con i tuoi, Pasqua con chi vuoi"*—"Christmas with your family, Easter with whomever you want"—most families make every effort to be together.

Mountains of long-stemmed artichokes, purple-green asparagus, fat pods of fava beans, and tiny peas fill the market stalls. Baby lamb or fresh kid is roasted, grilled, or stewed. In the Abruzzo and Puglia, chunks of stewed lamb are topped with a layer of eggs and cheese that forms a golden, custard-like topping. Eggs, symbolic of fertility and rebirth, are used in many dishes, as is cheese, especially fresh, creamy ricotta.

Every region seems to have its own special egg-and-cheese-rich pie or bread. *Fiadone* from Abruzzo, *torta Pasqualina* from Liguria, *pizza chena* or *pizza rustica* from Campania, *torta di Pasqua* from Umbria, and *crescia* from the Marches are just a few.

Easter desserts are rich in eggs and cheese, such as *pupi con l'uova*, baby dolls with an egg or Easter Baby Dolls (page 36); *colomba*, a sweet bread shaped like a dove; *Casatiello Dolce*, Grandma's Easter Egg Wreath (page 34); and cheesecake (see page 224). Marzipan is molded into baby lambs, complete with curly wool, as well as hearts, fish, and fruits. Beautifully decorated chocolate eggs, often with a gift hidden inside, finish the meal. Usually the gift is a small toy, but suitors sometimes have the eggs custom-made to conceal a more valuable gift like a watch or ring.

Easter Monday, known as *Pasquetta*, or Little Easter, is also a holiday. An Italian friend told me that it is like the first day of spring and the Fourth of July all rolled into one. People take the day off and go on picnics.

Whoever prepares the Easter dinner makes sure there will be plenty of leftovers to eat on *Pasquetta*. Monday morning, pasta is baked in big pans, then these are wrapped in towels and blankets to keep them warm. Everybody heads to the countryside to walk in the grass, play soccer with friends, or just sit in the sunshine and enjoy an informal meal. Sicilians like to barbecue, especially lamb and homemade sausages.

Roast Pork with Hazelnuts

Hazelnuts are so plentiful in Piemonte that they are used in all kinds of dishes. Enhanced by chopped hazelnuts, even a simple pork roast becomes festive. This dish would most likely be braised on top of the stove, but since our American pork is so lean, it tastes better when it is cooked in the oven. Don't overcook it! Pork is fully cooked, moist, and tender when cooked medium and still slightly pink in the center.

SERVES 8

2 tablespoons chopped rosemary
2 large garlic cloves, finely chopped
2 tablespoons olive oil
Salt and freshly ground black pepper
One 3-pound boneless pork loin roast, rolled
  and tied

1 cup dry white wine
About 1 cup meat or chicken broth
½ cup hazelnuts, toasted, skinned, and coarsely
  chopped (see page 243)

1. Preheat the oven to 425°F.

2. Finely chop the rosemary and garlic. Combine it with the oil and salt and pepper to taste. Rub the mixture all over the pork. Place the meat fat side up in a roasting pan just large enough to hold it. Roast for 15 minutes.

3. Pour the wine over the meat. Cook for 45 to 60 minutes more, or until the internal temperature reaches 150°F on an instant-read thermometer. Transfer the meat to a cutting board and let it rest for 15 minutes before slicing.

4. Place the roasting pan over medium heat and bring the juices to a simmer. Add the broth and simmer for 5 minutes, scraping the browned bits from the bottom of the pan. Stir in the chopped nuts and remove from the heat.

5. Slice the meat and arrange the slices on a warm platter. Spoon the sauce over the pork and serve.

WINE MATCH: Barbaresco, Roagna

Grilled Leg of Lamb

AGNELLO ALLA BRACE

A boned and butterflied leg of lamb is the perfect cut of meat for broiling or barbecuing. A half leg, weighing 3 to 4 pounds after trimming, will be enough for eight people, and you might even have enough left over for tasty sandwiches the next day. I prefer broiling the lamb since the broiler pan catches the drippings, which can be used as a little sauce.

In Sicily, this herb marinade is used to coat lamb chops and chunks of leg of lamb cooked on a skewer. There we ate the flavorful meat with artichokes grilled over the same fire. The artichokes we have here are generally too tough to be cooked that way. A good alternative would be Stuffed Artichokes, page 208.

SERVES 8

6 garlic cloves, finely chopped
¼ cup olive oil
3 tablespoons fresh lemon juice
4 sage leaves, chopped
1 tablespoon chopped rosemary

1 teaspoon dried oregano
Salt and freshly ground black pepper
One 3½-pound boned and butterflied
   leg of lamb

1. In a shallow pan, combine the garlic, oil, lemon juice, herbs, and salt and pepper to taste. Add the lamb, turning to coat both sides. Let marinate at room temperature for 1 hour.

2. Preheat the broiler or a grill. Position the broiler pan or grill rack about 4 inches from the heat source.

3. Pat the meat dry. Broil or grill it until it is slightly resistant when pressed in the thickest part, 8 to 10 minutes per side, depending on thickness, for medium-rare. Let the meat rest for 10 minutes.

4. Thinly slice the meat across the grain. Serve hot or cold.

WINE MATCH: Rosso del Conte, Regaleai

Sardinian Lamb Stew

ISTUFAU

Tender lamb stew with dried tomatoes and a touch of vinegar is a specialty at many holiday feasts and wedding banquets in Sardinia. There it is made with mutton, but lamb is milder-tasting and just as good. Use neck and shoulder meat for stew. It is bony, but the meat becomes meltingly tender as it cooks.

A good wine vinegar will give the best flavor; balsamic is too sweet. For the tomatoes, use the kind that are sold dry and not marinated. If you can only find marinated ones, rinse them and blot dry before using for this recipe.

SERVES 6

3 pounds lamb neck or shoulder, cut into 2-inch pieces and trimmed of fat
3 tablespoons olive oil
Salt and freshly ground black pepper
2 medium carrots, chopped
1 medium onion, finely chopped

2 teaspoons finely chopped rosemary
1 garlic clove, finely chopped
½ cup red wine vinegar
¼ cup dried tomatoes, cut into narrow strips
2 cups meat broth
1 tablespoon chopped flat-leaf parsley

1. Pat the meat dry with paper towels.

2. In a Dutch oven, heat the oil over medium heat. Add the lamb, a few pieces at a time, and brown well on all sides. Do not crowd the pot, or the meat will not brown. Transfer the browned meat to a plate. Sprinkle with salt and pepper. Continue with the remaining lamb.

3. Spoon off all but about 1 tablespoon of fat from the pot. Add the carrots and onion and cook, stirring frequently, for 10 minutes, or until lightly browned. Stir in the rosemary and garlic. Add the vinegar and bring to a simmer. Cook for 1 minute, scraping the browned bits from the bottom of the pot.

4. Return the lamb to the pot. Add the tomatoes and broth. Bring to a simmer. Reduce the heat to low. Cover and cook, stirring occasionally, for 2 hours, or until the lamb is fork-tender and coming away from the bones. If there is a lot of liquid, remove the lid during the last half hour of cooking to reduce it.

5. Transfer the lamb to a warm serving platter. Tip the pot and skim off any fat from the surface of the liquid. Spoon the pan juices over the lamb and sprinkle with the parsley. Serve immediately.

WINE MATCH: Cannonau, Sella and Mosca

Roman Lamb, Hunter's Style

ABBACCHIO ALLA CACCIATORA

Abbacchio *is Italian baby spring lamb so young that it has never grazed on grass. It is a specialty in Rome, but since lamb that young can be very hard to find here and has only a brief season in early spring, I make this stew with more mature lamb. Of course, the cooking time is longer, but the flavor of the mature lamb is a better match for the zesty flavors of the rosemary, vinegar, garlic, and anchovy pesto that finish the sauce.*

Alla cacciatora means hunter style, but there are as many variations on what is hunter style as there are hunters. This is a Roman version. In southern Italy, hunter-style lamb or chicken is prepared with tomatoes, while in northern Italy, it is made with mushrooms and wine.

Roast potatoes and fresh asparagus would be my choice to go with this savory dish.

SERVES 8

4 pounds lamb neck and shoulder, cut into
   2-inch pieces and trimmed of fat
2 tablespoons lard or olive oil
Salt and freshly ground black pepper

4 sage leaves
3 garlic cloves
Two 2-inch sprigs rosemary
½ cup dry white wine

PESTO
6 anchovy fillets
1 teaspoon minced rosemary
1 garlic clove, minced

2 to 3 tablespoons red wine vinegar

1. Pat the meat dry with paper towels.

2. In a heavy Dutch oven or stew pot, heat the lard over medium heat. Add the lamb, a few pieces at a time, and brown well on all sides. Do not crowd the pot, or the meat will not brown. Transfer the browned meat to a plate. Sprinkle with salt and pepper. Continue with the remaining lamb.

3. Spoon off all but about 1 tablespoon of fat from the pot. Add the sage, garlic, and rosemary. Return the meat to the pot. Add the wine and cook for 1 minute, scraping the browned bits from the bottom of the pot. Reduce the heat to low, cover, and cook,

stirring occasionally, for 2 hours, or until the lamb is fork-tender and coming away from the bones. Add a little water if the liquid evaporates too rapidly.

4. Meanwhile, make the pesto: Mash the anchovies, rosemary, and garlic in a small bowl with a wooden spoon or with a mortar and pestle. Add enough vinegar to make a smooth paste.

5. Scrape the pesto into the stew and simmer for 5 minutes.

6. Transfer the lamb to a warm serving platter. Tip the pot and skim off any fat from the surface of the liquid. Spoon the pan juices over the lamb. Serve immediately.

WINE MATCH: Vitiano, Falesco

Crispy Lamb Chops

BRACIOLETTE CROCCANTE DI AGNELLO

At the Colle Picchioni farm and winery, olives, persimmon, and other fruit trees and rows of grapevines grow in profusion. There Paola Di Mauro and her son, Armando, make outstanding white and red wines under the Colle Picchioni label.

Paola prepared a multicourse feast when we visited her. We began with big platters of hand-made agnolotti stuffed with a mix of ground beef, pork, sausage, veal, and chicken, tossed with a bright bouquet of buttery carrots, cherry tomatoes, bell peppers, and tasty zucchini from her garden.

Next came crunchy, crispy lamb chops. We started eating them with knives and forks, then switched to fingers so we could get to every bit of meat on the bones. The meal ended with tender biscotti flavored with white wine.

SERVES 4

16 thin rib lamb chops
2 large eggs, beaten
Salt and freshly ground
　　black pepper

About 1½ cups dry bread crumbs,
　　preferably homemade
Olive oil for frying
Lemon wedges, optional

1. Trim the fat from the chops. Place them on a cutting board and pound the meat gently to about a ½-inch thickness.

2. In a shallow bowl, beat the eggs with salt and pepper to taste. Spread the bread crumbs on a plate.

3. Pour about ⅓ inch of oil into a deep skillet. Heat until a bit of the egg mixture sizzles and cooks quickly when dropped into the pan. Dip a chop in the eggs, then dredge quickly in the bread crumbs, patting them on so they adhere well. Carefully place the chop in the hot oil. Repeat with just enough chops to fit comfortably in a single layer in the pan. Cook for 3 to 4 minutes per side, turning once, until browned and crisp.

4. Drain the chops on paper towels. Keep warm in a low oven while you fry the remainder. Serve hot, with lemon wedges, if desired.

WINE MATCH: Vigna del Vassalo, Colle Picchioni

Sunday Chicken with Fresh Tomatoes

POLLO ALLA ANNA

Anne Amendolara Nurse is a cooking teacher and caterer, though that only begins to describe her gifts. A former opera singer, Anne is a spiritual godmother to many cooks, chefs, and food writers. She knows everyone and helps everyone, generously volunteering her time and energy to a number of worthy programs.

I love to watch Anne cook. She is a natural in the kitchen, especially when it comes to Italian food, although her American-style roast ham and baked beans are legendary. Anne told me that her mother used to make chicken this way for Sunday dinner or special occasions. Chicken was expensive in those days, so if there were extra guests, she would add tomato sauce to the pan juices and some partially cooked perciatelli, with a sprinkle of pecorino romano, when the chicken was almost cooked. That way, one small chicken could be stretched to feed eight.

SERVES 4 TO 6

1 broiler chicken (about 3½ pounds), cut into 8 pieces
⅓ cup chopped flat-leaf parsley
2 garlic cloves, finely chopped

Salt and freshly ground black pepper
2 cups chopped fresh tomatoes or halved or quartered cherry or grape tomatoes

1. Preheat the oven to 425°F. Oil a 13 × 9 × 2-inch roasting pan.

2. Rinse the chicken and cut away any excess fat. Pat the pieces dry.

3. Place the chicken pieces in the pan and scatter the parsley, garlic, and salt and pepper to taste over them, turning them to coat. Turn the chicken skin side down. Add the tomatoes to the pan. Bake for 30 minutes.

4. Turn the chicken pieces skin side up. Bake for 30 to 40 minutes more, or until the chicken is browned and cooked through.

5. Transfer the chicken pieces to a plate. Tilt the pan and skim off the excess fat. Spoon the juices over the chicken and serve hot.

WINE MATCH: La Segreta Rossa, Planeta

Roast Chicken and Potatoes with Bay Leaves

POLLO E PATATE ARROSTO AL ALLORO

Ligurians think of All Saints' Day, November 1, as the starting point of the Christmas season, so the evening meal is always a festive one. Ravioli is the usual first course, followed by crisp roast chicken.

They have an old saying in this region: "Santi senza becco, Natale meschinetto," meaning, "All Saints Day without a chicken [literally, without a beak], Christmas will be a poor one." Another version finishes the proverb with "Natale secco secco"—"Christmas will be very dry," while a third predicts "Natale maledetto"—"Christmas will be a bad one."

To ensure a happy Christmas or a good meal anytime, serve this roast chicken. With the chicken in the oven, roast some potatoes at the same time. I do them in a separate pan to ensure that they turn out crispy and browned. Be sure that you use a wide shallow pan for the potatoes and spread the potatoes in one layer, or they will steam rather than brown.

Serve the chicken with Porcini-Stuffed Zucchini (page 206) and follow with All Souls' Day Spice Cookies (page 246) for dessert.

SERVES 4

1 broiler chicken (about 3½ pounds)
About ¼ cup olive oil
Salt and freshly ground black pepper
2 ounces sliced pancetta (about 4 slices), chopped
2 garlic cloves, chopped

2 bay leaves
4 medium potatoes, peeled
½ cup dry white wine

1. Position one oven rack on the lowest level and the other just above it, and preheat the oven to 450°F. Have ready two roasting pans, one that is wide enough to hold the potatoes in a single layer and shallow enough to fit on the lower rack, and another just large enough to hold the chicken.

2. Wash the chicken and pat it dry. Remove the excess fat from the cavity. Fold the wing tips behind the back. Rub the skin with a little olive oil and sprinkle inside and out with salt and pepper.

3. Place half the pancetta and garlic and 1 bay leaf inside the chicken. Tie the legs together with kitchen twine. Put the chicken in the roasting pan.

4. Toss the potatoes with ¼ cup olive oil, the remaining pancetta, garlic, and bay leaf, and salt and pepper to taste. Spread in a single layer in the shallow roasting pan.

5. Place the potatoes on the lower oven rack and the chicken on the upper rack. Roast for 20 minutes. Toss the potatoes. Reduce the heat to 375°F and roast until the chicken is golden, 45 to 60 minutes more.

6. Pour the wine over the chicken. Cook for 10 minutes more, or until the juices run clear when the thigh is pierced with a fork. Remove the chicken from the pan. Cover to keep warm and let rest for 10 minutes before carving.

7. Meanwhile, check the potatoes. They should be tender when pierced with a knife.

8. Carve the chicken and serve with the potatoes and the pan juices.

WINE MATCH: Sagrantino di Monte Falco, Terre de Trinci

Chanukah Fried Chicken

POLLO FRITTO

Chanukah is the eight-day festival that marks the victory of the Jews, led by the Maccabee brothers, over persecution and religious oppression by the Greeks. When the Maccabees went to the Temple of Jerusalem, a miracle occurred. The oil for the eternally burning flame lasted for eight days, even though there was only enough oil for one day. An important part of the celebration is the lighting of the menorah, a nine-armed candelabrum.

For Chanukah, Jewish people in Italy and elsewhere celebrate with foods fried in oil like fritters, potatoes, pancakes, and this delicious chicken. Serve it with Rosy Mashed Potatoes (page 216) and spinach tossed with raisins and pine nuts. Hazelnut Biscotti (page 244) would be good for dessert.

SERVES 4

3 tablespoons fresh lemon juice

2 tablespoons olive oil

Salt and freshly ground black pepper

1 chicken (about 3½ pounds), cut into
  2-inch pieces

3 large eggs

½ teaspoon grated lemon zest

About 1 cup all-purpose flour

Olive or vegetable oil for frying

Lemon wedges

1. In a large shallow bowl, beat the lemon juice, olive oil, 1 teaspoon salt, and pepper to taste with a fork. Add the chicken pieces and turn to coat them with the marinade. Let stand for 1 hour.

2. In a medium bowl, beat the eggs with the lemon zest and salt and pepper to taste until blended. Add a tablespoon or two of the marinade and beat well. Spread the flour on a sheet of wax paper.

3. Heat about ½ inch oil in a deep heavy skillet over medium heat until a bit of the egg mixture sizzles and cooks quickly when dropped into the oil. Drain the chicken pieces. Starting with the legs and other dark meat, which take longer to cook, roll the chicken in the flour, then dip it in the eggs, turning to coat on all sides. Place the pieces, a few at a time, in the hot oil, being careful that the oil does not bubble up too high. Cook until browned and crisp on all sides, about 20 minutes for dark meat and

15 minutes for white meat. Use tongs to turn the pieces so that you don't break the crust. Drain on paper towels. Keep the first batch warm in a low oven while you fry the remaining chicken.

4. Serve hot with lemon wedges.

WINE MATCH: Barbera d'Asti, Michele Chiarlo

Harvest Chicken with Peppers

POLLO CON PEPERONI

Sukkot is a week-long Jewish festival that celebrates the harvest and the end of the High Holy Days that begins with Rosh Hashanah and ends with Yom Kippur. In gardens and courtyards, on terraces and balconies, wherever there is an open space, each family constructs a hut made of branches and leaves. The hut, called a sukka, represents the impermanence of the Israelites' homes as they roamed the desert for forty years. They are decorated with fruits and vegetables, representing the abundance of the season. Prayers are said and meals are taken inside the shelter. It is a joyous holiday, and many of the foods that are prepared feature fruits and vegetables.

SERVES 4

1 chicken (about 3½ pounds), cut into 8 pieces
2 tablespoons olive oil
Salt and freshly ground black pepper
2 medium onions, chopped

1 pound fresh tomatoes, peeled, seeded, and
    chopped, or 2 cups chopped canned peeled
    Italian tomatoes, with their juice
2 green bell peppers, cut into bite-size pieces
2 garlic cloves, chopped
½ cup cured black olives, pitted

1. Rinse the chicken pieces and pat them dry.

2. Heat the oil in a large deep skillet over medium heat. Add the chicken pieces and brown well on all sides. Sprinkle with salt and pepper. Transfer to a plate and cover to keep warm. Spoon out all but 2 tablespoons of the fat from the pan.

3. Add the onions to the pan and cook until golden, about 10 minutes. Stir in the tomatoes, peppers, and garlic. Season with salt and pepper.

4. Return the chicken to the pan, turning the pieces once or twice. Cover and lower the heat. After about 10 minutes, remove the lid and check to see if there is enough liquid. If not, add a little warm water. Cook the chicken for 10 minutes more.

5. Add the olives. Cook for 10 minutes more, or until the chicken is tender and the sauce is thickened. Check for seasoning. Serve hot.

WINE MATCH: Santa Cristina, Antinori

NATALE

Until recent years, Christmas Day in Italy was a quiet religious holiday without the trappings of gifts and glitter. Families would go to Mass and then get together for a festive dinner. Afterward, there was the inevitable *passagiata*, or evening stroll. One tradition was to visit some of the Christmas crêches set up in churches, banks, shopping galleries, and the lobbies of corporate offices. Everyone marveled at the beautifully sculpted and painted scenes, complete with realistic figures of people going about their daily chores—the butcher, vegetable vendor, baker, and women doing laundry or cooking. There were angels, and the Magi and their entourage dressed in period clothes, surrounded by tiny animals, lights, and flowing water.

But in recent years, Christmas Day customs are changing. The Zampognari, shepherds who came down from the hills to the major cities to play *"Tu Scendi Dalle Stelle,"* probably the most beloved Italian Christmas song on their homemade bagpipes, are being replaced with Santa Claus, known in Italy as Babbo Natale. Though children still receive their gifts from the Befana, an old lady on a broom, on the Epiphany (January 6), many also receive small gifts from Father Christmas on Christmas Day. In Rome, lights and tinsel are strung across the Corso and other main shopping streets. Christmas trees are more apparent every year, and American Christmas music is played everywhere.

Fortunately, though, Italian food traditions are still held dear, though on a less elaborate scale, since most women work outside of their homes. Capon or turkey often is the centerpiece of the dinner. Some cooks poach the capon and serve the magnificent broth with fresh cappellini or other pasta. The bird itself is served with *mostarda,* jewel-like fruits preserved in a spicy mustard syrup. In other regions, the bird is roasted and served with a stuffing.

In my family, with its Neapolitan origins, the turkey stuffing was made with rice, sausages, peppers, mushrooms, celery, and onions. In Friuli–Venezia Giulia and other northern regions, the stuffing is often made with chestnuts and apples, while in Piedmont, it is veal with Parmigiano-Reggiano and truffles.

In Liguria, pasta called *natalin* is cooked in capon broth with little sausage meatballs and served for Christmas. Soup made with cardoons is the traditional first course in the Abruzzo. One of the prettiest Christmas pasta dishes, ravioli called *casonsei,* is stuffed with beets and soft cheese and drizzled with butter and poppy seeds.

Desserts like *panettone,* a specialty of Milano, and *panforte,* from Siena, in Tuscany, were originally strictly regional, but now are eaten all over Italy thanks to commercial production. Panettone is a tall, slightly sweet bread studded with raisins, nuts, and candied fruits. Panettone is served with sparkling dessert wine, like Asti Spumante, for dessert, toasted and topped with butter or mascarpone cheese for breakfast, and it is also good in desserts like bread pudding. Panforte is a flat, chewy fruit and nut cake. It is good in small wedges, with strong dark coffee.

In Sicily and throughout southern Italy, *cassata* is the typical Christmas cake. And practically every region lays claim to zuppa inglese as a traditional dessert. Cups of warm zabaglione are enjoyed for breakfast. *Struffoli* are essential for Christmas in Naples, while in Emilia-Romagna, people make *pinza,* a delicious cake filled with fruit preserves, dried fruit, and nuts. In Verona, *pandoro,* a golden star-shaped yeast cake, is the tradition.

Christmas Capon

Moist, flavorful capon is the traditional holiday bird in many parts of Italy. Often it is poached and the flavorful broth is used to make soup with tortellini or capelletti as a first course. Here it is roasted stuffed with truffle-flavored meats, a specialty of the Piedmont region.

Truffles, a type of fungus that grows on the roots of certain trees, have never been successfully cultivated. Because they are difficult to find, and becoming scarce due to environmental changes, they are extremely expensive. Both white and black truffles grow in Piedmont, but the white truffles are the real prize. They are never cooked, but are shaved raw over dishes like buttered fettuccine or risotto, polenta, or scrambled eggs. The warmth of the cooked food releases the aroma of the wafer-thin slices of truffle.

For this dish, however, a small, less expensive black truffle will do. Even the kind preserved in tiny jars are good for this stuffing, or you can just leave it out and the stuffing will still taste good.

SERVES 8

1 capon (about 8 pounds)

Salt and freshly ground black pepper

STUFFING

6 ounces ground pork

6 ounces ground veal

1 small canned or fresh black truffle, minced, optional

½ cup chopped carrots

½ cup freshly grated Parmigiano-Reggiano

½ cup fine dry bread crumbs

1 garlic clove, minced

½ teaspoon chopped thyme

⅛ teaspoon freshly grated nutmeg

1 large egg, beaten

Salt and freshly ground black pepper to taste

1 cup dry white wine

1. Preheat the oven to 325°F.

2. Remove the giblets from the cavity of the capon (reserve for another use, if desired). Rinse the capon well and dry it thoroughly inside and out. Sprinkle with salt and pepper.

3. To make the stuffing, mix together all of the ingredients in a large bowl, blending well. Just before you are ready to cook the capon, stuff it with the mixture, filling the cavity only about two-thirds full. Tie the legs together with kitchen twine.

4. Place the capon on a rack in a roasting pan. Roast for 25 to 30 minutes per pound, or about 3½ hours for an 8-pound bird. After an hour, begin basting every 20 minutes with the wine and pan juices. The capon is done when the temperature in the thickest part of the thigh and in the center of the stuffing registers 165°F on an instant-read thermometer.

5. Remove the capon from the oven and cover loosely with foil. Let stand for 15 minutes.

6. Meanwhile, strain the pan juices and skim off the fat.

7. To serve, reheat the juices. Carve the capon. Arrange the capon and the stuffing on a warm serving platter and drizzle with the pan juices.

WINE MATCH: Barolo, Marcarini

Roast Turkey with Chestnut Stuffing

TACCHINO ARROSTO

In Friuli–Venezia Giulia, in the northeast of Italy, herbed roast turkey stuffed with chestnuts is the traditional Christmas Day meal. Turkey is also served on Saint Carlo's Day, November 4, commemorating the establishment in 1816 of an annual market in the town of Aiello. The market is still held on that day and always attracts many visitors from the neighboring towns, as well as from nearby Austria and Slovenia, who come to shop at the market, which is something like a country fair. They eat turkey dishes and participate in turkey-related games and a twelve-kilometer "turkey march."

Chestnuts make this stuffing special. If you can, roast them yourself, or use the kind sold in cans or jars. Read the label carefully so that you can be sure the chestnuts are not sweetened.

Start the meal with Souffléd Chicken Soup (page 46) and serve Christmas Salad (page 198) with the turkey. End the meal with Struffoli (page 252) and fresh fruit.

SERVES 8

STUFFING

6 cups day-old Italian bread cut into
   1-inch cubes
1 cup milk
2 tablespoons unsalted butter
2 tablespoons olive oil
2 large onions, chopped
4 ounces pancetta, coarsely chopped
2 tablespoons chopped sage
1 cup peeled cooked fresh chestnuts or
   unsweetened canned or vacuum-packed
   chestnuts, coarsely chopped

1 small apple, peeled, cored, and chopped
Salt and freshly ground black pepper

1 tablespoon chopped rosemary
1 tablespoon chopped sage
1 small fresh turkey (12 to 14 pounds)
Salt and freshly ground black pepper
1 cup dry white wine

1. To make the stuffing, put the bread in a large bowl and add the milk. Let soak, stirring occasionally, for 10 minutes.

2. Melt the butter with the oil in a large skillet over medium heat. Add the onions and pancetta and cook, stirring often, until the onions are golden and the pancetta is lightly browned, about 10 minutes. Stir in the sage. Remove from the heat.

3. Squeeze out the bread, discarding the milk, and place it in a large bowl. Add the chestnuts and apple. Scrape the contents of the skillet into the bowl. Add a little salt and a generous grinding of pepper and mix well with a wooden spoon. Let cool. (The stuffing can be made ahead. Cover and refrigerate for up to 24 hours.)

4. Preheat the oven to 350°F.

5. Chop the rosemary and sage together. Remove the gizzards and neck from the turkey cavities. Wash and dry the turkey and sprinkle inside and out with salt and pepper. Carefully slide your fingers as far as you can between the flesh and the skin covering the breast and legs. Spread the herbs between the meat and skin.

6. Loosely fill the neck and body cavities with the stuffing. Place the turkey on a rack in a large roasting pan. Roast for 1 hour.

7. Begin basting the turkey every 20 to 30 minutes with the wine; when all the wine is used, baste with the juices that have accumulated in the pan. Roast the turkey for 2½ to 3 hours more; if it begins to brown too much, cover it with a foil tent. The turkey is done when the temperature of both the thigh meat at the thickest part and the stuffing in the center register 165°F on an instant-read thermometer. Transfer the turkey to a platter or cutting board. Let it rest, covered with foil, for at least 15 minutes.

8. Meanwhile, place the roasting pan over low heat. Add a little water (or chicken broth) and cook, scraping the browned bits from the bottom of the pan, until the juices are slightly reduced. Strain the juices.

9. Carve the turkey and transfer the stuffing to a bowl. Serve hot, with the pan juices.

TIP: If you prefer not to put the stuffing in the turkey, bake it alongside the bird in a buttered 2-quart casserole for 30 to 45 minutes, or until crusty on top and hot. An unstuffed turkey will take 30 to 60 minutes less cooking time.

WINE MATCH: Merlot, Vistorta

Braised Quail with Porcini

QUAGLIE IN TEGAME CON FUNGHI PORCINI

In November, the windows of pastry shops in Verona feature a sugary cake covered with a golden yellow icing shell topped with little chocolate birds, which imitate a favorite savory dish of the season, tiny game birds served on a mound of soft, buttery polenta. The sauce is made with dried porcini, meaty mushrooms with a deep woodsy flavor. Serve the quail with Polenta (page 129).

SERVES 6 TO 8

1 ounce dried porcini mushrooms (about ¾ cup)

8 quail, thawed if frozen

4 thin slices pancetta, cut in half

8 sage leaves

Salt and freshly ground black pepper

2 tablespoons unsalted butter

1 tablespoon olive oil

1 small onion, finely chopped

1 tender celery rib, finely chopped

1 carrot, finely chopped

½ cup dry white wine

2 teaspoons tomato paste

1. Soak the mushrooms in 2 cups of warm water for at least 30 minutes. Lift the mushrooms out of the water, reserving the liquid. Rinse the mushrooms under cool running water, paying special attention to the stem ends, where soil collects. Coarsely chop the mushrooms. Strain the reserved mushroom liquid through a piece of cheesecloth or a paper coffee filter. Set aside.

2. Rinse the quail inside and out and pat them thoroughly dry. Look them over for any pinfeathers and remove them. Place a piece of pancetta, a sage leaf, and a pinch of salt and pepper inside each one.

3. In a large skillet, heat the butter and oil over medium heat. Add the quail and cook, turning occasionally, until nicely browned on all sides. Remove the quail from the skillet and add the onion, celery, and carrot. Cook for 5 minutes, or until tender.

4. Add the wine and simmer for 1 minute. Stir in the mushrooms, tomato paste, and reserved mushroom liquid.

5. Return the quail to the pan and sprinkle with salt and pepper. Bring the liquid to a simmer. Reduce the heat to low, cover, and cook, turning and basting the quail occasionally, until the birds are very tender when pierced with a fork, about 1 hour.

6. If there is too much liquid in the pan, transfer the quail to a serving platter and keep warm. Turn the heat to high and boil the liquid until it is reduced. Spoon the sauce over the quail and serve immediately.

WINE MATCH: Barolo Rocche, Vietti

Santo Stefano

The day after Christmas is Saint Stephen's Day, and a special meal is served, called the First Feast. Ravioli made with escarole, bor- age, veal, brains, and mushrooms are among the typical dishes served.

Rabbit with Tomatoes, Wine, and Rosemary

CONIGLIO ALLA PROCIDANA

Procida is one of the smaller islands in the Bay of Naples. My father's parents came from there, and I love to wander around the island and imagine what my life would have been like if I had been born there. There are beautiful lemon and orange groves, and hidden beaches and coves. If you climb to the top of Mount Procida, there are splendid views over the bay to Naples, the nearby island of Ischia, and Mount Vesuvius in the distance.

Rabbit is a specialty of the island, and this is the way my grandmother used to prepare it. Sometimes she added extra tomatoes to the pan and served the sauce over fettuccine, with the rabbit itself as the second course. We usually had this on Palm or Easter Sunday.

SERVES 4 TO 6

1 rabbit (about 3 pounds), cut into 8 to 12 pieces
¼ cup olive oil
4 or 5 ripe plum tomatoes, peeled, seeded, and chopped
One 2-inch sprig rosemary

¼ cup chopped basil
½ cup dry white wine
Salt
1 small dried peperoncino, crumbled, or a pinch of crushed red pepper

1. Rinse the rabbit pieces in cold water and pat dry.

2. Heat the oil in a large nonreactive skillet. Add the rabbit pieces and cook over medium-low heat, turning occasionally, until lightly browned on all sides, about 15 minutes.

3. Add the tomatoes, rosemary, basil, wine, salt to taste, and peperoncino. Bring to a simmer. Partially cover the pan and cook, stirring the rabbit from time to time, for 1 hour, or until the rabbit is very tender. Add a little water if the sauce is too dry.

4. Remove the lid. If a lot of liquid is left in the pan, raise the heat and cook, basting the rabbit with the sauce until it is reduced and slightly thickened. Serve with the sauce.

WINE MATCH: Perdera, Argiolas

Vegetables

VERDURA

When I was growing up in Brooklyn, you could always tell the houses where Italians lived by their gardens. Vegetables shared the space with roses, daisies, and marigolds. Beds of tomatoes, lettuce, peppers, and eggplants were bordered with vines of zucchini and melons. Parsley and basil grew in window boxes and in fire escape planters. Instead of willow, oak, and maple trees for shade, Italian families grew fig, peach, or apple trees.

Fresh vegetables are at the center of most meals in Italy. They are served raw in salads, cooked in oil and garlic for pasta sauces, chopped or pureed into soups, and fried or roasted for side dishes to meat or fish. Most of the time vegetables are prepared simply, baked with butter and Parmigiano-Reggiano or steamed and dressed with olive oil.

Unlike French or American cooks, Italians like their cooked vegetables to be very tender and often soft. The term *al dente*, meaning, literally, to the tooth, is appropriate for pasta or risotto, but it could never be applied to vegetables cooked in the Italian manner. Beans and lentils are always creamy and soft, never crunchy or underdone.

Italian salads are usually served as a side dish with the main course. The dressing is very simple: fine extra virgin olive oil, good wine vinegar or sometimes fresh lemon juice and salt are all that are used.

Reinforcement Salad

INSALATA DI RINFORZO

Insalata di rinforzo, literally, salad of reinforcement, is the unusual name for this Neapolitan dish. One explanation for its name is that reinforcements, in the form of more olives, anchovies, pickles, or vegetables, can be added to the salad so that it will last for all the parties and dinners throughout the Christmas holidays. The second is that its sturdy ingredients replace the meat that was not supposed to be eaten on Christmas Eve.

The ingredients are flexible, and you can add shredded carrots, chopped parsley, or matchsticks of crunchy vegetables like zucchini, cucumbers, or radishes.

SERVES 8

1 cauliflower (about 1½ pounds)
Salt
⅓ cup extra virgin olive oil
2 tablespoons wine vinegar, or to taste
Freshly ground black pepper
1 cup pickled red and yellow peppers, drained
 and cut into strips (or use half sweet peppers
 and half hot peppers)

½ cup black olives, pitted and sliced
½ cup sour gherkins, chopped
2 tender celery ribs, sliced
8 to 12 anchovy fillets, chopped

1. Trim the cauliflower and cut it into 1-inch florets. Bring a large pot of water to a boil. Add the cauliflower and salt to taste. Cook until the cauliflower is tender, 3 to 5 minutes. Drain, rinse the cauliflower under cold running water, and drain well.

2. In a large bowl, whisk the oil, vinegar, and salt and pepper to taste. Add the cauliflower and the remaining ingredients and toss well. Cover and refrigerate for at least 3 hours, and up to 2 days.

3. Remove the salad from the refrigerator about 30 minutes before serving.

The Epiphany

Children all over Italy look forward to the Epiphany on January 6, Twelfth Night, because on that day the Befana, an old witch, arrives on her broom, bearing sweets and gifts. In Rome's Piazza Navona, there is a magical atmosphere, with excited children and their parents dressed in their holiday finery browsing the stalls that have been set up there since before Christmas. The stalls sell toys and trinkets, games like La Gioca del Oca (The Goose Game), Befana dolls in a range of sizes, traditional sweets like nougat and torrone, colored candies, and chunks of candy coal. Of course, there are Pokémon games and Power Rangers too, or whatever television is featuring that year.

The story goes that La Befana was once just a typical housewife. One day, the Magi, or Three Kings, stopped at her little home on their way to see the newborn Baby Jesus. They invited the old woman to join them on their quest, but she declined, saying she had too much cleaning to do. She soon regretted her decision and now she wanders the world on her broom on Three Kings Day, seeking the Christ Child. Her name is a corruption of the word *Epiphania*. She arrives in the early morning hours and flies down the chimney of each house, leaving rewards in the shoes and socks of good children, and hunks of coal and other punishments for those who have misbehaved. Children who are expecting the worst have been known to fortify themselves before going to sleep with hearty foods like beans and bread to help them resist a poke in the belly from her bony finger.

Christmas Salad

INSALATA NATALIZIA DI ENNA

Escarole, a member of the chicory family of leafy greens, is a favorite southern Italian vegetable. It resembles romaine lettuce in the shape and size of the leaves, but its color is darker. Since it is at its best in winter, when other greens are scarce, escarole is often cooked in hearty soups, with beans or lentils, and braised as a side dish. Whenever my mother boiled escarole, my father drank the cooking liquid because, he insisted, it was healthful. Somehow, though, he could never convince us kids to try it.

In this cooked salad, escarole and celery are garnished with orange wedges and pomegranate seeds to make a beautiful holiday presentation. The pomegranate seeds are not essential, but they do give the salad a very festive look.

SERVES 8

1 medium head escarole (about 1 ¼ pounds)
3 celery ribs, sliced
½ cup chopped green olives
2 tablespoons capers, drained and chopped
¼ cup extra virgin olive oil

2 tablespoons fresh lemon juice
Salt
1 or 2 oranges, peeled and cut into wedges
Seeds from half a pomegranate, optional

1. Discard any bruised escarole leaves and trim off the base. Separate the leaves and wash individually under cool running water. Stack the leaves and cut them into bite-size pieces.

2. Bring a large pot of water to a boil. Add the escarole and cook for 10 minutes, or until tender. Scoop out the escarole with a slotted spoon, place it in a strainer, and drain well.

3. Add the celery to the boiling water and cook for 5 minutes. Drain well.

4. In a large serving bowl, combine the escarole, celery, olives, and capers. Whisk together the oil, lemon juice, and salt to taste. Toss the vegetables with the dressing to coat them completely. Let marinate for 15 minutes.

5. Garnish the salad with the orange wedges and sprinkle with the pomegranate seeds. Serve warm.

Beans for the Befana

FAGIOLI DELLA BEFANA

No matter what type of beans you use—and you could use just about any kind in this recipe—be sure to cook them slowly so they turn out tender and creamy. Plan ahead so that the beans can soak for several hours at least before you begin cooking them.
Serve with grilled spareribs, steak, or chicken and broccoli rabe.

MAKES ABOUT 6 CUPS, SERVES 10 TO 12

1 pound dried cannellini, Great Northern, or cranberry beans, picked over and rinsed
1 large fresh tomato, peeled, seeded, and chopped, or 2 cans Italian peeled tomatoes, drained and chopped
6 sage leaves

4 garlic cloves, peeled
1 tiny dried peperoncino, crumbled, or a pinch of crushed red pepper
¼ cup extra virgin olive oil
Salt

1. Put the beans in a large bowl with cold water to cover by 2 inches. Let soak for at least 4 hours at room temperature, or overnight in the refrigerator.

2. Drain the beans and put them in a large pot with water to cover by 1 inch. Bring to a simmer. Skim off the foam that rises to the surface. Add the tomato, sage, garlic, peperoncino, and olive oil. Cook over very low heat until the beans are tender, about 1½ hours. (Cooking time will depend on the age and variety of the beans.) Add a little water if the level sinks below the surface of the beans.

3. When the beans are tender, stir in salt to taste. Let stand for 10 minutes before serving. (The beans can be made a day or two ahead of time. Store in the refrigerator and reheat gently.)

Poor Man's Fava Beans for the Feast of Saint Joseph

FAVE DEI POVERI

I don't know why this is called "poor man's" fava beans. It is simple food, but it is fit for a king. Serve it as a main dish with good bread. To make this a meatless main course, leave out the pancetta and add 2 tablespoons olive oil.

Dried fava beans are sold with and without skins. Since the skins are tough, buy the skinless variety.

SERVES 6

8 ounces dried skinless fava beans
2 slices pancetta, chopped
2 garlic cloves, chopped
Salt
4 dried tomatoes, diced
1 onion, finely chopped

¼ cup olive oil
1 pound chicory, Swiss chard, or escarole, trimmed, washed, and cut crosswise into bite-size pieces
Freshly ground black pepper

1. In a large pot, combine the fava beans, pancetta, and garlic. Add water to cover by 1 inch and bring to a simmer. Cover and cook until very tender, about 1 hour, adding a little more water if needed to keep the beans just covered. When the beans are tender, add salt to taste. Remove from the heat.

2. Meanwhile, in a large skillet, cook the tomatoes and onion in the oil over medium heat for 7 minutes, or until the onion is tender. Add the greens and salt and pepper to taste. Stir well. Cover and cook for 10 to 15 minutes, or until the greens are tender.

3. Mash the fava beans with a potato masher. Place them in a wide bowl. Top with the greens. Serve hot.

Swiss Chard and Fresh Fava Beans

BIETOLE E FAVE

A variety of fresh vegetables are cooked together in this delicious spring stew from the Marches. Phil and Jackie Cicconi recommend serving it as a side dish with steak or sausage or as a main dish with good bread.

I sometimes find good-quality frozen fava beans in Italian, Indian, or Middle Eastern markets. Do not substitute dried beans for the fresh—if you cannot find fresh favas, you can use fresh or frozen peas or lima beans.

SERVES 4 TO 6

3 green onions, thinly sliced

2 garlic cloves, minced

1 small dried peperoncino, crumbled, or a pinch of crushed red pepper

¼ cup olive oil

1 pound Swiss chard, trimmed, washed, and cut crosswise into 4-inch lengths

2 pounds fresh fava beans, shelled (about 1 cup)

Salt and freshly ground black pepper

1. In a large skillet, cook the onions, garlic, and peperoncino in the oil until the onions are wilted, about 3 minutes.

2. Add the Swiss chard, fava beans, salt and pepper to taste, and ¼ cup water. Cook, stirring often, until the vegetables are tender, 15 to 20 minutes. Serve hot.

Eggplant Parmigiana

PARMIGIANA DI MELANZANE

This Italian-American classic is an old, old favorite throughout southern Italy. In Lecce, in Puglia, it is always served on August 26, the Feast of Sant'Oronzo. On the island of Ischia, near Naples, it is served for the Feast of Sant'Anna, the protector of pregnant women, on July 26. At night, candles are lighted and placed on the windowsills and on the cliffs surrounding a statue of the saint. People climb into small boats decorated with flowers and lights and have picnics on board. Eggplant parmigiana is always on the menu. A prize is awarded for the best-decorated boat, and the evening concludes with spectacular fireworks.

I have found many variations on this dish. Some cooks dip the eggplant slices in flour and beaten eggs before frying them, while others make a bread crumb coating. Others add little meatballs to the layers of eggplant and cheese, and some use a meat ragu instead of tomato sauce. I like the simplicity of this version best. It can be a first or main course or a side dish, though for the last, it should be served in very small portions.

SERVES 6 TO 8

2 medium eggplants (about 1 pound each)
Salt
Olive or vegetable oil for frying

2½ cups tomato sauce, such as Tuscan Tomato
    Sauce (page 56) or Sugo Finto (page 57)
12 ounces fresh mozzarella, cut into thin slices
½ cup freshly grated pecorino romano or
    Parmigiano-Reggiano

1. Trim off the top and base of each eggplant. Cut the eggplant into ¼-inch-thick slices. Lay the slices in a colander, sprinkling each layer with salt. Let the eggplant slices stand for 30 minutes over a plate to eliminate their juices.

2. Rinse the eggplant slices and pat them dry. Pour about ½ inch oil into a large deep skillet and heat over medium heat. In batches, fry the eggplant slices in a single layer, turning once, until browned on both sides. Drain the slices on paper towels.

3. Preheat the oven to 350°F.

4. Spread a little tomato sauce in a shallow 2-quart baking dish. Make a layer of eggplant slices, overlapping them slightly. Top with a layer of mozzarella, another layer of sauce, and a sprinkle of Parmigiano. Repeat the layering, ending with eggplant, sauce, and grated cheese. Bake for 45 minutes, or until the sauce is bubbling and the mozzarella is melted. Let stand for 10 minutes before serving.

Summer Vegetable Stew

CIAMBOTTA

In Puglia, in southern Italy, this vegetable stew is served for the Feast of Saint Peter and Paul in late June. You can add zucchini or other summer squash, celery, green beans, or whatever you have a mind to. It always turns out great and it is good hot or at room temperature. Sometimes I leave out the cheese and stir in a handful of chopped fresh basil or parsley. It also makes a great hero sandwich, stuffed into a crisp roll.

SERVES 6

1 medium eggplant, trimmed and cut into bite-size pieces

2 medium red bell peppers, cored, seeded, and cut into bite-size pieces

1 large onion, diced

2 large ripe tomatoes, diced

2 medium potatoes, peeled and cut into bite-size pieces

2 tablespoons olive oil

Salt and freshly ground black pepper

¼ cup freshly grated pecorino romano

1. In a large pot, combine all of the ingredients except the cheese. Add ¼ cup water, cover, and cook, stirring occasionally, until the vegetables are very tender.

2. Just before serving, stir in the cheese. Serve hot or at room temperature.

Broccoli Rabe with Garlic and Anchovies

CIME DI BROCCOLI SOFFRITI

In southern Italy, broccoli rabe cooked with garlic, olive oil, and a bit of hot pepper is an essential part of the Christmas Eve seafood dinner. The anchovies are tasty, but not required. Regular broccoli and cauliflower are also good cooked this way.

This also makes a fine sauce for pasta. Or pile it on slices of toasted Italian bread and serve it as an appetizer.

SERVES 4 TO 6

1 bunch broccoli rabe (about 1½ pounds), rinsed
Salt
⅓ cup olive oil

4 garlic cloves
1 small dried peperoncino, crumbled, or a pinch of crushed red pepper
8 anchovies, optional

1. Bring a large pot of water to a boil. Meanwhile, trim off about 1 inch from the base of the broccoli rabe stems. Remove any bruised or yellow leaves.

2. Drop the broccoli rabe into the boiling water. Add salt to taste. Cook for 5 minutes, or just until partially cooked. Drain.

3. In a large saucepan, heat the oil with the garlic over medium-low heat. Add the peperoncino and the anchovies, if using. When the garlic is golden (and the anchovies are melted), add the broccoli rabe. Cook, stirring well to coat the broccoli with the garlic oil, for about 5 minutes, or until it is very tender. Serve hot or at room temperature.

Fresh Tomatoes and Rosemary

POMODORI AL ROSAMARINO

One of my favorite childhood memories is of spending time with my grandfather in his vegetable garden. It was just a tiny space surrounded by cyclone fencing in his Brooklyn backyard, but Grandpa had an amazing green thumb. I loved the sweet brown figs, fragrant white peaches, and big juicy tomatoes that we picked and ate while they were still warm from the sun.

When tomatoes are abundant and ripe, try this sauté from my friends the Cicconis. They recommend them with grilled steaks or roasted meat. Another way to enjoy them is to break some eggs into the pan of tomatoes and cook them all together. Serve the tomatoes with lots of crusty Italian bread to dip in the pan juices.

Don't even think about using those "hard ripe slicing tomatoes" that never get more than a pale pink color. The flavor just won't be the same.

SERVES 4

4 medium ripe tomatoes
¼ cup olive oil
2 garlic cloves, finely chopped
2 tablespoons chopped rosemary

1 small dried peperoncino, crumbled, or
   ¼ teaspoon crushed red pepper
Salt and freshly ground black pepper

1. Slice the tomatoes horizontally in half. Cut around the stem end of each and remove it.

2. In a large skillet, heat the oil with the garlic, rosemary, and peperoncino over medium heat for 1 minute. Arrange the tomato halves cut side down in the pan in a single layer. Sprinkle with salt and pepper. Cook for 7 to 10 minutes, or until the tomatoes are browned on the cut sides. Turn the tomatoes cut side up and sprinkle them with salt and pepper. Cook just until tender, about 5 minutes more. Do not overcook, or the tomatoes will fall apart.

3. With a slotted spatula, transfer the tomatoes to a serving platter. If there is a lot of juice left in the pan, increase the heat and cook until slightly thickened. Pour the juices over the tomatoes. Serve hot or at room temperature.

Porcini-Stuffed Zucchini

ZUCCHINI RIPIENI

No one is quite sure why June 13, the Feast of Saint Anthony of Padua, is celebrated in Liguria with stuffed zucchini. Saint Anthony was known for his frugality and sacrifice and one writer has suggested it may be that this luxurious dish with its mushrooms and cheese highlights the humble saint's sacrifices.

SERVES 8

½ cup dried porcini mushrooms
4 medium zucchini, about 6 inches long
   (about 1¼ pounds)
Salt
½ cup plus 2 tablespoons dry bread crumbs
¼ cup freshly grated Parmigiano-Reggiano
1 garlic clove, minced

1 teaspoon finely chopped fresh marjoram or
   ½ teaspoon dried
Pinch of freshly grated nutmeg
Salt and freshly ground black pepper
1 large egg, beaten
Olive oil

1. Place the mushrooms in a bowl with 2 cups warm water. Soak for 30 minutes.

2. Lift the mushrooms out of the soaking water. Rinse them well under cold running water, paying special attention to the base of the stems, where dirt may collect. Chop the mushrooms. (Reserve the soaking water for soup, sauces, or risotto: strain it through cheesecloth or a coffee filter and store in the refrigerator or freezer.)

3. Preheat the oven to 350°F. Oil a 12 × 9 × 2-inch baking dish.

4. Bring a medium saucepan of water to a boil. Add the zucchini and 1 teaspoon salt. Cook for 5 minutes, or until the zucchini are partially cooked. Drain and let cool.

5. Trim the zucchini stems. Cut them lengthwise in half. With a small spoon, scoop out the center of each half to form a shell; reserve the pulp. Arrange the zucchini shells cut side up in the prepared pan.

6. Chop the reserved pulp and place it in a bowl. Add ½ cup of the bread crumbs, the cheese, garlic, marjoram, nutmeg, and salt and pepper to taste. Add the egg and mix well. Spoon the mixture into the zucchini halves. Sprinkle with the remaining 2 tablespoons bread crumbs. Drizzle with olive oil.

7. Bake for 40 to 45 minutes, or until the crumbs are lightly toasted. Serve hot or at room temperature.

Stuffed Artichokes

CARCIOFI RIPIENI

Artichokes can be stuffed with ground meat, bread crumbs, seafood, or rice. This recipe, from my husband's grandmother, who came from Palermo, Sicily, substitutes anchovy fillets for the more common cheese.

SERVES 6

6 medium artichokes
Juice of 1 lemon
½ cup fine dry bread crumbs
¼ cup chopped flat-leaf parsley

4 anchovy fillets, finely chopped
1 garlic clove, very finely chopped
Salt and freshly ground black pepper
Olive oil

1. With a large knife, trim off the top 1 inch of the artichokes. Rinse them well under cold water. Fill a large bowl with cold water and add the lemon juice. Cut off the stems so that the artichokes will stand upright. Peel off the tough outer skin of the stems and set them aside. Bend back and snap off the small leaves around the base of each artichoke. With scissors, trim the pointed tops off the remaining leaves. Removing the chokes is optional: use a small knife with a rounded tip to scrape out the fuzzy leaves in the center. As each artichoke is finished, drop it into the bowl of lemon water.

2. Finely chop the artichoke stems. Mix them in a bowl with the bread crumbs, parsley, anchovies, garlic, and salt and pepper to taste. Add enough olive oil to moisten the crumbs evenly.

3. Gently spread the artichoke leaves apart. Holding an artichoke in one hand over the bowl, use your other hand to stuff it with the bread crumb mixture.

4. Place the artichokes in a pot just wide enough to hold them upright. Pour water to a depth of about ¾ inch around the artichokes. Drizzle the artichokes with 2 tablespoons olive oil. Cover the pot and place over medium heat. When the water comes to a simmer, reduce the heat to low. Cook until the artichoke bottoms are tender when pierced with a knife and a leaf pulls out easily, about 45 minutes, depending on the size and age of the artichokes. Add additional water if needed to prevent scorching.

5. Serve warm or at room temperature.

Stuffed Mushrooms

FUNGHI RIPIENI

With many varieties of mushrooms readily available today, reliable button mushrooms don't get much respect, even though they are excellent if treated well. You can use cremini mushrooms, but white button mushrooms are my first choice here. Larger buttons are good if you are serving them as a side dish, but small ones are best for appetizers, so they can be eaten in just one bite.

Mushrooms prepared this way go with many dishes. Serve with roast beef or veal or grilled steak or London broil.

SERVES 8

Two 10-ounce packages white mushrooms
1 cup dry bread crumbs, preferably homemade
    from Italian or French bread
1 garlic clove, minced
2 tablespoons chopped flat-leaf parsley

½ cup freshly grated Parmigiano-Reggiano or
    pecorino romano
Salt and freshly ground black pepper
Olive oil

1. Preheat the oven to 375°F. Oil a 12 × 9 × 2-inch baking pan.

2. Wipe the mushrooms clean with a damp towel. Snap or cut off the stems and set them aside. Place the caps rounded side down in the baking pan.

3. Trim off the ends of the mushroom stems if they seem dry. Set aside half the stems for another use (such as a soup or omelet). Chop the remaining stems and place them in a bowl. Add the bread crumbs, garlic, parsley, cheese, and salt and pepper to taste. Add enough olive oil to moisten the crumb mixture.

4. Lightly stuff the mushroom caps with the mixture. Do not press or pack the filling down. Drizzle the mushrooms with additional oil.

5. Bake for 35 to 45 minutes, or until the mushrooms are tender and the crumbs are crisp and browned. Serve hot or at room temperature.

Fried Cardoons

CARDI FRITTI

Cardoons look like overgrown grayish-green celery stalks. Although they grow in the wild in many parts of this country, they are not well known. Look for them in the fall and winter at ethnic produce markets that specialize in Italian foods.

In many regions of Italy, cardoons are an important part of the Christmas feast. In the Marches and Abruzzo regions, they are included in Minestra Maritata (page 50), and in Piemonte, tender ribs are served raw to dip in bagna caoda. My mother used to gather wild cardoons in the woods in Westchester County, New York. She prepared them this way, which is also a good treatment for fat asparagus.

Cardoons taste a lot like artichoke hearts, and they are, in fact, a member of the artichoke family. Choose small stalks that are unbruised. They darken easily once they are cut, so they need to be treated to a lemon water bath to help them stay light. Serve these as a side dish or as an appetizer with lemon wedges.

SERVES 8

1 lemon, cut in half
½ small bunch cardoons
3 large eggs
2 tablespoons freshly grated Parmigiano-
　Reggiano

Pinch of salt
Freshly ground black pepper
2 cups dry bread crumbs, preferably homemade
Olive oil for frying

1. Squeeze 1 lemon half into a large bowl of cold water. Separate the ribs of the cardoons. Trim the ends. With a paring knife, peel each rib to remove the long tough strings. Cut each rib into 3-inch lengths, dropping the pieces into the lemon water as you work to prevent them from darkening.

2. Bring a large saucepan of water to a boil. Squeeze the juice from the remaining lemon half into the water. Drain the cardoons and add them to the pan. Boil for 15 to 30 minutes, or until tender when pierced with a knife. Drain well and cool under running water. Pat dry.

3. In a shallow bowl, beat the eggs with the cheese. salt, and pepper to taste. Spread the bread crumbs on a sheet of wax paper. Dip the cardoons first in the egg, then roll them in the bread crumbs.

4. Heat about ½ inch oil in a large deep skillet over medium heat. Add the cardoons a few pieces at a time, leaving enough space between them so that they can fry without touching one another. Fry, using tongs to turn the pieces, until they are nicely browned on all sides, 3 to 4 minutes. Drain the cardoons on paper towels. Keep warm in a low oven while you fry the remainder. Serve hot.

Potato Croquettes

CROCCHÉ

Eating in the streets of Naples has a long tradition. For centuries, the common people were very poor and lived in crowded, dark ground-floor apartments called bassi. Since they had no cooking facilities, they bought food from the stalls throughout the neighborhoods. Fried foods were always popular, although there were even stands where you could buy a handful of cooked pasta. I do mean a handful: The proper way to eat spaghetti in these days was to tilt your head back, open your mouth, and hold the pasta in your hand overhead.

The pasta stands long ago became restaurants, but the fry stalls still exist, although now they are usually storefronts where you can buy fritters of vegetables, cheese, seafood, or alga marina, seaweed. My favorite are the crocché, bullet-shaped croquettes made with mashed potatoes and cheese and fried in a golden bread crumb crust. They are often part of a fritto misto, mixed fry of vegetables or fish, or may be served by themselves as a side dish with a roast.

In my home, we called these potato croquettes panzerotti, a name applied to several southern Italian dishes. It means big bellies, from the swollen shape—or could it be how you feel if you eat too many? Some cooks leave out the chopped salami or prosciutto and add mozzarella instead.

MAKES ABOUT 2 DOZEN

2 pounds boiling potatoes, scrubbed
3 large eggs, separated
½ cup freshly grated Parmigiano-Reggiano
¼ cup very finely chopped prosciutto or salami (about 2 ounces)
2 tablespoons chopped flat-leaf parsley

¼ teaspoon freshly grated nutmeg
Salt and freshly ground black pepper
About 2 cups dry bread crumbs, preferably homemade
Olive or vegetable oil for frying

1. Place the potatoes in a large saucepan with cold water to cover, cover, and bring to a boil. Cook over medium heat until the potatoes are tender when pierced with a fork.

2. Drain the potatoes and peel them. Press them through a food mill or ricer into a bowl.

3. Stir in the egg yolks, Parmigiano, prosciutto, parsley, and nutmeg. Add salt and pepper to taste.

4. Using about ¼ cup of the mixture, form it into a sausage shape about 1 inch thick and 2½ inches long. Repeat with the remaining potatoes.

5. In a shallow dish, beat the egg whites until frothy. Spread the bread crumbs on a sheet of wax paper. Dip the potato logs into the egg whites, then roll them in the crumbs, coating them completely. Place on a wire rack and let dry for 15 to 30 minutes. (This helps the croquettes to keep their shape.)

6. Pour about ½ inch oil into a large heavy skillet. Heat the oil over medium heat until a bit of the egg white sizzles when dropped in the oil. Add the croquettes, leaving at least ½ inch between them. Cook until crisp and brown, using tongs to turn the croquettes so that they brown evenly. Drain the croquettes on paper towels. Serve immediately, or keep warm in a 350°F oven while you fry the remainder.

Potato Cake

GATTÒ DI PATATE

This rich potato cake is a Neapolitan specialty. Gattò is a corruption of the French gâteau, meaning cake, and this was probably a creation of one of the French-trained chefs who cooked for the Neapolitan nobility. In my house, we ate it on most holidays, as a side dish with roast beef or turkey, but it also makes a fine appetizer or lunch main dish, served with a green salad.

For the fluffiest mashed potatoes, mash them with a ricer, a hand-held masher, or a food mill. Using an electric mixer or a food processor can make them gummy.

SERVES 6 TO 8

2 pounds boiling potatoes, scrubbed
5 tablespoons unsalted butter, softened
⅓ cup freshly grated Parmigiano-Reggiano
Salt and freshly ground black pepper
2 large eggs
½ cup milk

3 ounces sliced prosciutto, cut into narrow strips
3 ounces sliced salami, cut into narrow strips
8 ounces fresh mozzarella, sliced
2 tablespoons dry bread crumbs, preferably homemade

1. Place the potatoes in a pot and cover with cold water. Cover the pot and bring to a simmer. Reduce the heat to low and cook until the potatoes are tender when pierced with a knife. Drain the potatoes and let stand until cool enough to handle.

2. Preheat the oven to 375°F. Butter a 3-quart casserole or a 12 × 9 × 2-inch oval baking dish.

3. Peel the potatoes and mash them with a masher, ricer, or food mill. Stir in the butter, Parmigiano, and salt and pepper to taste. (Go easy on the salt, since there are a lot of other salty ingredients.)

4. Beat the eggs and milk. Stir into the potato mixture. Add the sliced meats.

5. Spread half the potato mixture in the prepared baking dish. Arrange the mozzarella slices on top. Add the remaining potatoes and spread the top to smooth. Sprinkle with the bread crumbs and dot with butter. (The potatoes can be made up to 24 hours ahead; cover and refrigerate.)

6. Bake the casserole for 45 minutes, or until heated through and lightly browned on top. (If the casserole dish is a deep one or if it has been refrigerated, baking time will be longer.)

7. Let stand for about 10 minutes before serving.

Rosy Mashed Potatoes

PATATE SCHIACCIATTE AL POMODORO

At a trattoria in Rome, the owner told me that these rosy mashed potatoes, with a hint of spicy chile, were a tradition there. Served as an antipasto, the potatoes were molded into a dome in a bowl, then inverted onto a serving plate and while warm, cut into wedges. Their bright color and unusual flavor are very festive.

SERVES 6

1½ pounds boiling potatoes, scrubbed
1 small onion, finely chopped
1 very small dried peperoncino, crumbled, or
   a pinch of crushed red pepper

¼ cup olive oil
2 cups peeled, seeded, and chopped fresh or
   canned Italian peeled tomatoes
Salt and freshly ground black pepper

1. Put the potatoes in a large saucepan with cold water to cover. Cover the pot and bring to a boil. Reduce the heat, and simmer for 20 to 25 minutes, or until the potatoes are tender when pierced with a knife. Drain the potatoes and let cool slightly.

2. Meanwhile, in a large skillet, cook the onion and peperoncino in the olive oil over medium heat until the onion is tender, about 7 minutes.

3. Stir in the tomatoes and salt and pepper to taste. Bring to a simmer, lower the heat, and cook for 15 to 20 minutes, or until the tomatoes are slightly thickened.

4. Peel the potatoes and mash them with a potato masher, ricer, or food mill. Stir the potatoes into the tomato sauce. Remove from the heat.

5. Lightly oil a 1-quart bowl. Add the potatoes and press them down with a spatula. Invert the potatoes onto a plate. Cut into wedges to serve.

Cakes and Tarts

TORTE E CROSTATE

Although Italians usually eat fruit after a meal, holidays and special occasions call for more elaborate desserts. Cakes and pies iced with chocolate or cream, layered with custard or fruit, and topped with nuts are sold in bakeries all year round. Then there are the regional classics that only appear in their season, like *panforte, pandolce, pandoro,* and *panettone* for Christmas. For Easter, there is *colomba* and *pupi.* Often these are shaped into figures that are symbolic of the season. The *colomba* is a dove that signifies the Holy Spirit, while *pupi* (dolls) symbolize fertility.

Sweets such as these are rarely baked at home. Italians tend to buy their desserts, one reason being that they are a source of local pride and widely available for purchase in pastry shops and caffès. Also, until recently, few homes had ovens that could be regulated with accuracy, so baking was chancy.

Ricotta cheese figures in many southern Italian cakes. It is baked into an endless variety of cheesecakes, either plain or combined with other ingredients, such as wheat berries or semolina.

Ricotta Layer Cake

CASSATA

The cassata *is the glory of Sicilian desserts, a layered extravaganza of sponge cake and ricotta cream, wrapped in colored almond paste and topped with candied fruit. It looks like a masterpiece and at first glance might seem difficult, but it really is very easy if you do it in stages.*

Working with almond paste, known as pasta reale *(royal paste), is a culinary art form in Sicily. Pastry shop windows are filled with the most exquisite fruits, vegetables, and creatures shaped from almond paste.*

I once watched Maria Grammatico, a renowned pastry and baking expert, make them, molding each shape with her hands and tinting them in soft pastel shades with food coloring. Maria learned the art while growing up in a Sicilian orphanage, where the nuns made pastries and sweets to supplement their living. Today Maria's pastry shop in Erice is a destination for travelers from around the world.

SERVES 10

4 ounces almond paste

FILLING
One 16-ounce container whole-milk or
   part-skim ricotta, drained (see page 219)
½ cup confectioners' sugar
1 teaspoon vanilla extract
2 ounces semisweet or bittersweet chocolate,
   chopped (½ cup)

ICING
2 large egg whites
¼ teaspoon grated lemon zest
1 teaspoon fresh lemon juice
2½ cups confectioners' sugar

1 to 3 drops green food coloring

½ cup chopped candied fruit, such as citron or
   orange peel

1 recipe Sponge Cake Layers (page 236)

Candied or dried fruits, such as cherries,
   pineapple, or oranges

1. Knead the almond paste briefly to soften it. Place it in a food processor and add 1 drop of food coloring. Process until evenly tinted a light green, adding more color if needed. Transfer to a work surface. With your hands, shape it into a log. Wrap in plastic wrap and set aside until ready to use.

2. To make the filling, combine the ricotta, confectioners' sugar, and vanilla in a food processor or a bowl and process or whip it with an electric mixer until smooth and creamy. Transfer to a bowl if necessary and stir in the chocolate and chopped candied fruit. (The filling can be made up to 24 hours ahead; cover and refrigerate.)

3. To assemble, place 1 cake layer on a flat serving plate. Spread the filling on top. Place the second cake layer on top.

4. Cut the almond paste lengthwise into 4 slices. Place one piece between two sheets of plastic wrap. With a rolling pin, flatten it into a long narrow ribbon, 3 inches wide and ⅛ inch thick. Remove the plastic wrap and trim off any rough edges. Repeat with the remaining almond paste. Standing them on one long side, wrap the ribbons around the cake, overlapping them slightly and pressing against the cake to cover the sides completely.

5. Gather any scraps of almond paste and reroll them. Cut the scraps into stars or hearts or ribbons with a fluted pasta cutter. Reserve for decoration.

6. To make the icing, whisk the egg whites, lemon zest, and lemon juice. Add the confectioners' sugar and stir until smooth.

7. Dot the icing over the top cake layer. Spread it smooth with a metal spatula. Decorate with the cut-out scraps of almond paste and the fruits. Cover and refrigerate until serving time, up to 24 hours.

TIP: The liquid in ricotta must be drained off before using it in baked goods. To drain it, line a fine-mesh sieve with cheesecloth or a paper coffee filter. Place the sieve over a bowl. Scrape the ricotta into the sieve. Place a sheet of plastic wrap and a small plate that fits inside the sieve on top. Weight the plate with a heavy can or similar object. Let the ricotta drain in the refrigerator for several hours, or overnight.

WINE MATCH: Tanit, Moscato Passito Liquoroso, MID

Zuppa Inglese

Rum-soaked layers of sponge cake alternate with smooth chocolate and vanilla pastry cream in this utterly delicious "English soup." Athough no one is quite sure of its origins, the dessert is believed to be an Italianization of the British trifle, a traditional Christmas dessert that is made with layers of cake soaked in sherry alternating with fruit and custard. Soft, spoonable, and served in a bowl, it came to be called a zuppa, *or a soup.*

A perfect dessert for special company, Zuppa Inglese can—and should—be made at least a day ahead of time for best flavor. You will need a large serving bowl about ten inches wide and four inches deep. Assembled in a clear glass bowl, this is quite a beautiful presentation. You can vary the flavors by substituting orange or cherry liqueur for the rum. A word of caution: Make Zuppa Inglese for a crowd, or you, like me, may find yourself unable to resist polishing off the leftovers!

SERVES 10 TO 12

PASTRY CREAM

1 quart milk
½ cup sugar
Pinch of salt
6 large egg yolks
½ cup all-purpose flour
2 teaspoons vanilla extract
4 ounces semisweet or bittersweet chocolate

1 recipe Sponge Cake Layers (page 236)
½ cup dark rum
½ cup apricot jam
1 cup heavy cream
Fresh strawberries or raspberries for garnish

1. To make the pastry cream, bring 3 cups of the milk, the sugar, and salt to a simmer in a heavy saucepan over medium heat, stirring to dissolve the sugar. Remove from the heat.

2. In a large heatproof bowl, whisk the egg yolks and the remaining 1 cup milk until blended. Place the flour in a sieve and sift it over the egg yolks, whisking until smooth. Beat in the hot milk a little at a time.

3. When all of the milk has been added, transfer the mixture to the saucepan and return it to the heat. Cook, stirring constantly, over medium heat, until the mixture

begins to boil. Reduce the heat and cook for 30 seconds more. Remove the pan from the heat and stir in the vanilla.

4. Divide the cream between two bowls. Break up and add the chocolate to one bowl and let stand until softened. Stir until the chocolate is completely melted and there are no streaks. Cover both bowls with plastic wrap, pressing the wrap against the surface of the cream to prevent a skin from forming. Refrigerate until cold. (The pastry cream can be made up to 24 hours ahead.)

5. To assemble, choose a large deep serving bowl with at least a 3-quart capacity. Split the cake layers horizontally in half so that you have 4 layers. Don't worry if they are not perfect. Stir together the rum and jam.

6. Spoon half of the vanilla pastry cream into the bottom of the bowl. Place a cake layer on top and brush with one-quarter of the rum mixture. Spoon half of the chocolate cream on top. Place another layer of cake on top and brush with the rum mixture. (Don't be concerned if the cake layers slide—remember, this will be more like a soft spoonable trifle than a layer cake.) Spoon the remaining vanilla pastry cream over it, place another cake layer on top, and brush with the rum mixture. Finish with the remaining chocolate cream, cake, and rum mixture. Cover tightly and refrigerate for 3 hours or up to 24 hours.

7. Just before serving, in a large bowl with chilled beaters, whip the cream until soft peaks form. Spoon the cream on top of the dessert. Garnish with strawberries.

WINE MATCH: Moscato d'Asti, Cascinetta

Chocolate Cake for Passover

TORTA DI CIOCCOLATO DI PESAH

Here is a lovely chocolate nut cake for Passover, or any special occasion. Try it plain, with a chocolate or fruit sauce, or split into layers and fill with whipped cream. Chop the chocolate very fine; the pieces should be about ⅛ inch.

SERVES 8 TO 10

Oil and fine matzoh meal (or flour) for the pan
1¼ cups whole almonds, toasted and cooled
⅔ cup sugar
5 large eggs, separated
1 teaspoon vanilla extract

6 ounces semisweet chocolate, very finely
  chopped
Pinch of salt
Cocoa powder for dusting

1. Preheat the oven to 350°F. Oil a 9 × 3-inch springform pan and dust it lightly with matzoh meal.

2. In a food processor or blender, combine the almonds and ⅓ cup of the sugar. Pulse or blend until the nuts are finely chopped.

3. In a large bowl, beat the egg yolks, vanilla, and the remaining ⅓ cup sugar until creamy. Stir in the nuts and chocolate.

4. In another large bowl, beat the egg whites with the salt on low speed until foamy. Increase the speed to high and beat until soft peaks form when the beaters are lifted.

5. Fold about one-third of the egg whites into the chocolate mixture to lighten it. Gradually add the remaining whites, folding gently with a rubber spatula to avoid deflating the whites.

6. Scrape the batter into the prepared pan. Bake for 35 minutes, or until the cake is slightly puffed around the edge but still moist in the center. Cool for 10 minutes on a wire rack.

7. Run a small knife around the inside of the pan. Remove the sides of the pan. Let the cake cool completely. It will sink slightly as it cools.

8. Just before serving, place cocoa powder in a small sieve and dust the top of the cake.

TIP: For most purposes, I prefer to chop good-quality chocolate bars into small pieces rather than using chocolate chips. To chop bars of chocolate easily, make sure they are at room temperature. Place the bar on a cutting board and chop it with a big chef's knife.

WINE MATCH: Bracchetto, Villa Banfi

Chocolate Chunk Cheesecake

TORTA DI RICOTTA

What dessert could be more delicious or easier to make than cheesecake? This creamy version studded with chocolate chunks was given to me by Barbara Riotto Garodnick. She learned it from her aunt's mother-in-law, Marietta Gisonda De Lillo, who was born in 1882. She brought the recipe with her from Grumo, a town near Bari, in Puglia. Barbara said the cheesecake is a family favorite served at holiday meals all year round.

Sometimes grated citrus zest or bits of candied fruit were added to the cake, but Barbara prefers it flavored with bittersweet chocolate chunks. I like it this way too. It reminds me of the delicious warm chocolate chip cheesecakes I tasted in Rome's Jewish Quarter.

SERVES 8 TO 10

Three 16-ounce containers whole-milk ricotta, drained (see page 219)
8 large eggs, at room temperature
1½ cups sugar
2 teaspoons vanilla extract

1 teaspoon grated lemon or orange zest
One 3- to 4-ounce bar semisweet or bittersweet chocolate, finely chopped
Confectioners' sugar for dusting

1. Preheat the oven to 400°F. Butter and flour a 10-inch springform pan. Tap out the excess flour.

2. Push the ricotta through a fine sieve into a large bowl. With a wire whisk, beat in the eggs one at a time. Beat in the sugar, vanilla, and zest until creamy and well blended. With a rubber spatula, stir in the chocolate.

3. Scrape the mixture into the prepared pan. Bake the cheesecake for 1 hour and 15 minutes, or until lightly golden on the surface and beginning to pull away from the sides of the pan. The center will still be soft.

4. Turn off the oven and prop the door open with a wooden spoon. Let the cake cool in the oven for 30 minutes.

5. Remove the cake and let cool completely on a rack. Cover tightly and store in the refrigerator for up to 3 days. Sprinkle with confectioners' sugar before serving.

TIP: If you like extra-smooth cheesecake (or other ricotta desserts), buzz the cheese briefly in a food processor or blender until creamy.

WINE MATCH: Asti Fontanafredda

Ricotta Tart

CASSATA AL FORNO

In Sicily, cassata *can mean any one of several things: a fancy dessert made with sponge cake layers, ricotta cream, and candied fruits; a simple baked cheesecake; a frozen layered ice cream dessert; or this pretty baked ricotta tart with a lattice top.*

If you don't have Marsala for the dough, substitute dry white wine, orange juice, or plain water.

SERVES 8

DOUGH

2½ cups all-purpose flour

½ cup sugar

½ teaspoon salt

8 tablespoons (1 stick) unsalted butter, cut into
   small pieces

2 large egg yolks

3 tablespoons dry Marsala

FILLING

One 32-ounce container whole-milk
   ricotta, drained (see page 219)

½ cup sugar

½ teaspoon ground cinnamon

½ cup golden raisins

2 tablespoons chopped candied orange peel

2 tablespoons chopped candied citron

Confectioners' sugar for dusting

1. To make the dough, combine the flour, sugar, and salt in a large bowl. Cut in the butter with a pastry blender or two knives until the mixture resembles coarse crumbs. Whisk the egg yolks and Marsala together. Pour the mixture over the flour and stir just until blended. If the dough seems dry, sprinkle on a few drops of cold water. Do not overwork the dough.

2. Divide the dough into two pieces, one a third larger than the other. Wrap each piece in plastic wrap and refrigerate for at least 30 minutes, or overnight.

3. Position a rack on the bottom level of the oven and preheat the oven to 350°F.

4. To make the filling, beat the ricotta, sugar, and cinnamon together in a bowl until smooth. Stir in the raisins and candied fruit.

5. To assemble the tart, on a lightly floured surface, roll out the larger piece of dough to a 12-inch circle. Drape the dough over the rolling pin and center it in a 9-inch fluted tart pan with a removable bottom. Gently press the dough against the sides of the pan, letting the edges hang over. With a rubber spatula, scrape the filling into the tart shell.

6. Roll out the remaining piece of dough to a 10-inch circle. With a fluted pastry cutter, cut the dough into ½-inch-wide strips. Lay half the strips across the filling, spacing them evenly. Rotate the pan 180 degrees and lay the remaining strips at right angles across the first ones, creating a lattice.

7. Bake the tart for 30 to 35 minutes, or until the top is browned and the filling is set. Cool the tart on a wire rack for 10 minutes. Remove the sides of the pan ring by placing the tart on a tall object such as a coffee can and slipping the ring down. Cool the tart completely on the wire rack.

8. Just before serving, sprinkle the tart with confectioners' sugar. Store in the refrigerator. Serve at room temperature.

WINE MATCH: Moscato di Trani, Rivera

Easter Wheat Berry Cheesecake

PASTIERA

La pastiera, or pizza gran, is the pride of Naples. Although it was once made only at East-ertime, today you can find enormous pans of it in just about every restaurant, pastry shop, and pizzeria all year round. Basically it is a cheesecake, but with the added texture of cooked wheat grains. It is flavored with cinnamon, bits of candied citron, and three kinds of orange flavoring: grated zest, candied peel, and orange flower water, a delicate essence. A tender, sweet pasta frolla *crust encases the filling, with a pretty lattice design on the top.*

The grain, orange flower water, and candied orange and citron can be found in Italian and Middle Eastern markets. The candied fruits that come already chopped in plastic containers in the supermarket have little flavor. Buy citron and orange peel in large pieces, then cut it into fine dice yourself.

SERVES 8

FILLING

4 ounces hulled wheat berries (about ½ cup)

½ teaspoon salt

8 tablespoons (1 stick) unsalted butter, softened

1 teaspoon grated orange zest

One 16-ounce container whole-milk ricotta

4 large eggs, at room temperature

⅔ cup sugar

3 tablespoons orange flower water

1 teaspoon ground cinnamon

½ cup very finely chopped candied citron

½ cup very finely chopped candied orange peel

DOUGH

3 cups all-purpose flour

½ teaspoon ground cinnamon

½ teaspoon salt

12 tablespoons (1½ sticks) unsalted butter, softened

1 cup confectioners' sugar

1 large egg

2 large egg yolks

2 teaspoons orange flower water

Confectioners' sugar for dusting

1. For the filling, place the wheat berries in a large bowl, add cold water to cover, and let soak overnight in the refrigerator.

2. To make the filling, drain the soaked wheat berries and place in a medium saucepan with cool water to cover. Add the salt and bring to a simmer over medium heat. Cook,

stirring occasionally, until the wheat is tender, 20 to 30 minutes. Drain and place in a large bowl. Stir in the butter and orange zest. Let cool.

3. To make the dough, combine the flour, cinnamon, and salt in a medium bowl. In a large bowl, beat the butter and confectioners' sugar until light and fluffy. Add the egg and yolks and beat until smooth. Beat in the orange flower water. Add the dry ingredients and stir until blended. Shape one-quarter of the dough into a disk. Make a second disk with the remaining dough. Wrap each piece in plastic wrap and chill for at least 1 hour, or overnight.

4. Preheat the oven to 350°F.

5. In a large bowl, combine the ricotta, eggs, sugar, orange flower water, and cinnamon and beat until blended. Stir in the wheat mixture, citron, and candied orange peel.

6. On a lightly floured surface, roll out the larger piece of dough to a 16-inch circle. Drape the dough over the rolling pin. Using the pin to lift it, transfer the dough to a 9 × 3-inch springform pan, pressing it evenly against the bottom and sides of the pan. Pour in the filling and smooth the top.

7. Roll out the smaller piece of dough to a 10-inch circle. With a fluted pastry cutter, cut the dough into ½-inch-wide strips. Lay half the strips 1 inch apart across the filling. Turn the pan 180 degrees and lay the remaining strips at right angles across the first ones, forming a lattice pattern. Press the ends of the strips against the dough covering the sides of the pan. Trim off all but ½ inch of the dough, fold the edge over the ends of the lattice strips, and press firmly to seal.

9. Bake the cheesecake for 1 hour and 10 minutes, or until browned on top and a toothpick inserted in the center comes out clean. Let cool on a rack for 15 minutes. Remove the side of the pan and let cool completely on the rack.

10. Serve at room temperature or chilled, sprinkled with confectioners' sugar. Store in the refrigerator.

WINE MATCH: Malvasia Delle Lipari, Colosi

Trieste Holiday Cake

PRESNITZ

Chef Mauro Mafrici of New York's I Trulli Restaurant gave me his family's recipe for presnitz, a dramatic holiday cake from his hometown of Trieste, in northeastern Italy. The cake is made with puff pastry, which you can make yourself or buy frozen. The pastry is rolled up around a filling of raisins, nuts, chocolate, and spices, like a jelly roll, then the roll is coiled into a spiral. The baked cake looks like a big golden snail. A small slice is very satisfying, and the cake keeps well for a long time.

Presnitz with slight variations goes by the name of gubana or potitza in different parts of Friuli–Venezia Giulia. Some versions are made with a yeast dough, while others use a simple pasta frolla (tart dough). When visiting the region, I was told that people sometimes douse their slice of presnitz with a shot of grappa before eating it.

SERVES 10 TO 12

FILLING

½ cup raisins
½ cup dark rum
4 tablespoons (½ stick) unsalted butter
¼ cup fine dry bread crumbs
1½ cups finely chopped walnuts
1 cup finely chopped candied orange zest
3 ounces semisweet chocolate, grated
½ cup pine nuts
½ cup sugar

1 tablespoon ground cinnamon
¼ teaspoon freshly grated nutmeg
Pinch of salt

One 16-ounce package frozen puff pastry
   sheets, thawed according to the package
   instructions
1 large egg, beaten with 1 tablespoon water

1. For the filling, toss the raisins in a small bowl with the rum and let stand for at least 30 minutes.

2. Place an oven rack in the center of the oven and preheat the oven to 325°F. Butter and flour a large baking sheet.

3. To make the filling, melt the butter in a small skillet over medium heat. Cook, swirling the pan occasionally, until the butter turns golden brown. Remove from the heat. Stir in the bread crumbs until the butter is absorbed.

4. In a large bowl, combine the bread crumbs, raisins, and rum with the remaining filling ingredients, mixing well with a wooden spoon.

5. On a lightly floured surface, arrange the 2 sheets of puff pastry and place next to each other, overlapping slightly to form one large rectangle. Press the seam together to seal. If necessary, brush the edges with a fingertip moistened with water so that they stick together. With a lightly floured rolling pin, roll out the dough to a 24 × 10-inch rectangle.

6. Place the pastry on a long piece of wax paper. Brush some of the egg over the pastry. Spread the filling over the pastry, leaving a 1-inch border all around. Fold one long side of the dough over the filling. Using the paper to help, tightly roll up the dough like a jelly roll. Pinch the ends to seal.

7. Using the paper to lift it, place the roll seam side down on the prepared baking sheet. Form the roll into a spiral. Carefully slide the paper out from under the roll. Brush the top with the egg.

8. Bake for 35 to 45 minutes, or until golden brown. Slide onto a rack to cool completely. Store leftovers at room temperature.

TIP: Dark rum gives a good flavor to many desserts.

WINE MATCH: Torcolato, Maculan

Double Chocolate Pudding Tart

CROSTATA DI SANGUINACCIO

Thick, rich chocolate pudding is a classic Neapolitan dessert, often served with plain cookies such as ladyfingers for dipping. Some versions are flavored with cinnamon, pine nuts, and candied fruits. I like it plain, served in a buttery pastry shell. Leave out the citron if you prefer a smooth pudding.

Sanguinaccio was once a specialty only made from December to Easter. One of its primary ingredients was pig's blood, used as a thickener. Before refrigeration, pigs were only slaughtered during the cold months, so the pudding was a seasonal treat. Today cornstarch does the job the pig's blood once did.

SERVES 6 TO 8

DOUGH

1⅓ cups all-purpose flour

3 tablespoons sugar

½ teaspoon salt

6 tablespoons (¾ stick) cold unsalted butter, cut into bits

1 large egg, lightly beaten

1 teaspoon vanilla extract

PUDDING

¼ cup cornstarch

¼ cup unsweetened cocoa powder

⅓ cup sugar

2 cups cold milk

3 ounces semisweet or bittersweet chocolate, broken up

2 tablespoons unsalted butter

2 tablespoons finely chopped candied citron, optional

1 teaspoon vanilla extract

¾ cup heavy cream

1 tablespoon pine nuts

1. To make the dough, combine the flour, sugar, and salt in a large bowl. With a pastry blender or two knives, blend in the butter until the mixture resembles coarse meal. Add the egg and vanilla and toss the mixture with a fork until the egg is incorporated. If the mixture seems dry, add a few drops of cold water. Gather the dough together and shape it into a disk. Wrap in plastic wrap. Refrigerate for at least 1 hour, or overnight.

2. On a lightly floured surface, roll out the dough to a 12-inch circle. Fit the dough into a 9- or 10-inch fluted tart pan with a removable bottom. Trim off the excess. Fold

the overhanging dough in over itself and press it into place. Chill the tart shell for at least 30 minutes.

3. Place an oven rack in the center of the oven and preheat the oven to 350°F.

4. Butter a sheet of aluminum foil just large enough to line the tart shell. Place foil buttered side down in the shell. Bake the shell for 15 minutes. Carefully remove the foil. With a fork, prick the bottom of the shell at 1-inch intervals. Bake for 10 minutes more, or until lightly browned. Let cool.

5. To make the pudding, combine the cornstarch, cocoa, and sugar in a medium saucepan. Gradually whisk in the milk. Place over medium heat and cook, stirring constantly, until the mixture comes to a boil. Reduce the heat and simmer for 1 minute, or until thick.

6. Remove the pot from the heat. Add the chocolate and butter and let stand until softened, then whisk until smooth. Pour into a bowl and stir in the citron and vanilla. Cover with plastic wrap placed directly on the surface to prevent a skin from forming, and let cool. Refrigerate until chilled.

7. Spread the pudding in the prepared pastry shell. Cover and refrigerate for 2 hours, or until ready to serve.

8. Just before serving, pour the cream into a large chilled bowl and whip it until soft peaks form. Spoon or pipe the cream around the edge of the tart. Remove sides of pan. Sprinkle with the pine nuts and serve.

TIP: Use semisweet or bittersweet chocolate for most baking. Milk chocolate should be reserved for eating. Do not use unsweetened baking chocolate unless the recipe calls for it specifically.

WINE MATCH: Bukkaram, De Bartoli

Orange Semolina Cake

MIGLIACCIO

Migliaccio *is something* like a *cheesecake, though the texture is more dense. The flavor, though, is lovely and delicate. This recipe comes from Naples and is enjoyed for Carnevale.*

SERVES 8

¼ cup fine semolina flour
½ cup sugar
One 16-ounce container whole-milk or
    part-skim ricotta
2 large eggs, separated

2 tablespoons orange liqueur
1 teaspoon grated orange zest
½ cup golden raisins
¼ teaspoon salt
Confectioners' sugar for dusting

1. Preheat the oven to 350°F. Butter an 8-inch round cake pan.

2. In a small saucepan, bring 1½ cups water to a boil. Drizzle the semolina into the water, stirring constantly with a wooden spoon. Stir in ¼ cup of the sugar. Cook, stirring often, until thickened, about 4 minutes. Remove the pan from the heat and let cool slightly.

3. In a large bowl, whisk the ricotta, egg yolks, liqueur, and zest. Stir in the raisins.

4. In a large bowl, beat the egg whites with the salt on low speed until foamy. Gradually beat in the remaining ¼ cup sugar on high speed and beat until the whites hold stiff peaks.

5. With a spatula, gently fold the egg whites into the ricotta mixture. Scrape the mixture into the prepared pan.

6. Bake the cheesecake for 1 hour or until puffed and golden on top. Remove from the oven. Let cool on a rack for 10 minutes. Invert onto a plate and let cool.

7. Serve at room temperature or chilled, sprinkled with confectioners' sugar.

TIP: Keep a sugar shaker filled with confectioners' sugar and another with unsweetened cocoa for a quick decoration for desserts. Mark them clearly so you don't get confused.

Sponge Cake Layers

PAN DI SPAGNA

A light sponge cake is the perfect base for many desserts with soft, creamy fillings. In this book, it is used to make Ricotta Layer Cake (page 218) and Zuppa Inglese (page 220). You can also fill the two layers with fruit preserves, whipped cream, or pastry cream, or serve them cut into wedges and topped with warm zabaglione. I always keep a pan di spagna in the freezer, ready to make a dessert in a hurry.

There is nothing difficult about making this cake, but it is important to follow the directions carefully. The cake relies on the egg foam for its structure, so be sure the eggs are at room temperature before you begin, and fold in the flour very delicately.

MAKES TWO 9-INCH LAYERS

⅔ cup sugar
1½ teaspoons vanilla extract

6 large eggs, at room temperature
1 cup sifted all-purpose flour

1. Preheat the oven to 375°F. Butter two 9-inch round cake pans. Line the bottom of the pans with circles of wax or parchment paper. Butter the paper, dust the pans with flour, and tap out the excess flour.

2. Put the sugar, vanilla, and eggs in a large electric mixer bowl. Using the whip attachment if you have one, begin beating the eggs on low speed, then gradually increase it to high and beat until the eggs are very thick, light, and fluffy, 5 to 7 minutes.

3. Place about one-third of the flour in a sieve and sift it over the egg mixture. Gradually and very gently fold in the flour with a rubber spatula. Rotate the bowl as you cut down with the spatula, lifting the bottom of the mixture over the top with each turn. Add the remaining flour in two additions, folding it in until there are no streaks.

4. Scrape the batter evenly into the prepared pans. Bake for 20 to 25 minutes, or until the cakes spring back when pressed lightly in the center and the top is lightly browned. Remove the pans from the oven and cool on cake racks for 10 minutes.

5. Run a small knife around the edges of the pans. Invert the cakes onto the racks and remove the pans. Carefully peel off the paper. Let the cakes cool completely. Use when cool, or wrap tightly in foil or plastic wrap and store at room temperature for up to 2 days.

Cookies, Fruit, and Nuts

Italians always seem to have a supply of biscotti in their pantry, ready to enjoy with morning coffee or afternoon tea, or as a postmeal treat with a glass of sweet wine. Breakfast cookies are plain and not too sweet, while those eaten for dessert are richer with nuts, chocolate, and icings.

Southern Italians often make cookies with almonds or almond paste. The nuts grow abundantly all over the south and have a fine, rich flavor. When the nuts will be ground into a paste, a few bitter almonds are commonly added to the mix to heighten the flavor of the sweet almonds.

Hazelnuts are more common in northern Italy, where they are used in cookies, cakes, and candies, especially *gianduja*, a blend of smooth dark chocolate and hazelnut puree.

For holidays and special occasions, a tray of plain and fancy cookies is a common sight, often garnished with Jordan almonds, confetti, and tinsel. Fresh and dried fruits and roasted nuts are often served at the end of a holiday meal.

Pine Nut–Almond Macaroons

PINOLI

After years of experimenting, I have found that the texture of these cookies depends on two things: the almond paste and the size of the macaroons. Two almond paste brands that I like are American Almond Products Company and Solo. Widely available in supermarkets, both have good almond flavor and stay soft, fresh, and moist because they are packed in cans. If you use less than a tablespoon of batter, the cookies turn out too crisp and flat. These are full and round and do not collapse after baking.

Be sure to coat the cookies completely with the nuts to prevent them from sticking to the pan.

Buy pignoli nuts in bulk at a health food store or ethnic market. Those in the little jars sold in supermarkets are overpriced and are generally not as fresh. These cookies are also good made with slivered almonds in place of the pignoli.

MAKES ABOUT 30

8 ounces almond paste
2 large egg whites, beaten, plus 1 tablespoon
   beaten white if necessary

1 cup confectioners' sugar, plus more for
   dusting
2 cups pignoli nuts

1. Preheat the oven to 350°F. Generously butter a large baking sheet.

2. Crumble the almond paste into a large mixer bowl. Add the 2 egg whites and the confectioners' sugar and beat until smooth. The batter should be very soft and sticky. If it is not, add up to another tablespoon of beaten egg white.

3. Place the pignoli nuts in a small bowl. Drop a scant tablespoon of the batter into the nuts. Roll into a ball and place on the prepared baking sheet. Repeat with the remaining batter and nuts, placing the balls about 1 inch apart.

4. Bake for 18 to 20 minutes, or until lightly browned. Let cool for 2 minutes on the pan. Transfer the cookies to racks to cool completely.

5. Dust the cooled cookies with confectioners' sugar. Store in an airtight container one week or in the freezer up to one month.

Vin Santo Rings

CIAMBELLINE AL VINSANTO

At the Selvapiana Winery in Tuscany, the Giuntini family enjoys these cookies at all their holiday gatherings. Made with just four ingredients, they are great with coffee. Or serve them with a glass of Selvapiana Vin Santo, the wine used in the recipe. Vin Santo is a moderately sweet dessert wine from Tuscany. Traditionally the dry cookies are dipped in wine to moisten and flavor them.

MAKES ABOUT 4 DOZEN

2½ cups unbleached all-purpose flour
½ cup sugar

½ cup extra virgin olive oil
½ cup Vin Santo

1. Preheat the oven to 350°F.

2. In a large bowl, combine the flour and sugar. Add the oil and wine and stir until thoroughly blended and smooth.

3. Pinch off a piece of dough about 1 inch in diameter. On a lightly floured surface, roll out the dough into a 4-inch rope about ½ inch thick. Pinch the ends together to form a ring and place on an ungreased baking sheet. Repeat with the remaining dough, placing the rings about 1 inch apart.

4. Bake the rings for 20 minutes, or until lightly colored. Transfer to racks to cool. Stored in an airtight container, these keep well for a long time.

WINE MATCH: Selvapiana Vin Santo

Glazed Vanilla Rings

TARALLI DOLCI

Ring-shaped taralli *can be sweet or savory, big or tiny. This sweet version is iced with a vanilla glaze and dusted with colored sprinkles. Sometimes they are tinted with a blue or a pink glaze to celebrate the birth of a baby.*

MAKES ABOUT 6 DOZEN

3¼ cups unbleached all-purpose flour

2½ teaspoons baking powder

1 teaspoon salt

3 large eggs, at room temperature

½ cup sugar

8 tablespoons (1 stick) unsalted butter,
  melted and cooled

1 teaspoon vanilla extract

GLAZE

1½ cups confectioners' sugar

1 teaspoon vanilla extract

Multicolored sprinkles

1. Preheat the oven to 375°F. Butter and flour two large cookie sheets.

2. Stir together the flour, baking powder, and salt.

3. In a large bowl, whisk the eggs and sugar until light. Stir in the butter and vanilla. Gradually stir in the dry ingredients to make a soft dough.

4. Break off a 1-inch piece of dough. Roll the dough between your hands or on a countertop into a 4-inch rope about ½ inch thick. If the dough is sticky, lightly flour your hands and the countertop. Pinch the two ends together to make a ring and place on a prepared baking sheet. Repeat with the remaining dough, placing the rings about 1 inch apart.

5. Bake the rings for 12 to 14 minutes, or until just beginning to color. Transfer to wire racks to cool.

6. To make the glaze, in a small bowl, stir together the sugar, 4 teaspoons water, and the vanilla until smooth. If necessary, stir in up to 2 teaspoons more water. Spread the glaze over the cookies and immediately dust them with sprinkles. Let dry on racks.

Saint Agatha's Day

Every culture and religion has traditions that may seem at least irreverent and often downright gruesome or macabre. The Saint Agatha's Day celebration, which falls on February 5, certainly fits into this category.

Small cakes known as *minni di vergine*, literally, virgin's breasts, are traditional. The rounded pastries filled with almond paste or preserves made from green squash were originally made by cloistered nuns in Palermo at the end of the eighteenth century. The nuns, who often had joined the convent because society at that time offered women few other opportunities, produced pastries and other sweets on holidays for wealthy patrons. The idea was to honor the holy day by bringing something symbolic of the sacred occasion to the secular public. It was also a way for the women, whose lives were so circumscribed, to have an outlet for their creativity and earn money toward their keep.

The story goes that in the year 251, Agatha spurned the attentions of an unwelcome suitor. Like Penelope, the wife of Ulysses, she put him off by asking him to wait until she had finished weaving a special robe. Though she wove the fabric for all to see by day, at night she secretly undid her work. Eventually, her trick became apparent and Agatha was cruelly martyred and her breasts were cut off. She is revered today as the patron saint of Catania, the protector of nursing mothers, and the patroness of weavers.

The citizens of Catania and the surrounding area celebrate her sacrifice with a three-day festival. The saint's remains, believed to protect the city from earthquakes and the eruption of nearby Mount Etna, are paraded through the streets. Her bier, decorated with flowers, is preceded by eleven *candelore*, man-size candles weighing more than 200 pounds each. Each candle represents one of the city's guilds. Shouting *"Evviva Saint'Agatha!"* (Long live Saint Agatha!), people stroll through streets decorated with colored lights. There are games of chance, music, and dancing.

Sesame Cookies

BISCOTTI REGINA

I love the nutty flavor of sesame seeds. Sesame bagels, bread sticks, and rolls are my favorites and after I have eaten them up, you will find me dabbing at the remaining seeds that have fallen to my plate.

So, of course, I find biscotti regina, *as these crusty Sicilian cookies are called, irresistible. I don't know if they were named for a queen or are simply the queen of cookies, though I suspect the latter. Sesame seeds were brought to Sicily by the Arabs, who called them* giugiulebbe, *from which derived the Sicilian* giugiulena.

My friend Sal Agro, also a big fan of biscotti regina, *makes regular trips from his home in Manhattan to his favorite bakery in Queens to stock up on them. At the bakery, he handpicks the cookies with the toastiest color for the most flavor.*

When Sal mentioned that his sister, Lina Aristorno, from Buffalo, New York, made homemade biscotti regina, *I had to have the recipe, which he graciously supplied. These really are the best I have ever tasted.*

Be sure to buy fresh, unhulled sesame seeds. Like nuts, the seeds have oils in them, which turn rancid if they are left in a warm place for too long. Store in the refrigerator or freeze.

MAKES ABOUT 4 DOZEN

4 cups unbleached all-purpose flour

1 cup sugar

1 tablespoon plus ½ teaspoon baking powder

½ teaspoon salt

½ pound (2 sticks) unsalted butter, cut into
  pieces, softened

2 large eggs, at room temperature

1 teaspoon vanilla extract

½ teaspoon grated orange zest

½ teaspoon grated lemon zest

½ cup milk

2 cups unhulled sesame seeds

1. Preheat the oven to 375°. Butter and flour two large baking sheets.

2. In a large electric mixer bowl, stir together the flour, sugar, baking powder, and salt. On low speed, add the butter a little at a time.

3. In a medium bowl, whisk the eggs, vanilla, and orange and lemon zest. Stir the egg mixture into the dry ingredients until well blended and the mixture forms a mass.

4. Place the milk in a shallow bowl. Spread the sesame seeds on a plate.

5. Pinch off a piece of dough the size of a golf ball and shape it into a sausage shape about 2½ inches long and ¾ inch thick. Roll the cookie in the milk, then in the sesame seeds. Place on a prepared baking sheet and flatten slightly. Continue with the remaining dough, placing the cookies about 1 inch apart.

6. Bake the cookies for 25 to 30 minutes, or until well browned and crisp. Let cool for 10 minutes, then transfer to a rack to cool completely. Store in an airtight container.

Toasting and Skinning Hazelnuts

Place the hazelnuts on a baking sheet. Bake for 10 to 15 minutes, or until the nuts are lightly toasted and the skins are beginning to split. Transfer the nuts to a towel and rub them to remove the skins. Let cool before chopping or grinding.

Hazelnut Biscotti

QUARESIMALI

The late food writer Richard Sax made the crunchiest quaresimali cookies I have ever tasted. He got the recipe from the very popular Veniero's Bakery in Manhattan, and he published a version in his cookbook Classic Home Desserts. The cookies seem to be made of nuts held together with a little bit of dough. Conversation comes to a halt when you serve these–the sound of crunching is too loud.

This is my version of Richard's cookies. Quaresimali are a specialty of the Lenten season because they are supposed to be so hard they are penance to eat. Somewhere along the way, though, they became a lot more flavorful. They have a double dose of spice in the form of ground cinnamon and several drops of cinnamon oil. The oil is hard to find, but I love the cinnamon candy flavor it adds. You can buy cinnamon oil at some gourmet shops and those that specialize in spices and extracts. There are several mail-order or online sources for it as well (see Sources, page 296).

If you don't have cinnamon oil, the cookies will still be delicious.

MAKES ABOUT 10 DOZEN

2 cups unbleached all-purpose flour
1¼ cups sugar
1¼ teaspoons ground cinnamon
1 teaspoon baking powder
¼ teaspoon salt

3 cups hazelnuts (about 12 ounces), toasted and skinned (see page 243)
3 large eggs, at room temperature
5 drops cinnamon oil, optional

1. Preheat the oven to 350°F. Butter and flour two large baking sheets.

2. In a large mixing bowl, stir together the flour, sugar, cinnamon, baking powder, and salt. Add the hazelnuts and mix well.

3. Beat the eggs with the cinnamon oil, if using. Stir the eggs into the dry ingredients until well blended. Divide the dough into 6 portions.

4. Moisten your hands with cool water. Shape one portion of the dough into a long log 1½ inches in diameter. Place the log on a prepared baking sheet. Repeat with the remaining dough, spacing the logs about 2 inches apart. They will spread as they bake.

5. Bake for 20 to 22 minutes, or until the logs are firm when lightly pressed and beginning to brown around the edges. Leave the oven on.

6. Slide the logs onto a cutting board. With a heavy chef's knife, cut the logs diagonally into ½-inch slices.

7. Place the slices on the baking sheets and bake until crisp and toasty brown, about 10 minutes. Cool the cookies on wire racks. Store in an airtight container.

All Souls' Day Spice Cookies

PAN DEI MORTI

On a visit to Milan in late October, every caffè and bakery I passed had these chewy spice cookies for sale. In one shop, they told me that pan dei morti, *bread of the dead as they are called in the local dialect, is an old Lombardian recipe. Sweet treats like these,* fave dei morti *(page 248),* ossa dei morti *("bones of the dead," meringue nut cookies),* pan di mei *(cornmeal cookies), and* amor polenta *(cornmeal cake) were made to bring some cheer to compensate for the sadness of the November 1 and 2 holidays, All Souls' and All Saints' Day.*

I tried numerous versions of the cookies. Some were made with figs and almonds, others contained raisins, citron, pine nuts, or walnuts. Crumbled amaretti cookies are another common ingredient. All were delicious, especially with a cup of steaming cappuccino, but these are my favorite.

MAKES ABOUT 40

2¼ cups unbleached all-purpose flour
1 tablespoon unsweetened cocoa powder
1½ teaspoons baking soda
½ teaspoon ground cinnamon
¼ teaspoon freshly grated nutmeg
Pinch of salt
¼ cup shortening, at room temperature
1 cup sugar

1 large egg
1 teaspoon grated orange zest
¼ cup orange juice
3 tablespoons honey
½ cup raisins
½ cup chopped walnuts or almonds
Confectioners' sugar for dusting

1. Preheat the oven to 350°F. Butter and flour two large baking sheets.

2. In a large bowl, stir together the flour, cocoa powder, baking soda, cinnamon, nutmeg, and salt.

3. In another bowl, beat the shortening and sugar until well blended. Beat in the egg, orange zest, juice, and honey. Stir in the flour mixture until well blended. Stir in the raisins and walnuts. The dough will be stiff.

4. Pinch off a piece of dough the size of a walnut. Shape it into a sausage shape about 2½ inches long. Place on a prepared baking sheet and flatten slightly. Repeat with the remaining dough, placing the cookies about 2 inches apart.

5. Bake the cookies for 12 minutes, or until puffed and just set. Let cool for 1 minute. Slide onto wire racks to cool completely. These taste best if allowed to mellow overnight. Store the cookies in airtight containers.

6. Just before serving, dust the cookies with confectioners' sugar.

TIP: If dried fruits like figs or raisins are too hard, you can revive them by soaking them briefly in warm water. Drain and pat dry before using.

Sweet Beans for the Day of the Dead

FAVE DEI MORTI

To commemorate Ognisanti, All Saints' Day, which Italians call simply I Morti, the dead, many Italians eat these fava bean–shaped cookies. Fava beans held an important role in ancient Roman beliefs. On the Feast of Feralia, the head of a Roman household would toss fava beans over his shoulder in the middle of the night so that they could be gathered up by any wandering spirits, who would then take their leave. Fava beans also were placed on the eyes of the dead before burial.

Not all associations with fava beans are quite so morbid. In the Veneto, November is the time of year when couples announce their engagement. One tradition has the groom giving his beloved an engagement ring tucked inside a small box with these sweet bean cookies.

Among the many variations of these tasty cookies are a Piemontese version made with both almonds and hazelnuts, one from the Veneto area made with cornmeal, and another from Sicily flavored with cloves.

Molding the dough into bean shapes requires patience. My husband said mine look more like lips than fava beans, but that did not stop him from eating them.

MAKES ABOUT 6 DOZEN

2½ cups blanched almonds
½ cup pine nuts
1 cup sugar
½ cup all-purpose flour
1 teaspoon grated lemon zest

¼ teaspoon ground cinnamon
1 large egg
1 large egg yolk
1 tablespoon grappa, rum, or brandy
Confectioners' sugar for dusting

1. Preheat the oven to 325°F. Butter and flour two large baking sheets.

2. In a food processor or blender, combine the almonds, pine nuts, and ½ cup of the sugar. Process or blend until the nuts are very finely chopped. Transfer to a large bowl. Stir in the remaining ½ cup sugar, the flour, lemon zest, and cinnamon.

3. Beat the egg and yolk in a small bowl. Add the eggs and grappa to the nut mixture and stir until the dough is evenly moist and forms a ball.

4. Pinch off a piece of dough the size of a grape. Roll it into a ball, then flatten it to form a kidney-bean shape. Place on a prepared baking sheet. Repeat with the remain-

ing dough, placing the cookies 1 inch apart. With the back edge of a dull knife, make a shallow lengthwise groove in each cookie.

5. Bake the cookies for 10 minutes, then reverse the positions of the baking sheets. Bake for 5 to 10 minutes more, or until lightly golden. Transfer to wire racks to cool.

6. Dust the cookies with confectioners' sugar before serving. Store in an airtight container.

TIP: Blanched almonds are simply shelled almonds that have been soaked in hot water to remove their brown skins. Some cooks say the skins are slightly bitter and should be taken off before the nuts are used in baking, while others say the skins enhance the almond flavor. I think it depends on the recipe. You can buy almonds with or without skins in most supermarkets.

Hazelnut Half-Moons

MEZZALUNE

Nutty and buttery, these half-moon-shaped cookies from Piemonte are perfect for Christmas. Walnuts or almonds can be substituted for the hazelnuts.

If you don't have a food processor, grind the nuts and sugar in a blender or nut grinder, then blend in the remaining ingredients by hand.

MAKES ABOUT 5 DOZEN

1 cup hazelnuts, toasted and skinned
⅓ cup sugar, plus more for rolling the cookies
2 cups all-purpose flour

½ pound (2 sticks) unsalted butter, cut into bits, at room temperature

1. Preheat the oven to 350°F. Butter and flour two large baking sheets.

2. In a food processor, combine the hazelnuts and sugar and process until the nuts are finely chopped. Add the flour and blend well. Add the butter and pulse to blend. Remove the dough and squeeze it together with your hands.

3. Pinch off a 1-inch piece of dough and form it into a ball. Shape it into a crescent. Roll in sugar. Place on the prepared baking sheet. Repeat with the remaining dough, placing the cookies about 1 inch apart.

4. Bake the cookies for 15 minutes, or until lightly browned. Let cool for 5 minutes on the baking sheets, then transfer to wire racks to cool completely. Store in an airtight container.

Little Old Ladies

VECCHIARELLE

When I was growing up in Brooklyn, a neighbor's mother used to make these red wine–flavored cookies covered with honey. At the holidays, she would bring us a heaping plateful, and my mother would give her struffoli *(page 252) in return.*

SERVES 12

4 cups unbleached all-purpose flour
2 teaspoons baking powder
1 teaspoon salt
1 large egg

¾ cup robust dry red wine
¼ cup cooking oil
Vegetable oil for frying
1 cup honey

1. In a large bowl, stir together the flour, baking powder, and salt.

2. In a small bowl, whisk the egg, wine, and oil until blended. Pour the mixture into the dry ingredients and stir until the flour is moistened and a dough forms.

3. Cut the dough into 8 pieces. Roll each piece into a ¾-inch-thick rope. Cut the ropes into ¾-inch lengths.

4. Holding a grater in one hand, use the thumb of your other hand to press and roll each piece of dough over the medium holes, roughening the surface on one side and forming an indentation on the other side.

5. Heat about 2 inches oil in a deep heavy pot until it reaches 370°F on a deep-frying thermometer or until a piece of dough sizzles in the oil (or use an electric deep fryer). Carefully lower just enough of the pieces of dough into the pot to form a single layer without crowding. Fry, stirring occasionally, until they are lightly golden, 2 to 3 minutes. Remove with a slotted spoon and drain well on paper towels. Repeat with the remaining dough. Transfer the cookies to a large bowl.

6. Heat the honey in a small saucepan over low heat until it thins and begins to simmer; do not boil. Immediately pour the honey over the cookies and toss well. Pile the cookies on a serving platter and scrape the remaining honey over the top. These keep well loosely covered at room temperature for up to 1 week.

Struffoli

I can't remember a Christmas without struffoli. Other families baked butter and spice cookies, but in our house, it was struffoli, little balls of egg dough fried and dipped in honey. My mom taught me how to make them when I was very young. To my mind, she made the best; other cooks' struffoli were hard and dense, but Mom's were always light and airy.

Mom's preparations began long before the holiday. We would go to a beekeeper on Staten Island, which was then still quite rural, and buy his unique honey. There were two kinds, one dark with a robust flavor and one pale and delicate tasting. He would mix the two to Mom's taste, and the resulting blend was especially delicious.

At home, I helped my mother mix the dough. After it was kneaded, she showed me how to make long ropes of dough, then cut them into mucchietti, little bits. I would pass them to Mom, who handled the frying, making sure to keep us kids far from the pot of hot oil. Finally, she would coat the crisp little puffs with the warmed honey. We could hardly wait until the struffoli cooled to try them, and soon we would all have sticky fingers as we snatched a few to taste.

Piled up into a cone shape on a platter, the struffoli became the centerpiece for our Christmas table. Some people like to arrange the struffoli in a wreath, which is also very pretty. Struffoli can be garnished with candied orange zest, cherries, or citron, though my mother always showered them with multicolored candy sprinkles.

Mom made her struffoli dough on a cutting board, making a well of flour and breaking the eggs into the center, as if she were making pasta, but it can be made in a food processor or mixer. Mom did not flavor the dough for her struffoli, but many cooks today add vanilla or lemon or orange zest, as I do.

In Naples, struffoli are often served in bowls made of croccante (page 266), caramelized nut or sesame candy.

SERVES 8

About 1 cup unbleached all-purpose flour
¼ teaspoon salt
2 large eggs
½ teaspoon grated lemon or orange zest
Vegetable oil for frying

1 cup honey
Multicolored candy sprinkles, diced candied
    orange peel, candied cherries, or toasted sliced
    almonds

1. In a large bowl, combine 1 cup flour and the salt. Add the eggs and zest and stir until well blended.

2. Turn the dough out onto a lightly floured board and knead until smooth, about 5 minutes. Add a little more flour if the dough seems sticky. Shape the dough into a ball, cover with an overturned bowl, and let rest for 30 minutes.

3. Cut the dough into ½-inch slices. Roll each slice between your palms into a ½-inch-thick rope and cut the rope into ½-inch nuggets. If the dough feels sticky, use a tiny bit of flour to dust the board or your hands. (Excess flour will cause the oil to foam up when you fry the *struffoli*.)

4. Pour about 1 inch oil into a wide heavy saucepan or a deep fryer. Heat the oil to 370°F on a deep-frying thermometer, or until a small bit of the dough dropped into the oil sizzles, swims rapidly around the pan, and turns brown in 1 minute. Being careful not to splash the oil, slip just enough *struffoli* into the pan to fit without crowding. Cook, stirring once or twice with a slotted spoon, until crisp and evenly golden brown, 1 to 2 minutes. Remove the *struffoli* with the slotted spoon and drain on paper towels. Continue with the remaining dough.

5. When all of the *struffoli* are fried, gently heat the honey just to a simmer in a large shallow saucepan. Remove from the heat; add the *struffoli*, and toss well.

6. Pile the *struffoli* on a dinner plate. Decorate with multicolored sprinkles.

7. To serve, break off a portion of *struffoli* with two large spoons or a salad server. *Struffoli* are typically picked off and eaten with the fingers.

TIP: For deep-frying sweets, use a mild-tasting vegetable or olive oil that will not interfere with their flavor.

Spiced Fig Cookies

CUCCIDATI

My Aunt Millie Castagliolia and her husband, Louis, made a big batch of these every Christmas. Grinding the figs, raisins, and nuts was quite a project because it was all done by hand with an old-fashioned meat grinder. Today, a food processor handles the job easily.

Use either dark or light figs. I prefer the kind from California, which are always moist and tender.

You can make the filling and dough a day ahead of shaping and baking. The most common shape for these is a sort of crown, but stars, flowers, or crescents are popular as well. The cookies keep well for a long time in a sealed tin and long after the holidays are over, you will be glad you have some.

MAKES 18

DOUGH

2½ cups unbleached all-purpose flour

⅓ cup sugar

2 teaspoons baking powder

½ teaspoon salt

6 tablespoons (¾ stick) unsalted butter

2 large eggs, at room temperature

1 teaspoon vanilla extract

FILLING

2 cups moist dried figs, stems removed

½ cup raisins

1 cup walnuts, toasted and chopped

½ cup chopped semisweet chocolate
(about 2 ounces)

⅓ cup honey

1 teaspoon grated orange zest

¼ cup fresh orange juice

1 teaspoon ground cinnamon

⅛ teaspoon ground cloves

1 egg yolk beaten with 1 teaspoon water,
for egg wash

Multicolored candy sprinkles, optional

1. To make the dough, combine the flour, sugar, baking powder, and salt in a large bowl. Cut in the butter pastry using a blender or two knives, until the mixture resembles coarse crumbs (or blend in using an electric mixer).

2. In a small bowl, whisk the eggs and vanilla. Add to the dry ingredients, stirring until the dough is evenly moistened. If the dough is too dry, blend in a little cold

water, a few drops at a time. Gather the dough into a ball and place it on a sheet of plastic wrap. Flatten it into a disk and wrap well. Refrigerate for at least 1 hour, or overnight.

3. To make the filling, process the figs, raisins, and nuts in a food processor until coarsely chopped; or grind them in a meat grinder with a medium disk. Transfer to a bowl and stir in the remaining ingredients. Cover and refrigerate if not using within an hour. (The filling can be made up to 24 hours ahead.)

4. Preheat the oven to 375°F. Butter two baking sheets.

5. Cut the dough into 6 pieces. On a lightly floured surface, roll each piece into a log about 4 inches long.

6. With a floured rolling pin, roll one log into a 9 × 5-inch rectangle. Trim the edges. Spoon a ¾-inch strip of the filling lengthwise down the dough slightly to one side of the center. Fold the dough over and press the edges together to seal. Cut the strip into 3 pieces. With a sharp knife, cut ¾-inch-long slits at ½-inch intervals in each piece. Curving them slightly to open the slits and reveal the filling, place the pastries 1 inch apart on a prepared baking sheet.

7. Brush the pastries with the egg wash. Drizzle with candy sprinkles, if desired. Repeat with the remaining dough and filling.

8. Bake the cookies for 20 to 25 minutes, or until golden brown. Cool on wire racks. Stored at room temperature in airtight containers, these keep indefinitely.

TIP: If you are planning to freeze cookies or cakes, do not decorate them with colored candy sprinkles. The color tends to run when they come in contact with moisture from the thawing food.

Christmas Chestnut Tortelli

TORTELLI DI NATALE ALLE CASTAGNE

Sweet roasted fresh chestnuts are a holiday favorite in Italy and many other European countries. The aroma of chestnuts roasting over a charcoal fire at street-corner stands is irresistible on a chilly day. Chestnuts are also good in desserts, or glazed and eaten like candy. I also like the ones in jars packed in a honey syrup; serve just with whipped cream or vanilla ice cream.

Chestnuts are no longer as popular here as they once were, since most of the American chestnut trees were destroyed in a blight that swept North America in the early 1900s. The fresh nuts we see here are imported, and it is too bad, since American chestnuts, though smaller than other varieties, have a sweeter and more intense flavor. The good news is that conservationists are successfully bringing back American chestnuts by crossbreeding them with blight-resistant varieties.

Peeling fresh chestnuts is a lot of tiresome work, so I rely on the kind that are cooked and vacuum-packed in plastic or glass jars. They are very good and very convenient, but read the label before you buy and make sure they do not have added sugar, as many canned chestnut products do.

These cookies are sometimes called ravioloni dolci or cassateddre and some cooks fry rather than bake them. Other variations drizzle them with honey or roll them in cinnamon sugar.

In parts of southern Italy, cooked chickpeas or ground almonds are substituted for the chestnuts (see variation). These cookies are called cuscini di Gesù Bambino, or Baby Jesus' pillows.

MAKES ABOUT 5 DOZEN

DOUGH

3½ cups all-purpose flour

2 teaspoons baking powder

1 teaspoon salt

8 tablespoons (1 stick) unsalted butter

2 large eggs, at room temperature

¼ cup olive oil

FILLING

1 cup (6 ounces) peeled cooked fresh, vacuum-packed, or canned chestnuts

½ cup sugar

2 teaspoons unsweetened cocoa powder

1 teaspoon instant espresso

2 tablespoons brandy or rum

2 ounces bittersweet or semisweet chocolate, chopped (½ cup)

¼ cup golden raisins

1 cup confectioners' sugar

1. To make the dough, combine the flour, baking powder, and salt in a large bowl. With a pastry blender or two knives held like scissors, cut in the butter until coarse crumbs form.

2. Whisk together the eggs, olive oil, and 2 tablespoons cold water. Add to the flour mixture and stir until evenly moistened. Squeeze the dough together with your hands. If it seems dry, stir in a little more cold water. Shape the dough into a disk and wrap it in plastic wrap. Let rest for 30 minutes at room temperature, or longer in the refrigerator. (The dough can be made up to 2 days ahead.)

3. To make the filling, combine the chestnuts, sugar, cocoa, espresso, and brandy in a food processor or blender and process until smooth. Transfer to a bowl and stir in the chocolate and raisins. (The filling can be made up to 2 days ahead; cover and refrigerate.)

4. Preheat the oven to 375°F. Butter and flour two large baking sheets.

5. Cut the dough into 4 pieces. Roll out one piece to a 10-inch circle about ⅛ inch thick. With a ravioli or biscuit cutter or a small glass, cut out 2½-inch circles.

6. Place a scant teaspoon of the filling to one side of each circle. Dip a fingertip in water and moisten the edge on one side. Fold the dough over to form a semicircle and pinch the edges firmly to seal. Repeat with the remaining dough and filling, placing the tortelli an inch apart on the prepared baking sheets.

7. Bake the tortelli for 15 minutes, or until crisp and very lightly colored. Remove from the oven.

8. Spread the confectioners' sugar on a piece of wax paper. Remove the tortelli from the baking sheets and roll in the sugar while still warm. Cool on wire racks. Stored in an airtight container, these keep well for at least 2 weeks.

VARIATION: In Calabria and other places in southern Italy, cooked chickpeas are used instead of chestnuts. Simply substitute an equal amount of cooked or canned drained chickpeas.

Rainbows

ARCOBALENI

I don't recall ever seeing these beautiful little layer cakes in Italy, but I always associate them with Italian pastry shops in America. They are called seven-layer cookies (though these only have six), Neapolitans, Venetians, or rainbows.

When I was a child, some relative or other would always bring us a box of fancy cookies at the holiday season. At weddings, these cookies were piled on trays. The colorful rainbow cookies stood out among the pignoli-crusted almond macaroons, Jordan almonds, and vanilla cookies topped with glazed cherries or big chocolate dots, all sprinkled with candy silver shot, confetti, and fine tinsel threads. My sister always opted for the pignoli cookies, but rainbows were my favorite, so my family would save them for me. I ate them one layer at a time so they would last longer.

If the only rainbow cookies you have ever tasted have been dry and garishly colored, please give this homemade version a try and see how good they can be. Despite their appearance, they are really not difficult to make. The cookies are moist and delicate, and even the colors are soft and appetizing. If you prefer not to use food coloring, just leave it out—they will still be pretty and taste just as good.

If you do not have three baking pans, or cannot fit three pans in the oven at one time, bake the layers in batches. Be sure to let the pan (or pans) cool in between and butter and re-line it each time.

These keep very well in the refrigerator or freezer, so you can make them ahead.

MAKES ABOUT 6 DOZEN

8 ounces almond paste
¾ pound (3 sticks) unsalted butter
1 cup sugar
4 large eggs, separated
¼ teaspoon salt
2 cups unbleached all-purpose flour

About 10 drops red food coloring, optional
About 10 drops green food coloring, optional
½ cup seedless raspberry jam
½ cup apricot preserves
One 6-ounce package chocolate chips (1 cup)

1. Preheat the oven to 350°F. Butter three identical 13 × 9 × 2-inch baking pans. Line the bottom of the pans with wax paper and butter the paper.

2. Crumble the almond paste into a large mixer bowl. Add the butter, ½ cup of sugar, the egg yolks, and salt and beat until fluffy. Beat in the flour.

3. In another large bowl, with clean beaters, beat the egg whites until foamy. Gradually beat in the remaining ½ cup sugar. Continue beating until the egg whites hold soft peaks when the beaters are lifted. Fold one-third of the whites into the yolk mixture to lighten it. Gradually fold in the remaining whites.

4. If using the food coloring, scoop one-third of the batter into one bowl and another third into another bowl. Fold the red into one portion of batter and the green into another. Spread the batter in the prepared pans, smoothing it out evenly with a spatula.

5. Bake the layers for 10 to 12 minutes, until just set and very lightly colored around the edges. Let cool in the pans for 5 minutes, then invert the layers onto cooling racks, leaving the wax paper attached. Let cool completely.

6. Using the paper to lift it, place the green layer paper side up on a large tray or cutting board. Peel off the paper. Spread with the raspberry jam. Set the white layer paper side up on top of the green layer. Remove the paper and spread with the apricot jam. Place the red layer paper side up on top. Peel off the paper. With a large heavy knife, trim the edges of the cake to make them straight and even all around.

7. Put the chocolate chips in a small heatproof bowl over, not in, simmering water and heat until the chips are softened. Stir until smooth. Pour the melted chocolate on top of the cake and spread it evenly with a spatula. Refrigerate until the chocolate is just beginning to set, about 30 minutes. (Don't let it get too hard, or it will crack when you cut it.)

8. Remove the cake from the refrigerator. Using a ruler or other straight edge as a guide, cut the cake crosswise into 9 strips, then cut lengthwise into 9 strips. Chill until the chocolate is firm, then separate.

9. Store in an airtight container in the refrigerator.

TIP: Commercially manufactured chocolate chips are useful for icing cookies because they are formulated to be harder at room temperature than bar chocolates.

Nonni's Wafer Cookies

PIZZELLE

Pizzelle are members of the family of thin wafer cookies that are known as brigidini in Venice, cialde in Montecatini, and ferratelle in other regions. In Italy, you often find these cookies for sale as souvenirs in resort towns or at street fairs.

Donna Capobianco Boland adapted this recipe for me from her grandmother's recipe. The original formula called for 5 pounds of flour, 2½ pounds of sugar, 5 wineglasses of oil, 1 bottle or more of anise extract, and 2 dozen eggs, as well as orange zest and a little juice. Donna told me that her grandmother, whom everyone called Nonni, made her pizzelle dough by hand on the huge wooden board she also used to make pasta. In addition to the 5 pounds of flour, she added more by the handful until the dough "felt right."

Donna experimented with the ingredients over and over until she got the recipe down to more manageable proportions and reliable quantities. Her pizzelle are light and crisp, with a delicate flavor. Though her husband and children approved, Donna wasn't sure she had gotten the recipe right until her Uncle Frank, Nonni's former chief assistant, sampled them and said they were just like her grandma's.

To make pizzelle, you need a special iron, either electric or the stove-top kind. An antique pizzelle iron, called a ferro, is a treasure passed down as an heirloom in many Italian families from one generation to the next.

Old pizzelle irons are very collectible and you can sometimes find them at antique sales. Often they were custom made as gifts for a bride. Browsing an Internet auction site one day, I spotted a charming one emblazoned with a man and woman toasting each other with goblets of wine. I now regret that I did not bid on it. It had a far more interesting pattern than my modern electric version. While mine is very easy to use, it leaves only a faint lacy imprint in the surface of the cooked pizzelle. If you are buying a pizzelle iron, try to find one with a deeply incised, interesting pattern.

Once you have bought your pizzelle maker, you will find all different uses for these cookies. Flat pizzelle are great as a garnish for ice cream or fruit desserts, or you can use them to make sophisticated ice cream sandwiches. The hot cookies stay soft and pliable for a few moments before they cool and crisp, so you can mold them into different shapes. Try wrapping them around tubes for cannoli, or tucking them into cups to make dishes to hold mousse or gelati. You can even use them to make ice cream cones.

Though they are usually flavored with vanilla or anise, I like to experiment and make pizzelle in other flavors. Try using different extracts, such as lemon, almond, or rum.

MAKES 3 TO 4 DOZEN
(ACCORDING TO THE DIMENSIONS OF THE PIZZELLE MAKER)

1 cup plus 3 tablespoons sugar
½ cup vegetable oil
3 large eggs, at room temperature
½ teaspoon salt

1 tablespoon grated orange zest
1½ teaspoons anise extract
3¼ cups unbleached all-purpose flour

1. In a large bowl, beat together the sugar and oil. Add the eggs, salt, orange zest, and extract and beat until well blended. Gradually stir in the flour until smooth. The dough will be soft and sticky.

2. Preheat a pizzelle maker following the manufacturer's directions.

3. Lightly flour your hands. Scoop up a spoonful of dough the size of a walnut and roll the dough between your palms to form a ball. Place the dough on the iron and cook until the pizzelle is golden brown, about 30 seconds on a stove-top iron, 1½ minutes on an electric iron. Transfer to a rack to cool. Repeat with the remaining dough. Store the pizzelle in a tightly sealed container.

How Santa Claus Came to America

Saint Nicholas is the patron saint of the city of Bari in the Puglia region. He is also revered throughout Europe as the protector of children. The story of how the saint, called San Nicola di Bari, came to be our modern-day Santa Claus is a long, fascinating tale.

Nicholas was born in the fourth century to wealthy parents in what is now Turkey. His parents died when he was quite young and he inherited their fortune. Nicholas was very kind and when he heard of a poor father who could not provide his three daughters with wedding dowries, dooming them to life in a brothel, he decided to help, without revealing his identity. One night, depending on the version of the story, he either climbed to the roof of the family's house and dropped a sack of gold down the chimney or tossed the money through the window. He repeated the action on two more occasions. The last time, the father, who had sat up waiting to see who his family's benefactor was, recognized Nicholas. Soon everyone in town knew of his good works. Eventually he was made the Bishop of Myra in Turkey, where he lived and died.

In 1087, sailors decided to take the Christian bishop's remains to safety away from Myra, which was then in the control of the Saracen infidels. His bones were removed and a great cathedral was built to house them in Bari. Many miracles were attributed to the bishop, and he eventually became a saint.

Nicholas is also considered the protector of sailors because, it is said, he once saved a ship from disaster when he was invoked during a fierce storm. His fame spread as far away as northern Europe. In the Netherlands, Saint Nicholas, there known as Sinterklaas, was depicted as a kindly old man with a long white beard, wearing his red bishop's robe. It became the custom to give children small gifts on his feast day, December 6.

Dutch settlers brought the story of Saint Nicholas with them to New Netherlands, what is now New York State. In 1809, on Saint Nicholas Day, Washington Irving published his *Knickerbocker Tales*, a humorous history of New York and the Dutch governor Peter Stuyvesant. Saint Nicholas is mentioned frequently, and Irving wrote, "nor was the day of St. Nicholas suffered to pass by, without making presents, hanging the stocking in the chimney, and complying with all its other ceremonies." Evidently the traditions we associate with Santa Claus and Christmas were already well established.

Clement Clark Moore, a classics professor and a member of a group of writers known as the Knickerbocker authors, which included Washington Irving, is believed to have written the poem "A Visit from Saint Nicholas" in 1822 as a gift for his children. Moore's poem inspired cartoonist Thomas Nast of *Harper's Weekly* to draw Saint Nicholas much as we know him today, as a jolly old fat man in a red suit.

Chocolate Figs

FICHI AL CIOCCOLATO

Figs are used frequently in southern Italian desserts, one reason being that they are so plentiful. Fig trees grow like weeds, sprouting out of walls and cracks in the sidewalks. By late summer, the trees are heavy with plump fruit, oozing thick, honey-like juices. Then they are eaten plain, with prosciutto or tangy cheese, or baked into tarts. There are always plenty available for drying to use in desserts all the rest of the year.

These chocolate-dipped figs are a delicious after-dinner confection, served with a glass of dessert wine, such as Sicilian Bukkaram.

SERVES 12

12 moist dried figs
About ¼ cup candied orange peel

½ cup semisweet chocolate, broken up

1. Holding each fig by the stem end, cut a slit in the base. Insert a piece of orange zest.

2. Place the chocolate in a small heatproof bowl set over, not in, simmering water. Heat until the chocolate is melted, stirring until smooth.

3. Dip the figs in the chocolate to coat the bottoms. Place them on a plate. Refrigerate until the chocolate is firm. Store in an airtight container in the refrigerator for up to 2 weeks.

Chocolate Spice Cookies

BISCOTTI DI CIOCCOLATO E SPEZIE

Linda Carucci's Grandma Guglietta learned to make these irresistible cookies from her comare, meaning close friend. Both ladies lived in Hartford, Connecticut, where they had settled with their families after arriving here from Naples. In fact, these cookies seem to be a soft version of the very hard spice cookies known as mostaccioli in southern Italy.

Linda says that the two would bake them by the dozen for cookie trays for weddings and other special occasions throughout the year. But Linda remembers them best at Christmastime, and to this day the combination of cloves and chocolate makes her think of Christmas with her grandmother.

Linda, who operates a cooking school called Linda Carucci's Kitchen and is a kitchen designer in Oakland, California, says the cookies improve a day or so after baking, as the rum and spice flavors mellow.

MAKES ABOUT 8 DOZEN

½ cup dark and/or golden raisins
3 tablespoons dark rum
2½ cups unbleached all-purpose flour
⅓ cup unsweetened cocoa powder
½ cup granulated sugar
½ cup packed light brown sugar
2 teaspoons baking powder
¾ teaspoon ground cinnamon

½ teaspoon ground cloves
¼ teaspoon baking soda (see Note)
¼ teaspoon salt
⅔ cup milk
2 large eggs, lightly beaten
¼ cup vegetable oil
1 tablespoon grated orange zest
½ cup chopped toasted walnuts

ICING

2 cups confectioners' sugar
3 tablespoons unsweetened cocoa powder

2 tablespoons dark rum
About 2 tablespoons milk

1. Preheat the oven to 350°F. Line three cookie sheets with parchment paper or foil.

2. In a small bowl, toss the raisins with the rum. Let stand for 15 minutes.

3. Sift together the flour, cocoa, both sugars, the baking powder, cinnamon, cloves, baking soda if using, and salt into a large bowl.

4. In a medium bowl, whisk the milk, eggs, oil, zest, raisins, and rum. Stir the mixture into the dry ingredients until well blended. Stir in the walnuts.

5. Drop the batter by teaspoonfuls about 1 inch apart onto the prepared baking sheets.

6. Bake for 10 minutes. Transfer the cookies to racks to cool.

7. To make the icing, sift the confectioners' sugar and cocoa into a bowl. With a rubber spatula, stir in the rum and 2 tablespoons milk. Add more milk if needed, until the icing is smooth and spreadable.

8. With a small spatula, ice the tops of the cookies. Let stand until firm. Store in an airtight container.

NOTE: Linda recommends eliminating the baking soda in the cookies if you are using Dutch-process cocoa powder for better flavor.

Almond Brittle

CROCCANTE (OR TORRONE)

A trip to an Italian street fair always meant chunks of this delicious caramel candy. We would buy long cellophane-wrapped bars of the candy and smack the bars against a hard surface to break them into bite-size pieces.

In Sicily, torrone or croccante is made with pistachios, hazelnuts, or even peanuts. It was introduced there by the Arabs, who originally made it with sesame seeds.

You can make a delicious simple dessert by smashing the torrone into bits and scattering it over ice cream. Finish with a drizzle of rum or liqueur.

SERVES 8 TO 10

Almond or vegetable oil
2 cups sugar
¼ cup honey

2 cups almonds (10 ounces)
1 lemon

1. Oil a marble surface or baking sheet.

2. In a medium saucepan, combine the sugar and honey and cook over medium-low heat, stirring occasionally, until the sugar begins to melt, about 20 minutes. Bring to a simmer and cook for 5 minutes more, or until the syrup is clear.

3. Add the nuts and cook for 3 minutes, or until the syrup is amber colored.

4. Carefully pour the hot syrup onto the prepared surface, using the lemon to smooth the nuts to a single layer. Let cool completely.

5. When the croccante is cool and hard, slide a thin metal spatula underneath it. Lift the croccante and break it into 1½-inch pieces. Stored in a tightly sealed container in a cool, dry place, croccante keeps indefinitely.

Italian Wine

Making homemade wine is a tradition many Italians in this country recall fondly, and a surprising number still make it today as a hobby. My mother remembers how she helped her father to press the grapes in an old-fashioned barrel press. The finished wine was buried in sand to keep the bottles cool. Occasionally the wine would re-ferment. The pressure created by carbon dioxide would cause the corks to pop out, spewing wine all over the cellar.

Today fine wine is made in every region of Italy and Italian wines are recognized for their high quality. Drinking wine is an important part of every day as well as feast day and special-occasion meals. Glasses of chilled dry sparkling wine called *spumante,* from producers such as Franciacorta and Bellavista, begin a meal on a festive note. In summer, Prosecco, a slightly sparkling white from the Veneto, is combined with fresh white peach puree to make the Bellini, an aperitif popularized at Harry's Bar in Venice.

Some of the finest Italian white wines come from the Friuli–Venezia Giulia region in the north, including varieties such as Pinot Bianco, Tocai Friulano, Pinot Grigio, and Sauvignon Blanc from producers Livio Felluga, Castello di Spessa, Puiatti, and Schioppetto, to name just a few.

Tuscany and Piedmont are renowned for their red wines. Tuscan reds include Chianti, Brunello di Montalcino, and Vino Nobile di Montepulciano from producers such as Antinori, Monsanto, Jacopo Biondi-Santi, and Banfi. Piedmontese reds include the three "B's"—barbera, barbaresco, and barolo from top producers such as Vietti, Ratti, and Michele Chiarlo.

Southern Italy has been capturing more and more recognition from wine lovers for the ever-improving quality of its wines in recent years. Producers such as Planeta and Regaleali in Sicily, Taurino in Puglia, and Villa Matilde in Campania are making wines the equal of those made anywhere else in the world.

A wide range of dessert wines is made all over Italy. Marsala and moscato di Panteleria are just two of the sweet wines from Sicily; Vin Santo, made from partially dried grapes and only mildly sweet, is from Tuscany; and low-alcohol sparklers like Moscato di Asti and Asti Spumante are from Piedmont.

It is not necessary to have a great deal of knowledge or spend a lot of money to enjoy good Italian wines. Find a friendly wine dealer in your area, ask a few questions, and most important, write notes about the wines sampled, or at least keep the labels, so that you will remember the next time you shop whether or not you liked the wine.

Little Sweets

ZUCCHERINI

According to Mira Sacerdoti, author of Cucina Ebraica in Italia, *these easy little cookies are made for Passover in Jewish homes all over Italy. In some cities, they are made with chicken or goose fat instead of olive oil and in others they are flavored with cinnamon instead of anise and lemon.*

Passover commemorates Israelite slavery in Egypt 3,000 years ago. God sent ten plagues to convince the cruel Pharaoh to release them. He instructed Moses to tell the Israelites to mark their homes with lamb's blood. In that way, the Israelites would be protected when the angel of death came to kill the firstborn of both men and animals. When the slaves were finally released, they left their homes so quickly they did not have time to bake their bread. Instead, they packed the raw dough and baked it on stones in the desert into flat bread called matzoh, or pane azzima in Italian.

The cookies are made with matzoh meal as a reminder of this event. They are simple and just right with a cup of tea or served with a fresh fruit salad. The recipe makes a lot, but each cookie is only a bite or two.

When shaping the cookies, handle them lightly and don't squeeze or pack the dough tightly. The cookies will be more tender.

MAKES ABOUT 10 DOZEN

3 large eggs, at room temperature
1 cup sugar
¼ cup olive oil
2 teaspoons grated lemon zest

3 cups fine matzoh meal
1 teaspoon anise seeds
½ teaspoon salt

1. Beat the eggs until foamy. Gradually add the sugar, beating until the mixture is thick and fluffy. Beat in the olive oil and lemon zest.

2. Stir in the matzoh meal, anise, and salt until well blended. Cover and let stand at room temperature for 1 hour.

3. Preheat the oven to 350°F. Line two baking sheets with foil.

4. Dampen your hands slightly. Pinch off a small piece of dough and roll it between your palms to form a ball about 1 inch in diameter. Handle the dough lightly or the cookies may become too dense and compact. Place the balls on the prepared baking sheets about 1 inch apart.

5. Bake the cookies 14 to 18 minutes or until lightly golden. Remove the baking sheets from the oven and cool 10 minutes. Transfer the cookies to wire racks and let cool completely.

Hot Roasted Chestnuts

CALDARROSTE

Saint Martin's Day, November 11, is celebrated all over Italy with hot roasted chestnuts and the newly made red wine. It marks not only the feast day of a beloved saint who was known for his kindness to the poor, but also the end of the growing season, the day the earth goes into repose for the winter season. In Sicily, the day is celebrated with music and dancing and, of course, a big feast, which ends with delicious doughnuts made with a mashed potato dough.

Roasted chestnuts are the finishing touch to every winter holiday meal. I put them in the oven when we sit down to dinner and by the time we are finished with our main course, they are ready to eat.

SERVES 8

1 pound fresh chestnuts

1. Preheat the oven to 425°F.

2. Wash the chestnuts and pat them dry. Place the chestnuts flat side down on a cutting board. Cut an X in each with the tip of a small sharp knife.

3. Place the chestnuts on a large sheet of heavy-duty aluminum foil. Fold up the edges to form a pouch. Place the pouch in a baking pan. Roast the chestnuts until tender when pierced with a small knife, 45 to 60 minutes.

4. Leave the chestnuts wrapped in the foil for 10 minutes, then serve hot.

Desserts

DOLCI

Fritters, pastries, and "spoon desserts," known as *dolci di cucchiaio,* make up the sweets in this chapter.

Zabaglione is the quickest and easiest of the spoon desserts and turns a bowl of berries or a slice of plain cake into a special treat. Frozen desserts like *biscuit tortoni* or *cremolata* are perfect for warm-weather parties.

Fried pastries are very common in Italy, probably because frying was the easiest way to make a dessert when homes were not equipped with ovens. Ribbons or balls of dough could be fashioned into *cartellate, zeppole,* or *struffoli.* Stuffed with a creamy ricotta filling, they became *cassatedde, sfinci,* or cannoli.

Surely the most unusual dessert I have come across anywhere is Chocolate Eggplant (page 278), a specialty from the town of Amalfi near Naples.

Frozen Almond Creams

BISCUIT TORTONI

I can't remember ever attending a wedding or anniversary party when I was a child where this dessert was not served. Usually it was presented in little pleated white paper cups that made me think of nurses' caps.

Delicious and so simple to make, this old-fashioned dessert is worth reviving. For a children's party, you could use paper muffin pan liners to mold the cream, but it looks much more sophisticated served in wine goblets, parfait glasses, or coffee cups.

SERVES 8

2 cups heavy cream
½ cup confectioners' sugar
1 teaspoon vanilla extract
½ teaspoon almond extract

2 large egg whites
Pinch of salt
¼ cup finely crushed amaretti cookies

1. In a large chilled bowl, with chilled beaters, whip the cream with the sugar and the extracts until soft peaks form.

2. In a medium bowl, with clean beaters, beat the egg whites with the salt on low speed until foamy. Gradually increase the speed and beat until soft peaks form. With a rubber spatula, gently fold the whites into the whipped cream.

3. Spoon the mixture into eight wine goblets or ramekins. Sprinkle with the amaretti. Cover with plastic wrap and freeze for at least 4 hours, or overnight.

4. Remove the tortoni from the refrigerator 15 to 30 minutes before serving.

Dancing the Giglio

At the Feast of Our Lady of Mount Carmel and Saint Paulinus every July in the Williamsburg section of Brooklyn, the descendants of the immigrants who settled there from Nola, near Naples, a hundred years ago continue the tradition of "dancing the giglio" through the local streets.

The giglio is an 85-foot-tall 4-ton tower made of pâpier-maché and wood that stands on a platform surrounded by a brass band. At a signal from the *capo*, or leader, two hundred strong men lift the tower on its platform in a series of three-minute intervals, called lifts. As the band plays songs including "O Giglio e Paradiso" ("The Lily of Paradise"), the festival's theme song, the men carry the tower as well as a smaller "boat" through the streets surrounding the parish church. They stop and turn, walk forward and then back, or execute other "dance steps" to the delight of the enthusiastic watchers lining the streets.

In 409, Paulinus was the Bishop of Nola. After invaders conquered the town, they took many of the young men to work as slaves, and Paulinus selflessly offered himself in exchange for the son of a poor widow. He was carried off, but was later freed through the efforts of a sultan who had heard of his bravery. When Bishop Paulinus returned to Nola in a boat, he brought with him the other men who had been enslaved. The townspeople greeted him with armfuls of lilies and for hundreds of years this event has been celebrated both in Nola, Italy, and more recently in Brooklyn, New York. Similar festivals were once held in Harlem and the Bronx, but as the Italian-American population diminished these celebrations came to an end.

Zabaglione

Many Italians consider zabaglione a healthful restorative, suitable for nursing mothers, cold sufferers, and anyone who is ailing. Others have called it an aphrodisiac, but you can decide that for yourself.

Zabaglione (pronounced tsah-bahl-YOH-neh) is both a dessert and a sauce. Serve it in a parfait or wineglass on its own, or spoon it warm over plain cake, fresh fruit, or ice cream. It is the ultimate quick dessert, what to make when you have nothing in the house to eat. The only problem is that it must to be made at the last minute if you want to serve it warm. Otherwise, try the chilled variation that follows.

Get out your hand-held electric mixer to make this, or enlist an assistant to take over the beating when your arm gets too tired.

SERVES 4 TO 6

4 large egg yolks
¼ cup sugar

¼ cup dry Marsala, Vin Santo, or other
    fortified wine

1. Bring about 2 inches water to a simmer in the bottom of a double boiler or in a medium saucepan.

2. In the top of the double boiler or in a heatproof bowl that will fit comfortably over the saucepan without touching the water, beat the yolks, sugar, and Marsala with a hand-held electric mixer or a whisk until well blended. Set over the simmering water and beat or whisk the mixture until it is pale, light, and fluffy and holds a soft shape when dropped from the beaters or whisk, 3 to 5 minutes. Serve immediately.

COLD ZABAGLIONE: Make the zabaglione as described above. Immediately place the bowl of zabaglione into a large bowl filled with ice water and whisk until cold. In a medium bowl, beat 1 cup heavy cream with 2 tablespoons confectioners' sugar and 2 tablespoons rum or almond or orange liqueur. Fold the cold custard into the whipped cream. Cover and refrigerate for up to 24 hours.

Toasted Almond Ice

CREMOLATA

Dancing the giglio (see page 273) is hard, sweaty work in the summer's heat. Though nothing is more refreshing than lemon ice, my real favorite has always been cremolata. *Made with almond-flavored milk, vanilla, and chips of toasted almonds, it is slightly richer than a water ice or granita, but much lighter than ice cream. You can buy* cremolata *and other Italian ices at Italian pastry shops around New York, but it is also very easy to make at home. I have given instructions for making it in the freezer compartment of the refrigerator, but you can use an ice cream freezer if you have one.*

MAKES 1 QUART

1 quart whole milk
1 cup sugar
1 teaspoon vanilla extract

¼ teaspoon almond extract
½ cup toasted almonds, coarsely chopped

1. Place 1 cup of the milk in a medium saucepan, add the sugar, and cook, stirring, until the sugar is dissolved. Transfer to a large bowl. Stir in the remaining milk and the extracts. Let cool.

2. Pour the milk mixture into ice cube trays or a shallow metal pan. Cover and freeze.

3. Just before serving, remove the *cremolata* from the freezer and let stand for 10 minutes, or just long enough to soften slightly.

4. Remove the cubes from the trays or cut up the frozen block with a knife and place the pieces in a large electric mixer bowl or food processor container. Beat or process until the mixture is creamy, smooth, and light. Fold in the chopped almonds. Serve immediately.

Wheat Berry Pudding for Saint Lucy

CUCCIA DOLCE DI SANTA LUCIA

Cuccia, *a sweet made with whole wheat berries, is traditional for the Feast of Santa Lucia on December 13.*

Lucia, whose name means light, lived in Sicily, though both Palermo and Siracusa claim her. She was a beautiful young girl who attracted the attention of a powerful man who wanted to marry her, but she steadfastly refused his attentions, eventually plucking out her own eyes and sending them to him to discourage him. Enraged, he denounced her as a Christian, and she was cruelly martyred. She is often depicted carrying her eyes on a plate and is revered as the protector of people who suffer from eye maladies.

Sicilians have a special reason to honor her memory. According to legend, a terrible famine struck Sicily and the starving people prayed to Lucia for help. Miraculously, a fleet of ships appeared in the harbor, their holds filled with precious grain. The people were so hungry that they cooked the unprocessed wheat without first milling it and ate it on the spot. Even today it is considered bad luck to eat foods made with processed wheat in the form of flour on Saint Lucy's Day. Flour substitutes are eaten instead. Arancini, *rice balls (page 12),* and panelle *made with chickpea flour (page 10) are tradi-tional, as well as this unusual pudding.*

Lucia is venerated well beyond Sicily. The poet Dante is said to have been cured through prayers to Santa Lucia of eye problems brought about by the tears he shed for his beloved Beatrice. Scandinavians, who probably learned about Lucia centuries ago from foreign sailors, celebrate her day with processions, gifts, and little cakes known as Lucia buns. She is depicted as a lovely young girl wearing a white gown and a crown of candles, representing light.

In northern Italy, it is Santa Lucia, instead of Babbo Natale *(Father Christmas) or the* Befana, *who brings Christmas gifts. In the Veneto, Lucia arrives on a donkey on the eve of her day. Children leave carrots or hay to attract the hungry donkey so that Santa Lucia will stop and bring them gifts.*

In Bergamo, where the streets of the town are lined with colorful stalls selling candy and toys, children drop letters expressing their wishes to Santa Lucia into a special mail-box. In Lombardy, children open presents on the morning of Saint Lucy's Day, while those who live in Verona receive special cookies shaped like a piglet or a pony or a flower.

About 6 ounces (¾ cup) hulled wheat berries, rinsed and drained

1 teaspoon salt

1 cup ricotta

¼ cup sugar

¼ teaspoon ground cinnamon

1 teaspoon grated orange zest

¼ cup chopped semisweet chocolate

1 tablespoon chopped candied citron

Orange slices or strawberries for garnish

1. Soak the wheat berries overnight, then place them in a saucepan with cold water to cover, add the salt, and bring to a simmer. Cover the pan and cook until the wheat is tender but still a little chewy, about 45 minutes. Drain off any water that remains.

2. In a large bowl, whisk together the ricotta, sugar, cinnamon, and orange zest. Stir in the chocolate and citron. Finally, stir in the drained wheat berries. Cover and chill.

3. To serve, scoop the *cuccia* into small dessert dishes and garnish with fruit.

Chocolate Eggplant

MELANZANE AL CIOCCOLATO

Maurizio Di Rosa told me about this unique recipe. Eggplant with chocolate is eaten on August 15, the Feast of the Assumption, around the town of Amalfi along the beautiful coast south of Naples. The day celebrates the Virgin Mary's rise to heaven and coincides with Ferragosto, considered the height of summer by Europeans.

At this time of year, everybody in Italy goes to the beach or the mountains to cool off, and the city streets are completely deserted. Frustrated tourists wander around the cities and towns aimlessly, since many businesses and sights are closed. Along the Amalfi Coast, this dessert is a specialty, made only at this time of year. Maurizio says you won't find it in restaurants or pastry shops—it is strictly homemade. When I have served it, no one has even come close to guessing what it was, but everyone loves it.

The dish was supposedly invented during the Middle Ages by monks from the monastery in Tramonti near the Amalfi Coast. They made a black liqueur known as concerto d'Erbe and used the brew to coat slices of fried eggplant, also a local specialty. Eventually, chocolate came to be substituted for the liqueur.

Maurizio, who comes from nearby Naples, said that the best recipe for this unusual dish is the one in Arthur Schwartz's book Naples at Table. This recipe is adapted from Arthur's. It is really two recipes in one, since the fried eggplant with its light egg coating is delicious on its own or can be used to make Eggplant Parmigiana (page 202).

SERVES 8 TO 10

EGGPLANT

1 medium eggplant (1 pound)

3 large eggs

¼ teaspoon salt

Flour for dusting

Extra virgin olive oil for frying

12 ounces semisweet or bittersweet chocolate, melted

¼ cup coarsely chopped almonds or whole pine nuts

5 to 6 tablespoons finely minced candied citron or mixed citron and candied orange peel

¼ cup crushed Jordan almonds

1. Peel the eggplant and cut it into ¼-inch-thick slices. (Do not salt.)

2. In a shallow bowl or pie plate, beat the eggs, 2 tablespoons water, and the salt. Place the flour on a sheet of wax paper.

3. In a large skillet, heat about ⅓ inch oil over medium heat until a piece of eggplant sizzles immediately when added. Dip an eggplant slice in the flour and shake off the excess. Using a fork, dip the eggplant in the egg, coating the slice entirely, and add to the pan. Coat a few more eggplant slices and fry until the edges are golden brown. Turn the eggplant and cook until the coating is golden on both sides and the eggplant is tender. Drain the slices on paper towels. Repeat with the remaining eggplant.

4. Cover the bottom of a platter large enough to hold the eggplant in two layers with half the eggplant slices, overlapping them slightly. Pour on half of the melted chocolate and spread it evenly with a spatula. Sprinkle with the pine nuts and half the candied fruits.

5. Arrange a second layer of eggplant over the first and pour on the remaining chocolate. Garnish with the remaining candied fruit and the crushed Jordan almonds. Serve at room temperature. Store in the refrigerator up to 1 day.

Saint Joseph's Fritters

SFINCI DI SAN GIUSEPPE

For Anna Tasca Lanza, whose family owns the Regaleali winery in Sicily, March 19 is not only Saint Joseph's Day but also her father's name day. In Italy, Catholics are given names of saints, and so your name day is the saint's feast day, and it is celebrated like a birthday. Friends and family members come from all over to join in the celebration.

When we visited, a big bonfire was lit in the fields on the eve of Saint Joseph's Day, symbolizing the preparations for the new crops that sprout in the spring. The next day, big tables were set up in the courtyard and we feasted on special dishes like grilled artichokes, sausages, and lamb; little fried timbales of pasta; arancini; and panelle. For dessert, we ate freshly made fritters like these. Usually filled with ricotta cream or pastry cream, they also can be served plain, dusted with confectioners' sugar.

SERVES 8

RICOTTA CREAM

One 16-ounce container whole-milk or
   part-skim ricotta
½ cup confectioners' sugar
½ teaspoon vanilla extract

2 tablespoons chopped semisweet chocolate
1 tablespoon chopped candied orange peel or
   citron

DOUGH

4 tablespoons (½ stick) unsalted butter
1 teaspoon salt
1 cup all-purpose flour
4 large eggs

Olive or vegetable oil for frying
Candied orange peel for garnish
Confectioners' sugar for dusting

1. To make the filling, stir the ricotta, sugar, and vanilla until smooth. Stir in the chocolate and citron. (Can be made up to 24 hours ahead. Cover and refrigerate.)

2. To make the dough, heat the butter, 1 cup water, and salt until the butter melts and the mixture comes to a boil. Remove from the heat. Add the flour all at once and stir well with a wooden spoon until the flour is completely incorporated.

3. Return the saucepan to medium heat and cook, stirring constantly and turning the dough over itself often, until it begins to leave a thin film on the bottom of the saucepan, about 3 minutes. Transfer the dough to a large bowl.

4. Add the eggs one at a time, beating thoroughly after each addition with a wire whisk. At first the dough will resist absorbing the eggs, but continue to beat and it will become smooth.

5. In a deep heavy saucepan or a deep-fryer, heat about 3 inches of oil to 370°F on a deep-frying thermometer, dropping a tiny bit of dough into the oil. If it sizzles and moves around rapidly, the oil is ready. Scoop up about 1 rounded tablespoon of the batter. With another spoon, push the batter off into the oil, being careful not to splash it. Add a few more spoonfuls of batter, but do not crowd the pan. The batter will puff up and double or triple in size. Cook, turning the puffs often, until golden brown: when they are almost done, they will break open—cook for 1 or 2 minutes longer. Remove the puffs with a slotted spoon or skimmer and place them on paper towels to drain. Repeat with the remaining batter.

6. When all of the puffs have been fried, split them part way open with a small knife. Place a scoop of the ricotta cream in each. Garnish the cream with strips of candied orange peel.

7. Serve warm, or chill until serving time. (These are best eaten soon after they are made.) Just before serving, sprinkle the fritters with confectioners' sugar.

San Gennaro

San Gennaro was the bishop of Benevento, a small city northeast of Naples, in the early part of the fourth century. Gennaro was actually his last name, a Neapolitan translation of *Ianuario*, making him a descendant of the Gens Januaria family of ancient Rome. During the reign of the emperor Diocletian, he was persecuted for his religious beliefs and condemned to death. Though he survived burning and being thrown into a den of wild animals, eventually Gennaro was beheaded. His followers collected two vials of his blood and gave them to the archbishop of Naples, and his remains were placed in the catacombs of Capodimonte.

When Mount Vesuvius erupted in the fourteenth century threatening to destroy Naples, the residents fled to the crypt where Gennaro's remains rested and prayed to the saint to protect them. The eruption stopped, and San Gennaro was named the patron saint of Naples.

A famous, and controversial, mystery surrounds the vials of the saint's blood. Three times a year—on San Gennaro's Day, September 19; the first Sunday in May, which was the day his relics first came to Naples; and December 16, the anniversary of Naples' deliverance from destruction by Vesuvius—the archbishop of the city displays the vials to the faithful gathered in the cathedral. The people pray, and the dried blood liquefies, signifying that San Gennaro is watching over the city. The process can take seconds or days, but it is rare that it does not occur.

The Feast of San Gennaro has been celebrated every year since 1926 in New York's Little Italy. More than 3 million people attend the street festival, which lasts about ten days.

Doughnuts

At the Feast of San Gennaro, in September, and the Feast of Saint Anthony, in June, in New York's Little Italy, colorful booths line the streets selling all kinds of food, from sausages and peppers or meatball heroes to corn on the cob, cotton candy, pastry, zeppole, and even roasted turkey legs. The turkey is not traditional, but the zeppole are. They are made with a simple yeast dough that is dropped into a cauldron of hot oil, and as soon as they are brown and puffy, they are scooped out and dusted with confectioners' sugar. The trick is to get them when they are freshly made. Everyone walks around holding a greasy bagful, with confectioners' sugar dusting their shirtfronts.

When Donatella Arpaia told me that she served zeppole at her elegant New York restaurant Bellini, I knew that they would be far better than anything I might find at the feast. Donatella serves them with a rich, warm chocolate sauce.

Many people prefer to serve these fritters for Saint Joseph's Day, rather than the very rich sfinci (see page 280).

SERVES 6

1 teaspoon active dry yeast

1 tablespoon sugar

1½ cups unbleached all-purpose flour

1 teaspoon salt

Confectioners' sugar for dusting

1. In a large bowl, sprinkle the yeast over 1 cup warm (110° to 115°F) water. Add the sugar and stir with a wooden spoon until the yeast dissolves. Add the flour and salt and mix until the flour is completely moistened. Cover the bowl with plastic wrap and let rise in a warm place for 1 to 2 hours.

2. Pour about 2 inches oil into a deep heavy saucepan or deep-fryer and heat over medium heat until the temperature reaches 370°F on a deep-frying thermometer, or a drop of the dough sizzles and turns brown in 1 minute when slipped into the oil. Drop the dough by tablespoons into the hot oil; do not crowd the pan. Cook until golden brown and puffed, about 2 minutes. Remove the zeppole with a slotted spoon and drain them on paper towels. Repeat with the remaining dough.

3. Sprinkle generously with confectioners' sugar, or put the zeppole in a paper bag with the sugar and shake them until well coated. Serve immediately.

Zucchini Flower Fritters

FRITTELLE DI FIORE DI ZUCCA

My husband's birthday falls on August 24, and every year I make him a special dinner. He always asks for his favorite starter, zucchini flowers stuffed with mozzarella and anchovies and fried in a crisp batter. When you cut into them with a fork, the thin shell of the crunchy crust shatters to reveal creamy melted cheese accented with the tangy little fish.

Charles discovered these rich delicacies many years ago on a trip to Rome, at Ristorante il Matriciano, and now he can't get enough of them. (The recipe is in my book The Antipasto Table, Ecco Press.) *He would eat them every day if I made them. He loves the delicate flavor of the flowers in pasta, in risotto, and other dishes too. We can usually buy the flowers during the summer months at our local Greenmarket, but if you know people who grow their own zucchini (or other squash), so much the better.*

It is not often that you meet someone who cites zucchini flowers as one of his favorite foods. So you can imagine my surprise when I read that the Feast of San Bartolomeo is celebrated on August 24 in the Veneto with—you guessed it—zucchini flowers! In this case, they are made into sweet fritters, which are eaten as dessert.

SERVES 8

16 zucchini or other squash blossoms
1 cup unbleached all-purpose flour
1 tablespoon sugar
1 teaspoon baking powder
½ teaspoon salt
2 large eggs

1 tablespoon Marsala
1 teaspoon grappa
½ teaspoon grated lemon zest
Oil for frying
Confectioners' sugar for dusting

1. Wipe the flowers gently with a damp paper towel.

2. In a large bowl, mix together the flour, sugar, baking powder, and salt. In a medium bowl, beat the eggs until foamy. Stir in ½ cup cold water, the Marsala, grappa, and lemon zest. Stir the liquid ingredients into the dry ingredients.

3. In a deep heavy saucepan or deep-fryer, heat about 2 inches oil until the temperature reaches 370°F on a deep-frying thermometer, or a drop of batter added to the oil sizzles and cooks quickly without burning.

4. Dip a flower into the batter, turning it to coat well. Drain off the excess, then slip the flower into the hot oil. Coat and add more flowers, leaving enough room in the pan so that the flowers do not touch or stick together. Turn the flowers and cook for 2 minutes, or until nicely browned. Remove with a slotted spoon and drain on paper towels. Fry the remaining flowers in the same way.

5. Serve immediately, sprinkled with confectioners' sugar.

Honey Pinwheels

CARTELLATE

Luigi Sada, in his book La Cucina Pugliese, *calls these crisp pastry spirals "the flower in the button-hole of Pugliese sweets . . . the symbol of happiness, of rejoicing, of feasting." He goes on to say that no one can say for sure where the sweets originated, but they were mentioned in a document dating from 1762. Cartellate are sometimes called the "dahlias of Saint Nicholas" because of their color and shape, and their association with the nuns of the hospice for pilgrims of Saint Nicholas of Bari.*

At one time honey was expensive and not always available, so cooks would use a syrup made from figs to drizzle over the cartellate. *The syrup was made in late August, when the trees were heavy with big plump figs bursting open from the sweet juices within. The figs were cooked in large pots until the juices were reduced and thickened, then strained in a clean sack. The syrup would last a long time and was used as a sweetener all year round.*

Alternatively, the pastries were drizzled with mosto cotto *(grape must or juice), cooked down to a thick, sweet syrup as dark as molasses. Making and bottling* mosto cotto *was an important ritual with superstitious touches in many families. Only women who were members of the family and not having their menstrual period were allowed to participate in its preparation. Otherwise, it was feared, the cooked must would break down, forming two layers in the bottle, one of the syrup and the other of water. Sada points out that the fig syrup is more economical than syrup made from grape must—if you are lucky enough to have access to a healthy fig tree, I would add.*

A handful of specialty stores and on-line shopping sources now sell mosto cotto, *also called* vino cotto, *and fig syrup, but I like honey.*

MAKES 32

2 cups all-purpose flour
2 tablespoons extra virgin olive oil
½ teaspoon salt

Vegetable oil for frying
2 cups honey

1. In a large mixer bowl, combine the flour, oil, salt, and ½ cup water and beat until a dough forms. Turn the dough out onto a lightly floured surface and knead until smooth. Shape the dough into a ball. Wrap it in plastic and let rest at room temperature for 1 hour.

2. Divide the dough into 4 pieces. Flatten one piece of dough slightly. Dust it with flour and pass it through a pasta machine set at the widest opening. Continue to stretch the dough, passing it through each successive setting of the pasta machine, flouring it each time.

3. With a fluted pastry cutter, cut the rolled-out dough into strips 10 inches long and 1¼ inches wide. Lightly fold each strip lengthwise in half. Do not press it together. With the wavy edges up, wind the strips into loose spirals about 2 inches wide. Pinch the ends to seal. Place on an oiled baking sheet. Repeat with remaining dough.

4. Let the pinwheels dry at room temperature for 2 hours.

5. Pour about 2 inches oil into a deep heavy saucepan or deep-fryer and heat the oil until it reaches 370°F on a deep-frying thermometer, or a small piece of dough sizzles and cooks rapidly when added to the pan. Carefully slip a few pinwheels at a time into the pan and fry until golden, about 1 minute. Remove with a slotted spoon and drain on paper towels. Repeat with the remaining pinwheels.

6. Heat the honey in a small saucepan until it thins. Arrange the *cartellate* in a single layer on individual plates. Drizzle with the warm honey.

WINE MATCH: Primitivo di Manduria Amabile, Savese

Ricotta Pockets

CASSATEDDE DI SANTA NINFA

When I told Arthur Schwartz, host of a popular radio show called Food Talk in New York and an Italian cooking expert, that I was writing a book of family holiday recipes, he immediately replied, "Don't forget to include a recipe for cassatedde. My listeners always ask for it." Sure enough, the next time I was on his show talking about Italian food, someone called in and asked for a recipe for cassatedde.

I had never eaten them but I knew I had to find a recipe. It wasn't so easy, though. Everybody wanted one, but nobody had a recipe to give me. I looked in a number of reference books and found pastries called cassatedde, cassadeddre, and cassateddre, filled with everything from candied or dried fruit to nuts to chocolate to mashed sweetened chickpeas, but the recipe I was seeking was for a small pastry turnover filled with ricotta.

Food writer Marie Bianco, a friend who writes for New York Newsday, saved the day. Marie learned how to make the ricotta-filled turnovers I sought from Giuseppina Bianco (they are not related), who lives in the Sicilian town of Santa Ninfa. In Santa Ninfa, cassatedde are made with goat's milk ricotta rather than cow's milk and the pastries are fried in dark green oil pressed from luscious Sicilian olives.

Marie makes the pastry in the traditional way, making la fontana, the well of flour, to which she gradually adds the liquid ingredients. It can also be prepared in a heavy-duty mixer. Since there are several steps involved, it is helpful to make these with friends or other family members. One can roll out and fill the dough, another can fry the pastries, and someone else can roll them in the sugar.

Cassatedde are at their best when they are freshly fried and still warm, but they do reheat well in a 325°F oven. The recipe makes a lot, so plan to make them for a crowd.

MAKES 4 DOZEN

DOUGH

5 cups bleached all-purpose flour

½ pound (2 sticks) margarine or unsalted butter, melted and cooled

3 large eggs, lightly beaten

1 cup dry Marsala

FILLING

One 3-pound container whole-milk ricotta, drained overnight (see page 219)

1 cup sugar

2 ounces semisweet chocolate, finely chopped

Grated zest of 1 lemon

4 tablespoons (½ stick) margarine or unsalted butter, melted and cooled

Flour

Olive oil for frying

About 2 cups sugar

1. To make the dough, mound the flour on a large work surface and make a well in the center, keeping the sides as high as possible. Pour ½ cup of the margarine into the well and, with a fork, gradually flick in flour from around the edges, a little at a time, mixing until the margarine is absorbed. Add the remaining margarine using the same technique. Add the eggs the same way. Gradually stir in the Marsala. Knead the dough until smooth, about 10 minutes. The dough should be stiff; if it is too dry, knead in 1 to 2 tablespoons water. Cover the dough with an inverted bowl and let rest in the refrigerator for at least 30 minutes, or overnight.

2. To make the filling, pass the ricotta through a fine sieve or blend it in a food processor until smooth. Transfer to a bowl if necessary and stir in the sugar, chocolate, and lemon zest.

3. Cut the dough into quarters. On a lightly floured surface, roll out one piece into a 12-inch square. Brush with 1 tablespoon of the margarine. Tightly roll up the dough into a long rope. Cut the rope into 12 pieces. Place the pieces on a plate, cover, and refrigerate. Prepare the remaining dough in the same way.

4. Dip both cut sides of one piece of dough lightly in flour. Roll out the dough into a 5- to 6-inch circle. Place about 2 tablespoons of the ricotta filling on one half of the circle. Dip a finger in cold water and lightly moisten the edges. Fold the dough in half and seal by pressing the edges firmly with your fingertips. Repeat with the remaining dough and filling, placing the turnovers on large baking sheets or trays. Pour 1 inch oil into a deep heavy skillet and heat to 370°F on a deep-frying thermometer, or until a small piece of dough dropped in the oil sizzles and turns brown within 1 minute. Add the turnovers, a few at a time, and cook until golden brown, about 4 minutes, turning once. Drain on paper towels.

5. Roll the turnovers in sugar and let cool on wire racks.

VARIATION: In Sicily, *cassatedde* are fried, but they can be baked if you prefer. Preheat the oven to 375°F. Place the turnovers about 1 inch apart on large greased baking sheets. Brush them with margarine or butter and sprinkle with sugar. Bake for 15 minutes, or until browned and puffed. Transfer the turnovers to wire racks and let cool.

Cream Puffs

BIGNÉ

Cream puffs, known as bigné, *are magnificent in Naples. Lined up on refrigerator trays in the Caffè Gambrinus, they look like big golden clouds dusted with confectioners' sugar snow. The crisp exterior conceals a soft, sweet filling which can be made of pastry cream, ricotta cream, ice cream, or simply whipped cream and a big juicy strawberry in season.*

My mother always made cream puffs filled with vanilla pastry cream, and I could never decide if I liked them better freshly made and crisp, or when they had been filled earlier and allowed to soften.

MAKES 1 DOZEN

8 tablespoons (1 stick) unsalted butter
½ teaspoon salt
1 cup all-purpose flour
4 large eggs, at room temperature

½ recipe Pastry Cream (page 220) or Ricotta Cream (page 280), your favorite ice cream, or whipped cream
Confectioners' sugar for dusting

1. Preheat the oven to 400°F. Butter a large baking sheet. Dust the baking sheet with flour and tap out the excess.

2. In a medium saucepan, heat the butter, 1 cup water, and the salt over medium-low heat until the butter melts and the mixture comes to a boil. Remove from the heat. Add the flour all at once and stir well with a wooden spoon until the flour is completely incorporated.

3. Return the saucepan to medium heat and cook, stirring constantly and turning the dough over itself often, until it begins to leave a thin film on the bottom of the saucepan, about 3 minutes. (This helps to dry the dough so the cream puffs will be crisp.) Transfer the dough to a large bowl.

4. Add the eggs one at a time, beating thoroughly after each addition. Continue to beat until smooth and shiny.

5. Drop the dough by rounded spoonfuls onto the prepared baking sheet, forming 12 mounds spaced about 3 inches apart. Pat the tops to make a nice round shape.

6. Bake until golden brown, 40 to 45 minutes. Turn off the oven and remove the puffs. With a small knife, poke a hole in the side of each puff to allow the steam to escape. Return the puffs to the oven for 10 minutes to dry.

7. Using a serrated knife, cut the puffs part way in half horizontally. Open like a book and scoop out the soft dough from the inside. Transfer to a wire rack and let cool completely. (The puffs can be made ahead of time and frozen, tightly sealed, in a plastic bag. Crisp on a baking sheet in a low oven before using.)

8. Just before serving, spoon in the filling and dust with confectioners' sugar.

The Grape Harvest

All over Italy, October is the time to celebrate the grape harvest. One of the most famous celebrations occurs in Marino, in the Castelli Romani area south of Rome. In the center of town, the magnificent Fountain of the Four Moors, which was sculpted out of local stone in 1632 by Pompeo Castiglia, recalls the victory of the Castelli Romani in the Battle of Lepanto. For the feast, the fountain is rigged to spout wine instead of water.

Crispy Cream-Filled Pastry Tubes

CANNOLI

On our first trip to Taormina, in Sicily, Charles and I stopped at a caffè for a snack. We could see the young baker filling a freshly made batch of cannoli, so we ordered some. Normally, cannoli are too sweet for me and, unless they are freshly filled, the crusts are too soggy. One bite of these, though, and I was in cannoli heaven. Not only were the shells so crisp they shattered when we took a bite, they had a special flavor of their own. The cream was rich and, though quite sweet, had a delicious tangy flavor. I asked a few questions and found out that the shells had been fried in fresh lard and the cream filling was made from ricotta di pecora, sheep's milk ricotta, which has a lot more flavor than the cow's milk ricotta we find here.

To make our American ricotta taste like the Sicilian, I blend it with a few tablespoons of fresh goat's cheese, which adds a rich tang similar to Sicilian sheep's milk cheese.

The dough for cannoli must be rolled very, very thin so that they will turn out very crisp. A pasta machine does an exceptional job of this, but the dough can also be rolled out with a rolling pin. Since the lard available here is not very good, unless it is home-made, I fry the shells in olive oil.

Wooden broom handles or bamboo canes at one time were cut up for use in forming the cannoli tubes. If you are handy or know someone who is, you can make cannoli tubes out of a 1-inch wooden dowel, cut into 4-inch lengths. Metal cannoli tubes can be bought at many kitchen equipment stores, or you can mail-order them through one of the sources on page 296. They normally come four to a set and are inexpensive. If you enjoy making cannoli, invest in 12 of the forms so that you can shape all of the dough before frying them. It will make the job much easier.

In Sicily, cannoli are essential for Carnival, but they are eaten all year round. Cannoli shells can be made up to 2 days ahead, then stored in tightly sealed plastic or metal containers. The filling can be made a day in advance, but the shells should be filled just before serving.

MAKES 12 TO 16

PASTRY SHELLS

2 cups unbleached all-purpose flour

1 tablespoon sugar

1 teaspoon unsweetened cocoa powder

½ teaspoon ground cinnamon

½ teaspoon salt

3 tablespoons vegetable oil

About ½ cup dry white wine

1 large egg white, beaten

Lard, olive oil, or vegetable oil for frying

One 32-ounce container whole or part-milk
  skimmed ricotta, drained (see page 219)
¼ cup soft fresh goat cheese, optional
1 cup confectioners' sugar, or to taste
1 teaspoon vanilla extract
½ teaspoon ground cinnamon

¼ cup chopped semisweet chocolate
2 tablespoons chopped candied citron or orange
  peel, optional

¼ cup finely chopped unsalted pistachios
Confectioners' sugar for dusting

1. To make the shells, mix the flour, sugar, cocoa, cinnamon, and salt in a food processor or electric mixer bowl. Blend in the oil. Add enough of the wine to make a soft
dough. Turn the dough out onto a lightly floured board and knead it until smooth and
well blended, about 2 minutes. Shape the dough into a ball, cover with an inverted
bowl, and let rest at room temperature for 30 minutes to 1 hour.

2. Lightly oil the cannoli tubes. Cut the dough into 4 pieces. Starting at the middle
setting, run one piece of dough through the rollers of a pasta machine. Lightly dust
the dough with flour as needed to keep it from sticking. Continue to pass the dough
through the machine, skipping every other setting, until you reach the narrowest or
next-to-narrowest setting, depending on the machine. The dough should be about 4
inches wide and thin enough to see your hand through but still hold its shape. (You
can also roll out the dough on a floured board with a rolling pin, but be sure to roll it
very thin.)

3. Cut the strip of dough into lengths about 1 inch shorter than your cannoli tubes.
Holding each piece of dough like a diamond shape, place a tube lengthwise on it, from
point to point. Fold the two opposite sides of the dough around the tube, being careful not to stretch or pull the dough tightly, which would make it more difficult to
remove the pastry from the tube after frying. Dab a little egg white on the dough
where the edges overlap—avoid getting egg white on the tube, or it will stick—and
press to seal. Set aside.

4. Roll and cut out the dough. You can re-roll the scraps if they are still soft. If you do
not have enough cannoli tubes for all of the dough, lay the pieces on sheets of plastic
wrap and keep them covered until you are ready to use them.

5. Add enough lard or oil to a deep heavy saucepan or deep-fryer to reach a depth of
2 inches and heat to 370°F on a deep-frying thermometer. Line a baking pan with

paper towels. Carefully lower a few of the cannoli tubes into the hot oil; do not crowd the pan. Fry the cannoli until golden, about 2 minutes, turning them so that they brown evenly. With tongs, remove the cannoli tubes, holding each one straight up so that the oil flows back into the pan, and drain on the prepared baking pan. While they are still hot, carefully slide the cannoli shells from the tubes: Grasp each tube with a pot holder and pull the cannoli shell off the tube with a pair of tongs, or with your hand protected by an oven mitt or towel. Cool the shells completely on the paper towels.

6. Repeat with the remaining dough. If you are reusing them, let the cannoli tubes cool before wrapping them in the dough. (The shells can be made up to 2 days before serving; store in a sealed container in a cool, dry place.)

7. To make the filling, using a rubber spatula, push the ricotta through a fine sieve. Or put it in a food processor and blend it until creamy. Transfer to a bowl if necessary. Add the goat cheese, if using, sugar to taste, vanilla, and cinnamon and stir until smooth. Stir in the chocolate and the candied fruit, if using. (The filling can be made up to 24 hours before serving; cover and refrigerate.)

8. To assemble, fill a pastry bag fitted with a ½-inch plain tip or a heavy-duty plastic storage bag with the ricotta cream. If using a plastic bag, cut about ½ inch off one corner. One at a time, insert the tip in the cannoli shells and gently squeeze the bag, filling them from both ends. Smooth the cream with a small spatula. Sprinkle the cream with the chopped pistachios and dust the shells with confectioners' sugar. Serve within 1 hour.

Creamy Rice Fritters

FRITTELLE DI RISO

These delicious fritters taste like creamy rice pudding in a crisp crust. The recipe is from Elda Batacchi, who lives in Tavarnuzze, outside Florence. Her daughter-in-law, Carmela, told me that Elda fries up big batches of fritters for Saint Joseph's Day and Palm Sunday. She serves them with a little bowl of sugar so everyone can dip them for extra sweetness.

SERVES 8

1¼ cups milk
1 cup medium-grain rice, such as Arborio
2 tablespoons unsalted butter
¼ cup sugar
¼ teaspoon salt
4 large eggs, separated

1 teaspoon grated orange zest
1 cup all-purpose flour
1 teaspoon baking powder
Vegetable oil for deep-frying
Confectioners' sugar for dusting

1. Combine the milk and 1 cup water in a medium saucepan and bring to a simmer over medium heat. Add the rice, butter, sugar, and salt. Cook, stirring frequently, until the liquid has been absorbed and the rice is tender. Scrape the mixture into a large bowl. Let cool slightly.

2. Stir the egg yolks and orange zest into the rice until well blended. Stir in the flour and baking powder.

3. In a large mixer bowl, beat the egg whites until soft peaks form. Gently fold one-third of the whites at a time into the rice.

4. Heat about 3 inches oil in a deep heavy saucepan or deep-fryer to 370°F on a deep-frying thermometer. Or test the oil by slipping a drop of the rice mixture into the oil. If it sizzles and rises to the surface of the pan, the oil is ready. Gently push the rice mixture by heaping tablespoons into the hot oil. Do not crowd the pan, or the fritters will stick together. Cook the fritters, turning often, until browned and puffed, about 3 minutes. Drain on paper towels.

5. Sprinkle the fritters with confectioners' sugar and serve immediately.

WINE MATCH: Moscadello, Villa Banfi

Sources

BAKING SUPPLIES AND EQUIPMENT, CHICKPEA FLOUR

King Arthur Flour Company
The Baker's Catalog
P.O. Box 876
Norwich, VT 05055-0876
800–827–6836
Website: www.kingarthurflour.com

SPICES

Penzeys, Inc.
P.O. Box 933
Muskego, WI 53150
Phone: 800–741–7787
Website: www.penzeys.com

FRESH MOZZARELLA

Mozzarella Company
2944 Elm Street
Dallas, TX 75226
Phone: 800–798–2954
Website: www.mozzoco.com

CANDIED CITRON AND ORANGE PEEL, WHEAT BERRIES, SPICES, DRIED BEANS, CHICKPEA FLOUR, NUTS, DRIED FRUITS

Kalustyan's
123 Lexington Avenue
New York, NY 10016
Phone: 212–683–8458

OIL, VINEGAR, PASTA, CHEESES

Zingerman's
422 Detroit Street
Ann Arbor, MI 48104
Phone: 734–633–DELI
Website: www.zingermans.com

Dean & DeLuca
121 Prince Street
New York, NY 10012
Phone: 212–254–8776

PANETTONE, CHEESES, OILS, PASTA

Esperya USA
3 Westchester Plaza
Elmsford, NY 10523
Phone: 877–907–2525
Fax: 914–592–1787
Website: www.esperya.com

Bibliography

Alberini, Massimo. "Basilicata Strangolapreti fritti e grano dolce." *La Cucina Italiana* Agosto 1994.

Barolini, Helen. *Festa*. New York: Harcourt Brace Jovanovich, 1988.

Barr, Nancy Verde. *We Called It Macaroni*. New York: Knopf, 1990.

Cafiero, Antonio. *Sorrento e le sue delizie*. Sorrento: Franco di Mauro Editore, 1993.

Castello, Antonio. *Sapori e piaceri d'Italia*. Roma: Editrice Sallustiana, 1996.

Cavalcanti, Ottavio. *Il libro d'oro della cucina e dei vini di Calabria e Basilicata*. Milano: Mursia Editore, 1979.

Celotto, Antonio F., and Maculan, Guerrino. *I santi a tavola*. Bassano del Grappa: Tassotti Editore, 1998.

Correnti, Pino. *Il libro d'oro della cucina e dei vini di Sicilia*. Milano: Mursia Editore, 1976.

Dolcino, Esther and Michelangelo. *Le ricette liguri per Tutte le occasioni*. Genoa: Nuova Editrice Genovese, 1990.

———. *La cucina della nonna*. Scafati: Luigi Panella Editore, Pengraf, 1994.

———. *La cucina di genova e della Liguria*. Genoa: Valenti Editore.

Francesconi, Jeanne Carola. *La cucina Napoletana*. Roma: Newton Compton Editore, 1992.

Field, Carol. *Celebrating Italy*. William Morrow, 1990.

Freson, Robert. *Savoring Italy*. New York: HarperCollins, 1992.

Girardi, Robert. *Vaporetto 13*. New York: Delta, 1997.

Grammatico, Maria, and Simeti, Mary Taylor. *Bitter Almonds*. New York: William Morrow, 1994.

Lanza, Anna Tasca. *The Heart of Sicily*. New York: Clarkson Potter, 1993.

Lo Pinto, Maria and Miloradovich, Milo. *The Art of Italian Cooking*. New York: Doubleday, 1948.

Machlin, Edda Servi. *The Classic Cuisine of the Italian Jews*. New York: Everest House, 1981.

Malizia, Giuliano. *La cucina Ebraico-Romanesca*. Roma: Tascabili Economici Newton, 1997.

Parenti, Giovanni Righi. *La grande cucina Toscana*. Volumes 1 and 2. Milano: SugarCo Edizioni, 1986.

Ricette di osterie del Veneto quaresime e oriente. Bra: Slow Food Editore, 1996.

Ristoranti trattorie e cose buone d'Italia. Milano: Editoriale Giorgio Mondadori, 1997.

Sada, Luigi. *La cucina Pugliese*. Roma: Newton Compton Editore, 1994.

Serra, Anna and Piero. *La cucina della Campania*. Napoli: Franco di Mauro Editore, 1983.

Simeti, Mary Taylor. *Pomp and Sustenance: Twenty-five Centuries of Sicilian Food*. New York: Knopf, 1989.

Schwartz, Arthur. *Naples at Table*. HarperCollins, 1998.

Valli, Emilia. *La cucina Friulana*. Padua: Franco Muzzio, 1992.

Recipes by Holidays, Feast Days, and Celebrations

New Year's Eve and Day:
 about, 167
 bollito misto for, 171
 good luck lentil soup, 49
 old slipper tradition for, 171
 roast pork porchetta style, 170–71
 zampone with lentils, 168–69

Epiphany, about, 197

San Biagio (Saint Blaise), about the feast of, 23

Saint Agatha's Day, about, 241

Carnevale (Carnival):
 about, 96
 crispy cream-filled pastry tubes for, 292–94
 lasagne, 96–97
 orange semolina cake, 234
 polenta, 129
 sausage, fava bean, and cabbage soup, 52

Valentine's Day, red risotto for, 126–27

Ash Wednesday, about the Herring Group, 81

Saint Joseph's Day:
 about, 53
 creamy rice fritters, 295
 fritters, 280–81
 pasta for, 106–7
 poor man's fava beans for, 200
 soup, 54

Lent, hazelnut biscotti, 244–45

Passover:
 artichoke risotto for, 124–25
 chocolate cake for, 222–23
 little sweets, 268–69

Holy Week, Tuscan rosemary raisin bread, 22–23

Good Friday:
 fresh pasta ribbons in a hot garlic bath, 87
 pasta, 91
 in Puglia, 149

Palm Sunday or Easter:
 about, 173

baby dolls, 36–37

creamy rice fritters, 295

egg wreath, Grandma's, 34–35

pie, savory, 28–29

pie from Abruzzo, 30–31

prosciutto bread, 26–27

rabbit with tomatoes, wine, and rosemary, 194

roast leg of lamb with garlic, rosemary, and little potatoes, 172–73

soup, Roman, 43

stuffed eggs, 20

tart, Ligurian, 38–40

wheat berry cheesecake, 228–29

Easter Monday, asparagus and prosciutto frittata, 16–17

San Marco (Saint Mark's Day), Venetian risotto with peas for, 122–23

The Tonnara, the capo's tuna, 146–47

Porto Cesareo Fish Festival, linguine with white clam sauce, 120–21

Saint Anthony's Feast Day:
doughnuts, 283
porcini-stuffed zucchini, 206–7

Saint Vitus's Day:
eel for, 148
focaccia for, 32–33

Saint John the Baptist, ravioli for the feast of, 88–90

Saint Peter and Paul Feast Days, summer vegetable stew, 203

Feast of Our Lady of Mount Carmel and Saint Paulinus, dancing the giglio, 273

Saint Rosalie's Day:
chickpea-flour fritters, 10–11
snails for the feast of, 150

Feast of the Redeemer, about, 158

Sant'Anna Feast Day, eggplant parmigiana, 202

Feast of the Assumption, chocolate eggplant, 278–79

San Lorenzo Day, potato tortelli, 92–93

San Bartolomeo's Feast Day, zucchini flower fritters, 284–85

Feast of the Whites, veal roll-ups, 160–61

Sant'Oronzo Feast Day, eggplant parmigiana, 202

Rosh Hashanah:
harvest chicken with peppers, for Sukkot, 186
red risotto for, 126–27

San Gennaro's Feast Day:
about, 282
doughnuts, 282

Grape Harvest, about, 291

All Saints' Day, roast chicken and potatoes with bay leaves, 182–83

Day of the Dead (All Souls' Day):
    fettuccine and chickpeas for, 80
    spice cookies, 246–47
    sweet beans for, 248–49

Saint Martin's Day, hot roasted chestnuts, 270

Saint Catherine's Day, pecorino di fossa, 59

Chanukah, fried chicken, 184–85

Saint Lucy's Day:
    chickpea-flour fritters, 10–11
    golden rice balls, 12–14
    wheat berry pudding for, 276–77

Christmas Eve:
    about, 114–15
    baccalà stew, 152–53
    baked clams, 18–19
    baked stuffed lobster tails, 151
    broccoli rabe with garlic and anchovies, 204
    fried baccalà, 154
    Ligurian seafood salad, 137–39

linguine with lobster for, 116–17
linguine with red mussel sauce for, 118–19
marinated eel skewers for, 148–49
seafood salad, 134–35
shrimp with garlic and toasted
    bread crumbs, 144

Christmas Day:
    about, 187
    beet ravioli, 94–95
    capon, 188–89
    chestnut tortelli, 256–57
    chicken soup with escarole and little
        meatballs, 48
    chocolate spice cookies, 264–65
    feast day meat loaf, 165
    fried cardoons, 210–11
    how Santa Claus came to America, 262
    married soup, 50–51
    reinforcement salad, 196
    roast turkey with chestnut stuffing, 190–91
    salad, 198
    Selvapiana seven P pasta for, 112–13
    struffoli, 252–53

Recipe Index

Recipe titles in Italian are in italics.

abbacchio alla cacciatora,
    178–79
Abruzzo, Easter pie from,
    30–31
agnello al forno, 172–73
agnello alla brace, 175
agnolotti, 84–86
All Souls' Day spice cookies,
    246–47
almond(s):
    in All Souls' Day spice
        cookies, 246–47
    brittle, 266
    creams, frozen, 272
    ice, toasted, 275
    in pasta for Saint Joseph's
        Day, 106–7
    –pine nut macaroons, 238
    in sweet beans for the Day
        of the Dead, 248–49
almond paste:
    in rainbows, 258–59
    in ricotta layer cake, 218–19
anchovies, 107
    broccoli rabe with garlic
        and, 204
    in cherry bombs, 6
    in fresh pasta ribbons in a
        hot garlic bath, 87

in pasta for Saint Joseph's
    Day, 106–7
in reinforcement salad, 196
in San Vito's focaccia, 32–33
in stuffed artichokes, 208
antipasti, 5–20
    asparagus and prosciutto
        frittata, 16–17
    baked clams, 18–19
    cherry bombs, 6
    chickpea-flour fritters,
        10–11
    golden rice balls, 12–14
    olives with fried bread
        crumbs, 15
    stuffed Easter eggs, 20
    stuffed olives from the
        Marches, 7–9
arancini, 12–14
arcobaleni, 258–59
artichoke(s):
    risotto, 124–25
    stuffed, 208
asparagus and prosciutto
    frittata, 16–17

*babbaluci del festino di Santa
    Rosalia,* 150
baby dolls, Easter, 36–37

baccalà (salt cod):
    fried, 154
    stew, 152–53
baccalà fritta, 154
baked stuffed lobster tails,
    153
basil, in pesto Genovese, 64
bay leaves, roast chicken and
    potatoes with, 182–83
bean(s):
    for the Befana, 199
    green, summer spaghetti
        with, 111
    in Saint Joseph's Day soup,
        54
    sweet, for the Day of the
        Dead, 248–49
    see also chickpea(s); fava
        bean(s)
béchamel sauce, 61
    in cannelloni, 82–83
beef, ground:
    in feast day meat loaf, 159
    in golden rice balls, 12–14
    in Grandma Amico's Sicilian
        baked pasta, 108–10
    in meatballs, for Sunday
        meat and tomato sauce,
        69

beef, ground (*continued*)
meatballs, little, chicken soup with escarole and, 48
in meatballs with raisins and pine nuts, 72–73
in meat ravioli, 84–86
in meat sauce Bologna style, 71
in Mother Leone's meat sauce, 62–63
in Sicilian ragu, 65
beef round, in Sunday meat and tomato sauce, 68–70
beet(s):
ravioli, Christmas, 94–95
in red risotto, 126–27
bietole e fave, 201
bigné, 290–91
biscotti, hazelnut, 244–45
biscotti di cioccolato e spezie, 264–65
biscotti regina, 242–43
biscuit tortoni, 272
Bologna, *see* meat sauce Bologna style
Boniface VIII, Pope, timbale of, 98–99
borage, in Saint Joseph's Day soup, 54
braciole, in Sunday meat and tomato sauce, 68–70
braciolette croccante di agnello, 180
braised quail with porcini, 192–93
bread, 21–40
Easter baby dolls, 36–37
Grandma's Easter egg wreath, 34–35

olive rolls, 24–25
prosciutto, 26–27
San Vito's focaccia, 32–33
soup, 45
tips for, 25, 27, 33, 40
Tuscan rosemary raisin, 22–23
bread crumbs:
in baked stuffed lobster tails, 151
in cherry bombs, 6
in Christmas capon, 188–89
fried, olives with, 15
in fried cardoons, 210–11
in Good Friday pasta, 90
in Grandma Amico's Sicilian baked pasta, 108–10
homemade, making, 19
in pasta for Saint Joseph's Day, 106–7
in stuffed artichokes, 208
in stuffed mushrooms, 209
toasted, shrimp with garlic and, 144
broccoli, in married soup, 50–51
broccoli rabe:
with garlic and anchovies, 204
in married soup, 50–51
brodetto pasquale alla romana, 43
broth, *see* chicken soup and broth
butter, browned, polenta with soft cheese and, 130–31
butter and sage sauce, 60

cabbage:
in married soup, 50–51
sausage, and fava bean soup, 52
cakes, 217–25, 228–31
chocolate, for Passover, 222–23
orange semolina, 234–35
ricotta layer, 218–19
Trieste holiday, 230–31
zuppa inglese, 220–21
see also cheesecake; sponge cake layers
caldarroste, 270
cannellini beans, in Saint Joseph's Day soup, 54
cannelloni, 82–83
cannoli, 292–94
capon, Christmas, 188–89
Capo's tuna, 146–47
cappon magro, 137–39
carciofi ripieni, 208
cardi fritti, 210–11
cardoons, fried, 210–11
Carnival lasagne, 96–97
carpone di Natale, 188–89
cartellate, 286–87
casonsei, 94–95
cassata, 218–19
cassata al forno, 226–27
cassatedde di Santa Ninfa, 288–89
cauliflower, in reinforcement salad, 196
cavatelli, 104–5
Chanukah fried chicken, 184–85
cheese:
soft, polenta with browned butter and, 130–31
see also specific cheeses

cheesecake:
  chocolate chunk, 224–25
  Easter wheat berry,
    228–29
cherry bombs, 6
chestnut(s):
  hot roasted, 270
  stuffing, roast turkey with,
    190–91
  tortelli, Christmas, 256–57
chicken, 159, 181–86
  Chanukah fried, 184–85
  with fresh tomatoes,
    Sunday, 181
  in meat ravioli, 84–85
  with peppers, harvest, 186
  and potatoes with bay
    leaves, roast, 182–83
chicken soup and broth, 42
  bread, 45
  with escarole and little
    meatballs, 48
  Roman Easter, 43
  in a sack, 44
  souffléd, 46–47
chickpea(s):
  in Christmas tortelli,
    256–57
  and fettuccine for the Day
    of the Dead, 80
  -flour fritters, 10–11
  in Saint Joseph's Day soup,
    54
chicory, in poor man's fava
    beans for the feast of
    Saint Joseph, 200
chocolate (chips):
  cake for Passover, 222–23
  chunk cheesecake, 224–25
  eggplant, 278–79

figs, 263
  pudding tart, double,
    232–33
  in rainbows, 258–59
  spice cookies, 264–65
  in spiced fig cookies, 254–55
  in Trieste holiday cake,
    230–31
Christmas beet ravioli, 94–95
Christmas capon, 188–89
Christmas chestnut tortelli,
  256–57
Christmas Eve seafood salad,
  134–35
Christmas salad, 198
*ciambella di Pasqua alla
  nonna*, 34–35
ciambelline al vinsanto, 239
ciambotta, 203
cima alla genovese, 162–64
cime di broccoli soffriti, 204
clam(s):
  baked, 18–19
  cleaning of, 136
  opening of, 19
  sauce, white, linguine with,
    120–21
  storage of, 158
cod:
  dried, about, 155
  salt, *see* baccalà
code di aragoste amollicate,
  151
coniglio alla procidana, 194
cookies, 237–61
  All Souls' Day spice,
    246–47
  chocolate spice, 264–65
  Christmas chestnut tortelli,
    256–57

glazed vanilla rings, 240
hazelnut biscotti, 244–45
hazelnut half-moons, 250
little old ladies
  (*vecchiarelle*), 251
little sweets, 268–69
Nonni's wafer (*pizzelle*),
  260–61
pine nut–almond
  macaroons, 238
rainbows, 258–59
sesame, 242–43
spiced fig, 254–55
struffoli, 252–53
sweet beans for the Day of
  the Dead, 248–49
tips for, 254
Vin Santo rings, 239
cornmeal, *see* polenta
cotechino with lentils, 168–69
crab:
  blue, sauce, linguine with,
    117
  or lobster linguine quick,
    128
  storage of, 158
cream:
  -filled pastry tubes, crispy,
    292–94
  puffs, 290–91
  in Selvapiana seven P pasta,
    112–13
creamy rice fritters, 295
cremolata, 275
crispy lamb chops, 180
croccante (or *torrone*), 266
crocché, 212–13
croquettes, potato, 212–13
crostata di sanguinaccio,
  232–33

cuccia dolce di Santa Lucia,
276–77
cuccidati, 254–55

desserts, 271–95
   chocolate eggplant, 278–79
   cream puffs, 290–91
   creamy rice fritters, 295
   crispy cream-filled pastry
     tubes, 292–94
   doughnuts, 283
   frozen almond creams,
     272
   honey pinwheels, 286–87
   ricotta pockets, 288–89
   Saint Joseph's fritters,
     280–81
   toasted almond ice, 275
   wheat berry pudding for
     Saint Lucy, 276–77
   zabaglione, 274
   zucchini flower fritters,
     284–85
double chocolate pudding tart,
   232–33
doughnuts, 283
dumplings, potato, 109–10

Easter wheat berry
   cheesecake, 228–29
eel skewers, marinated,
   148–49
egg(s):
   in asparagus and prosciutto
     frittata, 16–17
   in bread soup, 45
   Easter, stuffed, 20
   pasta, fresh, 76–79
   in souffléd chicken soup,
     46–47

in soup in a sack, 44
wreath, Grandma's Easter,
   34–35
eggplant:
   chocolate, 278–79
   parmigiana, 202
   in summer vegetable stew,
     203
   in vegetable ragu, 58
escarole:
   chicken soup with little
     meatballs and, 48
   in Christmas salad, 198
   in married soup, 50–51
   in poor man's fava beans for
     the feast of Saint Joseph,
     200
   in Saint Joseph's Day soup,
     54

fagioli della Befana, 199
fake sauce *(sugo finto),* 57
fava bean(s):
   for the feast of Saint
     Joseph, poor man's, 200
   fresh, Swiss chard and,
     201
   in Saint Joseph's Day soup,
     54
   sausage, and cabbage soup,
     52
fava dei poveri, 200
favata, 52
fave dei morti, 248–49
feast day meat loaf, 165
fettuccine and chickpeas for
   the Day of the Dead, 80
fettuccine e ceci, 80
fiadone, 30–31
fichi al cioccolato, 263

fig(s):
   chocolate, 263
   cookies, spiced, 254–55
filling, ricotta, for ravioli, 90
fish, 133
   Monzù's swordfish pie,
     156–58
   storage of, 158
   see also seafood; *specific
     fish*
focaccia, San Vito's, 32–33
focaccia di San Vito, 32–33
fresh pasta ribbons in a hot
   garlic bath, 87
fresh tomatoes and rosemary,
   205
fried:
   baccalà, 154
   cardoons, 210–11
   chicken, Chanukah, 184–85
   crispy lamb chops, 180
frittata, asparagus and
   prosciutto, 16–17
*frittata di asparagi e
   prosciutto,* 16–17
frittelle di fiore di zucca,
   284–85
frittelle di riso, 295
fritters, chickpea-flour, 10–11
fritters, dessert:
   creamy rice, 295
   Saint Joseph's, 280–81
   zucchini flower, 284–85
fruit, chocolate figs, 263
funghi ripieni, 209

gamberi aragonati, 144
garlic:
   bath, hot, fresh pasta
     ribbons in, 87

broccoli rabe with
anchovies and, 204
roast leg of lamb with
rosemary, little potatoes
and, 172–73
shrimp with toasted bread
crumbs and, 144
gattò di patate, 214–15
Genovese, pesto, 64
ghiotta di Natale, 152–53
glazed vanilla rings, 240
gnocchi di patate, 100–101
goat cheese:
in crispy cream-filled
pastry tubes, 292–94
in polenta with soft cheese
and browned butter,
130–31
Good Friday pasta, 91
good luck lentil soup, 49
Grandma Amico's Sicilian
baked pasta, 108–10
gravy, 70
grilled leg of lamb, 175

half-moons, 250
roast pork with, 174
toasting and skinning of,
243
halibut, in Ligurian seafood
salad, 137–39
ham:
fresh, porchetta style roast,
171
in savory Easter pie,
28–29
in timbale of Boniface VIII,
98–99
harvest chicken with peppers,
186

hazelnut(s):
biscotti, 244–45
honey pinwheels, 286–87

ice, toasted almond, 275
impanata di pesce spada,
156–58
insalata di frutti di mare,
134–35
insalata di rinforzo, 196
insalata di scungilli, 140–41
insalata natalizia di enna, 198
istufau, 176–77

lamb, 159, 175–80
chops, crispy, 180
hunter's style, Roman,
178–79
stew, Sardinian, 176–77
lamb, leg of:
with garlic, rosemary, and
little potatoes, roast,
172–73
grilled, 175
lasagna di carnevale, 96–97
lasagne, Carnival, 96–97
leek, in Selvapiana seven P
pasta, 112–13
lentil(s):
in Saint Joseph's Day soup,
54
soup, good luck, 49
zampone with, 168–69
Ligurian:
Easter tart, 38–40
seafood salad, 137–39
linguine:
with blue crab sauce, 117
Good Friday, 91
with lobster, 116–17

quick lobster or crab,
128
with red mussel sauce,
118–19
with white clam sauce,
120–21
linguine alle vongole, 120–21
linguine con aragosta, 116–17
*linguine con aragosta o
granchio*, 128
linguine con le cozze, 118–19
little old ladies, 251
lobster:
or crab linguine, quick, 128
in Ligurian seafood salad,
137–39
linguine with, 116–17
storage of, 158
tails, baked stuffed, 151

macaroons, pine nut–almond,
238
making the fountain, 79
manicotti, 102–3
marinated eel skewers, 148–49
married soup, 50–51
Marsala, in ricotta pockets,
288–89
mashed potatoes, rosy, 216
meat, 159–80
ravioli, 84–86
*see also specific meats and
meat sauces*
meatballs:
little, chicken soup with
escarole and, 48
with raisins and pine nuts,
72–73
in Sunday meat and tomato
sauce, 68–70

meat loaf, feast day, 165

meat sauce:

    Bologna style, 71

    Mother Leone's, 62–63

    Sunday meat and tomato
        sauce, 68–70

melanzane al cioccolato,
    278–79

mezzalune, 250

migliaccio, 234–35

minestra di buona fortuna,
    49

*minestra di legumi per San
    Giuseppe,* 54

minestra maritata, 50–51

minestra nel sacchetto, 44

miniuledde, 24–25

Monzù's swordfish pie,
    156–58

mozzarella:

    in Carnival lasagne,
        96–97

    in eggplant parmigiana,
        202

    in manicotti, 102–3

    in potato cake, 214–15

    in savory Easter pie, 28–29

    in timbale of Boniface VIII,
        98–99

mushroom(s):

    and sausage ragu, 74

    stuffed, 209

mushrooms, porcini:

    braised quail with, 192–93

    in sausage and mushroom
        ragu, 74

    -stuffed zucchini, 206–7

    in Umbrian ragu, 66–67

mussel(s):

    cleaning of, 156

sauce, red, linguine with,
    118–19

storage of, 158

Nonni's wafer cookies, 260–61

nuts, *see* almond(s); almond
    paste; pine nut(s);
    walnuts

nuts, for dessert:

    almond brittle, 266

    hot roasted chestnuts, 270

octopus, in Christmas Eve
    seafood salad, 134–35

olive(s):

    with fried bread crumbs, 15

    Marches-style stuffed, 7–9

    in reinforcement salad, 196

    rolls, 24–25

olive ascolana, 7–9

olive fritte, 15

orange semolina cake, 234–35

osso buco al vino rosso, 166–67

osso buco with red wine, 166–67

pancetta:

    in Selvapiana seven P pasta,
        112–13

    in veal roll-ups, 160–61

pan dei morti, 246–47

pan di ramerino, 22–23

pan di spagna, 236–37

pane di prosciutto, 26–27

panelle, 10–11

parmigiana di melanzane, 202

Parmigiano-Reggiano:

    in cannelloni, 82–83

    in Carnival lasagne, 96–97

    in Christmas beet ravioli,
        94–95

    in Christmas capon,
        188–89

    in eggplant parmigiana, 202

    in Grandma Amico's
        Sicilian baked pasta,
        108–10

    in Ligurian Easter tart,
        38–40

    in manicotti, 102–3

    in meat ravioli, 84–86

    in pesto Genovese, 64

    in potato croquettes,
        212–13

    in potato dumplings,
        100–101

    in potato tortelli, 92–93

    in ravioli for the feast of
        Saint John the Baptist,
        88–90

    in red risotto, 126–27

    in ricotta filling for ravioli,
        90

    in Selvapiana seven P pasta,
        112–13

    in stuffed mushrooms, 209

    in timbale of Boniface VIII,
        98–99

    in Venetian risotto with
        peas for San Marco,
        122–23

Passover, chocolate cake for,
    222–23

pasta, 75–121

    sauces for, *see* meat sauce;
        ragus; sauces; tomato
        sauce

    tips for, 27, 86, 90

pasta, dried, 105–13, 116–21

    Grandma Amico's Sicilian
        baked, 108–10

for Saint Joseph's Day,
106–7
Selvapiana seven P, 112–13
tips for, 121
see also linguine; spaghetti
pasta, fresh, 76–80, 82–90,
92–105
cannelloni, 82–83
Carnival lasagne, 96–97
fettuccine and chickpeas for
the Day of the Dead, 80
manicotti, 102–3
potato dumplings, 100–101
potato tortelli, 92–93
ribbons in a hot garlic bath
timbale of Boniface VIII,
98–99
see also ravioli
pasta, fresh egg, 76–79
pasta al forno, 108–10
pasta all'uovo, 76–79
pasta di San Giuseppe, 106–7
pastasciutta della vigilia, 91
pastiera, 228–29
*patate schiacciatte al
pomodoro*, 216
peas:
in Grandma Amico's
Sicilian baked pasta,
108–10
split, in Saint Joseph's Day
soup, 54
Venetian risotto with, for
San Marco, 122–23
pecorino di fossa, 59
pecorino romano:
in Carnival lasagne, 96–97
in eggplant parmigiana, 202
in Grandma Amico's Sicilian
baked pasta, 108–10

in potato dumplings,
100–101
in savory Easter pie,
28–29
in timbale of Boniface VIII,
98–99
peperoncini ripieni, 6
peperoncino:
in linguine with lobster,
116–17
in linguine with red mussel
sauce, 118–19
in scungilli in spicy tomato
sauce, 142–43
in Selvapiana seven P pasta,
112–13
tips for, 117, 119
peppers:
cherry bombs, 6
harvest chicken with, 186
red bell, in summer
vegetable stew, 203
in reinforcement salad,
196
pesto Genovese, 64
pies, savory, 21
Abruzzo-style Easter,
30–31
Easter, 28–29
Ligurian Easter tart,
38–40
Monzù's swordfish,
156–58
pine nut(s):
–almond macaroons, 238
meatballs with raisins and,
72–73
in pesto Genovese, 64
in sweet beans for the Day
of the Dead, 248–49

in Trieste holiday cake,
230–31
pinoli, 238
pink sauce, 61
pizza rustica, 28–29
pizzelle, 260–61
polenta, 75, 129
with soft cheese and
browned butter, 130–31
tip for, 131
pollo alla Anna, 181
pollo con peperoni, 186
pollo e patate arrosto al alloro,
182–83
pollo fritto, 184–85
*polpette con uva passa e
pinoli*, 72–73
polpettone, 165
pomodori al rosamarino, 205
poor man's fava beans, 200
poppy seeds:
in Christmas beet ravioli,
94–95
tip for, 95
porchetta, 170–71
porcini mushrooms, *see*
mushrooms, porcini
pork, 159, 168–71
with hazelnuts, roast, 174
porchetta style, roast,
170–71
zampone with lentils,
168–69
see also ham; prosciutto;
salami; sausage, Italian
pork, ground:
in Christmas capon,
188–89
in feast day meat loaf,
165

pork, ground (*continued*)
    in meatballs, for Sunday
        meat and tomato sauce, 69
    in meatballs with raisins
        and pine nuts, 72–73
    in meat sauce, Bologna
        style, 71
    in Mother Leone's meat
        sauce, 62–63
    in Umbrian ragu, 66–67
pork ribs:
    in married soup, 50–51
    sausage, fava bean, and
        cabbage soup, 52
potato(es):
    cake, 214–15
    croquettes, 212–13
    dumplings (gnocchi),
        100–101
    little, roast leg of lamb with
        garlic, rosemary and,
        172–73
    and roast chicken with bay
        leaves, 182–83
    rosy mashed, 216
    in summer vegetable stew,
        203
    tortelli, 92–93
poultry, 159
    see also capon, Christmas;
        chicken; turkey
presnitz, 230–31
prosciutto:
    and asparagus frittata,
        16–17
    bread, 26–27
    in married soup, 50–51
    in potato cake, 214–15
    in potato croquettes,
        212–13

pudding:
    tart, double chocolate,
        232–33
    wheat berry, for Saint Lucy,
        276–77
puff pastry, in Trieste holiday
    cake, 230–31
pulpette avvolte, 160–61
pupi con l'uova, 36–37

*quaglie in tegame con funghi
    porcini*, 192–93
quail, with porcini, braised,
    192–93
quaresimali, 244–45
quick lobster or crab linguine,
    128

rabbit with tomatoes, wine,
    and rosemary, 194
ragù alla siciliana, 65
ragù all'Umbra, 66–67
ragù bolognese, 71
ragù della domenica, 68–70
ragù de verdura, 58
ragù di Mama Leone, 62–63
ragù di salsiccia e funghi,
    74
ragus:
    meatballs with raisins and
        pine nuts in, 72–73
    Sicilian, 65
    Sunday meat and tomato
        sauce, 68–70
    Umbrian, 66–67
    use of term, 70
    vegetable, 58
    see also sausage and
        mushroom ragu
rainbows, 258–59

raisin(s):
    in All Souls' Day spice
        cookies, 246–47
    in chocolate spice cookies,
        264–65
    meatballs with pine nuts
        and, 72–73
    in orange semolina cake,
        234–35
    rosemary bread, Tuscan,
        22–23
    in spiced fig cookies, 254–55
    in Trieste holiday cake,
        230–31
ravioli:
    Christmas beet, 94–95
    for the feast of Saint John
        the Baptist, 88–90
    meat, 84–86
    ricotta filling for, 90
ravioli di San Giovanni, 88–90
reinforcement salad, 196
rice, 75
    balls, golden, 12–14
    fritters, creamy, 295
    see also risotto
ricotta:
    in Carnival lasagne, 96–97
    in chocolate chunk
        cheesecake, 224–25
    in crispy cream-filled
        pastry tubes, 292–94
    in Easter pie from Abruzzo,
        30–31
    in Easter wheat berry
        cheesecake, 228–29
    filling for ravioli, 90
    layer cake, 218–19
    in Ligurian Easter tart,
        38–40

in manicotti, 102–3

in orange semolina cake, 234–35

pockets, 288–89

in polenta with soft cheese and browned butter, 130–31

in ravioli for the feast of Saint John the Baptist, 88–90

in Saint Joseph's fritters, 280–81

in savory Easter pie, 28–29

in souffléd chicken soup, 46–47

tart, 226–27

in wheat berry pudding for Saint Lucy, 276–77

ricotta salata, in summer spaghetti with green beans, 111

risi e bisi, 122–23

riso rosso, 126–27

risotto, 122–27

artichoke, 124–25

with peas for San Marco, Venetian, 122–23

red, 126–27

tips for, 125, 127

risotto di carciofi, 124–25

roast(ed):

chestnuts, hot, 270

chicken and potatoes with bay leaves, 182–83

leg of lamb with garlic, rosemary and little potatoes, 172–73

pork, porchetta style, 170–71

pork with hazelnuts, 174

turkey with chestnut stuffing, 190–91

rolls, olive, 24–25

Roman:

Easter soup, 43

lamb, hunter's style, 178–79

rosemary:

fresh tomatoes and, 205

rabbit with tomatoes, wine and, 194

raisin bread, Tuscan, 22–23

roast leg of lamb with garlic, little potatoes and, 172–73

rosy mashed potatoes, 216

sage and butter sauce, *see* butter and sage sauce

Saint Joseph's Day soup, 54

salad:

Christmas, 198

reinforcement, 196

seafood, *see* seafood salad

salami:

Genoa, in savory Easter pie, 28–29

in potato cake, 214–15

in potato croquettes, 212–13

salsa Balsamella, 61

salsa di burro e salvia, 60

salsa di pomodoro alla Toscana, 56

Sardinian lamb stew, 176–77

sauces, 55–74

marrying pasta and, 63

pesto Genovese, 64

pink, 61

use of term, 70

see also béchamel sauce; butter and sage sauce; meat sauce; ragus; tomato sauce

sauces, seafood:

blue crab, linguine with, 117

lobster, linguine with, 116–17

red mussel, linguine with, 118–19

white clam, linguine with, 120–21

sausage, Italian:

fava beans, and cabbage soup, 52

in married soup, 50–51

in savory Easter pie, 28–29

sausage and mushroom ragu, 74

cavatelli with, 104–5

sciusceddu or *soffiello*, 46–47

scungilli:

salad, 140–41

in spicy tomato sauce, 142–43

scungilli in salsa piccante, 142–43

seafood, 133–45

handling of, 158

marinated eel skewers, 148–49

snails for the feast of Saint Rosalie, 150

see also clam(s); crab; lobster; mussel(s); scungilli; shrimp

seafood salad:

Christmas Eve, 134–35

Ligurian, 137–39

scungilli, 140–41

Selvapiana seven P pasta,
112–13
semolina orange cake,
234–35
sesame cookies, 242–43
sette p penne di Selvapiana,
112–13
sfinci di San Giuseppe,
280–81
shrimp, 145
    in Christmas Eve seafood
        salad, 134–35
    with garlic and toasted
        bread crumbs, 144
    in Ligurian seafood salad,
        137–39
Sicilian ragu, 65
snails for the feast of Saint
    Rosalie, 150
soppressata, in married soup,
    50–51
souffléd chicken soup, 46–47
soups, 41–54
    good luck lentil, 49
    married, 50–51
    Saint Joseph's Day, 54
    sausage, fava beans, and
        cabbage, 52
    see also chicken soup and
        broth
spaghetti:
    Good Friday, 91
    with green beans, summer,
        111
spaghetti con fagiolini, 111
spice(d) cookies:
    All Souls' Day, 246–47
    chocolate, 264–65
    fig, 254–55
spiedini di anguilla, 148–49

spinach:
    in Ligurian Easter tart,
        38–40
    in meat ravioli, 84–86
    in ravioli for the feast of
        Saint John the Baptist,
        88–90
sponge cake layers, 236
squid, in Christmas Eve
    seafood salad, 134–35
stews:
    baccalà, 152–53
    Sardinian lamb, 176–77
    summer vegetable, 203
stockfish, 155
struffoli, 252–53
stuffed artichokes, 208
stuffed mushrooms, 209
stuffing, chestnut, roast
    turkey with, 190–91
sugo finto, 57
summer spaghetti with green
    beans, 111
summer vegetable stew, 203
Sunday chicken with fresh
    tomatoes, 181
Sunday meat and tomato
    sauce, 68–70
sweet beans for the Day of the
    Dead, 248–49
Swiss chard:
    and fresh fava beans, 201
    in Ligurian Easter tart,
        38–40
    in poor man's fava beans
        for the feast of Saint
        Joseph, 200
    in ravioli for the feast of
        Saint John the Baptist,
        88–90

Swiss cheese, in savory Easter
    pie, 28–29
swordfish pie, Monzù's,
    156–58

tacchino arrosto, 190–91
taglierini in bagna caoda, 87
taralli dolci, 240
tart, Ligurian Easter, 38–40
tarts, sweet:
    double chocolate pudding,
        232–33
    ricotta, 226–27
timbales:
    of Boniface VIII, 98–99
    Grandma Amico's Sicilian
        baked, 108–10
timballo di Bonifacio VIII,
    98–99
toc'n braide, 130–31
tomatoes:
    fresh, and rosemary, 205
    fresh, Sunday chicken with,
        181
    in Grandma Amico's Sicilian
        baked pasta, 108–10
    in linguine with lobster,
        116–17
    in linguine with red mussel
        sauce, 118–19
    in Mother Leone's meat
        sauce, 62–63
    in quick lobster or crab
        linguine, 128
    rabbit with wine, rosemary
        and, 194
    in rosy mashed potatoes,
        216
    in Selvapiana seven P pasta,
        112–13

in Sicilian ragu, 65

in summer vegetable stew,
203

in vegetable ragu, 58

tomato sauce, 56, 65

spicy, scungilli in, 142–43

see also fake sauce *(sugo
finto)*; Sunday meat and
tomato sauce; Tuscan
tomato sauce

tonno del capo, 146–47

torrone, 266

torta di cioccolato di Pesah,
222–23

torta di ricotta, 224–25

torta pasqualina, 38–40

tortelli:

Christmas chestnut,
256–57

potato, 92–93

Trieste holiday cake
(presnitz), 230–31

tortelli di Natale alle castagne,
256–57

*tortelli di San Lorenzo, o
tortelli di patate,* 92–93

truffle(s):

black, in Umbrian ragu, 66–67

in Christmas capon, 188–89

tuna:

capo's, 146–47

in Ligurian seafood salad,
137–39

-stuffed Easter eggs, 20

turkey, 159

with chestnut stuffing
roast, 190–91

Tuscan rosemary raisin bread,
22–23

Tuscan tomato sauce, 56

Umbrian ragu, 66–67

uova ripiene pasquali, 20

vanilla rings, glazed, 240

veal, 159–67

cold stuffed breast of,
162–64

osso buco with red wine,
166–67

roll-ups, 160–61

shoulder, in cannelloni,
82–83

veal, ground:

in Christmas capon, 188–89

in feast day meat loaf, 165

in golden rice balls, 12–14

meatballs, little, chicken
soup with escarole and,
48

in meatballs with raisins
and pine nuts, 72–73

in meat sauce Bologna
style, 71

in Sicilian ragu, 65

in Umbrian ragu, 66–67

vecchiarelle, 251

vegetable(s), 195–216

ragu, 58

stew, summer, 203

see also specific vegetables

Venetian risotto with peas for
San Marco, 122–23

Vin Santo rings, 239

vongole aragonate, 18–19

walnuts:

in All Souls' Day spice
cookies, 246–47

in chocolate spice cookies,
264–65

in Good Friday pasta, 91

in spiced fig cookies,
254–55

in Trieste holiday cake,
230–31

wheat berry:

cheesecake, Easter,
228–29

in pesto Genovese, 64

pudding for Saint Lucy,
276–77

whelks, *see* scungilli

wine:

Italian, 267

Vin Santo rings, 239

wine, red:

in little old ladies, 251

osso buco with,
166–67

rabbit with tomatoes,
rosemary and, 194

yeast, proofing of, 33

zabaglione, 274

cold, 274

with lentils, 168–69

porcini-stuffed, 206–7

zampone con lenticchie,
168–69

zeppole, 283

zuccherini, 268–69

zucchini flower fritters,
284–85

zucchini ripieni, 206–7

zuppa di pane, 45

zuppa di pollo, 42

*zuppa di pollo con scarola e
polpettini,* 48

zuppa inglese, 220–21